BUFFALO DAYS

Col. Homer W. Wheeler

BUFFALO DAYS

The Personal Narrative of a Cattleman,
Indian Fighter and Army Officer

By
COLONEL HOMER W. WHEELER

Introduction to the Bison Book Edition
by Thomas W. Dunlay

University of Nebraska Press
Lincoln and London

Copyright © 1925 by Homer W. Wheeler
Renewal copyright © 1953 by Clara B. Wheeler
Introduction to the Bison Book Edition © 1990 by
the University of Nebraska Press
All rights reserved
Manufactured in the United States of America

First Bison Book printing: 1990
Most recent printing indicated by the last digit below:
10   9   8   7   6   5   4   3   2   1

Library of Congress Cataloging-in-Publication Data
Wheeler, Homer W.
Buffalo days: forty years in the Old West: the personal narrative of a cat-
tleman, Indian fighter, and Army officer / by Homer W. Wheeler: intro-
duction to the Bison Book edition by Thomas W. Dunlay.
p.   cm.
Reprint. Originally published: Indianapolis: Bobbs-Merrill, [c1925]
Includes bibliographical references.
ISBN 0-8032-9726-2
1. Wheeler, Homer W. 2. Pioneers—West (U.S.)—Biography. 3. Fron-
tier and pioneer life—West (U.S.) 4. West (U.S.)—History—1848–
1950. 5. Indians of North America—West (U.S.) 6. Indians of North
America—Wars—1866–1895. I. Title.
F594.W58   1925
978.03′092 — dc20   89-24967   CIP
[B]

Reprinted by arrangement with the Macmillan Publishing Company

Originally published as *Buffalo Days: Forty Years in the Old West: The
Personal Narrative of a Cattleman, Indian Fighter and Army Officer*

To

The loyal officers and men of the Fifth and
Eleventh United States Cavalry, with whom
for thirty-eight years I marched, fought and
bivouacked on the Great Plains of the West
this volume is affectionately dedicated.

INTRODUCTION TO THE BISON BOOK EDITION
by Thomas W. Dunlay

One of my most vivid memories of graduate school is of
a seminar on American Indians. One day a visiting professor
happened to remark that many of the most intelligent and
sympathetic written accounts of Indians from the nineteenth
century come from army officers. This was during the sixties,
and the member of the seminar who most vocally represented
the counter-culture refused to believe that U.S. Army officers
could have anything meaningful to say about Indians. He expressed his opinion so vehemently that the professor finally
told him very bluntly that he should learn something about the
subject before talking about it.

Most of those who are familiar with the literature of the
western Indian wars, and the memoirs of their white partici-
pants, would find the professor's assertion unremarkable. In
studying the secondary literature of the frontier military, one
becomes accustomed to the biographical sketch that runs:
"———, unlike most army officers, did not believe that 'the
only good Indian is a dead one.' " One begins to wonder about
that supposedly typical officer who did equate good and dead
Indians. He did exist, of course; General Phil Sheridan, one
of the highest-ranking in the post–Civil War army, is commonly credited with that remark, and one cavalryman published a description of Indians as "human *lice*."[1] In fact, army
officers on the frontier ran the gamut of attitudes in regard to
Indians; blanket, racist hostility was probably less common
than paternalism, and a genuine attempt to understand an alien
culture appears fairly often. Indifference was least likely.

An army officer who had worked with Apache scouts told
Frederic Remington that he and his fellows should not be called

"Indian fighters." His statement has often been quoted: "In reality I have been in only a few small affairs of that character, but I have done a power of Indian-thinking for which I will receive no credit. It would often be better and more truthful to call us 'Indian-thinkers' rather than 'fighters.' "[2]

At the head of the list of frontier military memoirs is, of course, John G. Bourke's *On the Border with Crook*. In terms of breadth, wit, and ethnographic sophistication, Bourke was an experienced combat veteran, a staff officer, and one of the pioneers of American anthropology. William P. Clark, out of his long experience with Indian scouts on the northern plains, produced not a memoir but *The Indian Sign Language*, which covers much more than the title subject.

Coming behind these two, several old warriors in the twentieth century wrote lively personal recollections of their youthful experiences. Some of the best, interestingly enough, were by men who had experience leading Indian scouts. Britton Davis's *The Truth about Geronimo* and Thomas Cruse's *Apache Days and After* are outstanding in this genre. Robert G. Carter's *On the Border with Mackenzie* may not appeal to present-day sensibilities, but it is an essential source on the southern plains wars.[3]

Hugh Scott, who went on to become chief of staff of the army, commanded Kiowa scouts on the southern plains and was, like W. P. Clark, an authority on sign language. His *Some Memories of a Soldier* covers a much broader period than most of the others mentioned here, but a large part of it relates to his frontier experience and his service with the scouts.[4]

Homer Wheeler's *Buffalo Days* fits in with the other works noted here. He wrote in old age, when the automobile, airplane, and radio were common, yet the frontier and the Indian wars were still vivid in the memories of living men. A good deal of nostalgia already surrounded "the winning of the West," and there was a market for books appealing to it. For many people, the West was already a never-never land of romance and adventure. Wheeler's memoirs were first published under the title *The Frontier Trail* in 1923 and then as *Buffalo Days* in 1925. Both titles, of course, tell us simply that the book is about the Wild West, which is all that most of its original readers asked. After more than sixty years, however, the public may want more substantial reasons for buying a paperback reprint that probably costs more than the hardbound original.

Homer Wheeler's frontier career was unique in some respects. Most of his contemporaries in the army came west after service in the Civil War or four years at West Point, first encountering the country and its inhabitants as officers with certain duties and a certain point of view. Wheeler had lived for several years on the frontier as a civilian, as a cattleman, sutler, and volunteer scout among people who often had a poor opinion of soldiers and whom the soldiers often regarded with contempt. The contempt did not extend to Wheeler, whose service as a scout gained such high regard among army officers that he was offered a second lieutenant's commission direct from civilian life. He joined the Fifth Cavalry in late 1875, the "Dandy Fifth" that had produced a host of Civil War generals and in Wheeler's time included such notables as Wesley Merritt, Eugene A. Carr, and Captain Charles King, whose literary efforts almost singlehandedly made the Cavalry-versus-Indian tale a staple of American popular culture.

Wheeler's military career was fairly typical of the period: it consisted of occasional campaigns against hostile Indians and long stretches of garrison duty that included a good deal of peaceful interaction with Indians. Army officer's perceptions of Indians developed out of a variety of experiences, not from constant hostilities. Wheeler gives us interesting firsthand accounts of the Red River War of 1874 and the Sioux campaign of 1876, notably the Battle of the Red Fork of the Powder River — the "Fight with Dull Knife's Band."

A portion of Wheeler's book not only exploits the interest in the Old West but might be characterized as "filler." More charitably, the old soldier retailed ideas and information common to westerners of his generation. People wanted to hear about Buffalo Bill Cody and Wild Bill Hickock, and Wheeler had known them at least slightly, although much of what he had to say about them was generally known. His judgments on the Little Big Horn battle probably represent common opinion among army officers of his time.

The significance of *Buffalo Days* lies in Wheeler's account of his command of Indian scouts and his general opinions about Native Americans. Commanding Indian scouts offered a special challenge to the frontier officer. Regular soldiers and Indian warriors both made war and killed their enemies, but their ideas about the best way to do this differed radically. General George Crook, who placed more faith in Indian scouts than any other military commander, believed that attempting to discipline them and supervise their every movement as if they were white soldiers would destroy their effectiveness: "They know better how to obtain the information which is needed . . . than we do, and should be allowed to use their own methods in getting it . . . Their best quality is their individuality and as soon as this is destroyed their efficiency goes with it."[5]

Various colonial powers employed "native" troops, of course, in much larger numbers and on a more permanent basis than the United States. France and Britain organized local military forces in many parts of Africa and Asia in order to assert their authority over other Africans and Asians. These were permanent organizations and their officers were specialists who served with the same troops for years, often learning their languages.

U.S. Army Indian Scouts, by contrast, were enlisted for six months as needed for an emergency, and their officers were on temporary assignment from their infantry or cavalry regiments. Some soldiers yearned to see the establishment of permanent Indian units that could make use of the fighting talents of the warriors, absorb energies that might otherwise have been turned against whites, police the frontier more efficiently than white troops, and promote peaceful assimilation. In 1889 Rudyard Kipling encountered a young lieutenant who had read about the British forces in India and wanted to see an Indian corps on the British model: ''Only . . . there is no frontier these days, and all our Indian wars are nearly over. Those beautiful beasts will die out, and nobody will ever know what splendid cavalry they can make.'' [6] One hopes the line about ''beautiful beasts'' came from Kipling and not from the unnamed officer.

Wheeler's command of his Southern Cheyenne company came during a period when the Indian wars were ''nearly over,'' and he could not recount any campaigns they had made. Instead, he told of what he tried to do with his company and what manner of men they were. Scout officers often congratulated themselves on their understanding of Indians. A modern anthropologist might consider their confidence excessive, but, in fact, their purposes were simply different from those of the student of Indian cultures. It is obvious that Wheeler regarded his Indian scouts as people, not animals or congenital criminals (two views of Indians not uncommon on the frontier). At the same time, his attitude was obviously paternalistic, typical of a regular officer of his generation in dealing with enlisted men. He seems to have been more ''regular'' than many officers involved in more active campaigning; ''Making Soldiers of Indians'' is, after all, the title of one of his chapters. Scout units tended to become more formal and more military as the need for their services diminished. In the 1890s the army attempted to integrate Indians into regular units by forming all-Indian companies in selected regular regiments. The experiment failed because of cultural differences and lack of commitment within the army hierarchy.[7] At the same time, the United States Scouts became an established part of the regular army with crossed-arrow insignia and special uniform details. The active scout units of the Indian wars had done without insignia and with cast-off uniforms or none at all.

A famous thesis on colonialism holds that Europeans sought

in colonial situations to relieve their own sense of inferiority by dominating others without considering human needs and feelings.[8] Such an attitude has never been lacking in Indian-white relations in the American West, in Wheeler's day or our own, but it was an attitude that a man in Wheeler's position could not afford. He never rid himself entirely, any more than any of us do, of the notion that he represented an incomparably superior culture, but he could never have enjoyed any success in a scout command without remembering that the men he commanded were intelligent fellow humans. Possibly he had to take more notice of them than he would if they had been white soldiers. It is a pity, certainly, that we do not have direct evidence from some of Wheeler's scouts as to how they regarded their relationship.[9] As it is, Homer Wheeler has left us a picture of his army and the American Indians that tells us more about the time, the place, and the people than we would know otherwise.

NOTES

1. Eugene B. Beaumont, "Over the Border with Mackenzie," *United Service* 12 (March 1885): 286.

2. Frederic Remington, "How an Apache War Was Won," in *Frederic Remington's Own West,* ed. Harold McCracken (New York: Dial Press, 1960), p. 49.

3. John G. Bourke, *On the Border with Crook* (Lincoln: University of Nebraska Press, 1972); William P. Clark, *The Indian Sign Language* (Lincoln: University of Nebraska Press, 1981); Britton Davis, *The Truth about Geronimo* (Lincoln: University of Nebraska Press, 1976); Thomas Cruse, *Apache Days and After* (Lincoln: University of Nebraska Press, 1987); Robert G. Carter, *On the Border with Mackenzie* (New York: Antiquarian Press, 1961). One of the best scout officers published only one brief account during his short life: Charles B. Gatewood, "Campaigning against Victorio in 1879," *The Great Divide* (April 1894), pp. 102–4.

4. Hugh L. Scott, *Some Memories of a Soldier* (New York: Century Company, 1928).

5. C. S. Roberts to W. S. Shipp, August 14, 1885, in John S. Bigelow, *On the Bloody Trail of Geronimo* (Los Angles: Westernlore, 1958), pp. 43–44.

BISON BOOK INTRODUCTION

6. Rudyard Kipling, *Rudyard Kipling's West: American Notes,* ed. Arrell M. Gibson. (Norman: University of Oklahoma Press, 1981), pp. 98–99.

7. For a further exposition of this subject, see Thomas W. Dunlay, *Wolves for the Blue Soldiers: Indian Scouts and Auxiliaries with the United States Army, 1860–90* (Lincoln: University of Nebraska Press, 1982), pp. 195–97.

8. O. Mannoni, *Prospero and Caliban: The Psychology of Colonization* (New York: Frederick A. Praeger, 1956). For more on white officers and Indian scouts, see Dunlay, *Wolves for the Blue Soldiers,* pp. 91–107.

9. For the recollections of Northern Cheyennes who were scouts in the same type of company at Fort Keogh, Montana, at about the time Wheeler commanded Southern Cheyennes, see Thomas B. Marquis, *Wooden Leg: A Warrior Who Fought Custer* (Lincoln: University of Nebraska Press, 1962), pp. 333–45, and the account of James Tangled Yellow Hair in Thomas B. Marquis, *Cheyenne and Sioux* (Stockton, California: Pacific Center for Western Historical Studies, 1973), pp. 38–45.

INTRODUCTION

No nation looking to a future can afford to ignore the history and traditions of its past. Especially is this true of our country, now faced with the necessity of absorbing a large alien element.

Events have marched so rapidly in the last thirty years that a generation has arisen which has forgotten that we once had a western frontier, great plains, over which rode the red Indian and roamed the wild buffalo. The history of the Rosebud, the Washita, the Little Big Horn, Sappa Creek, Powder River and the Arickaree Fork of the Republican is no longer told by the light of cavalry camp-fires. The generation that knew Custer, Crook, Mackenzie, Sheridan and the Forsyths is almost gone. The names of Roman Nose, Spotted Tail, Sitting Bull, Dull Knife, Red Cloud and Crazy Horse—chieftains whose flaunting eagle feathers once meant as much to tens of thousands of the red horsemen of the plains as did the white plume of Navarre to the French royalists at Ivry—now stir memories in the hearts of but a few old men.

Fifty-three years ago Homer W. Wheeler, a descendant of Revolutionary stock, left his boyhood home in Vermont for the great plains. He became a part of that wild life, marching, scouting, fighting, raising cattle, riding to the rescue of Sandy Forsyth in the Arickaree fight, known and trusted by Sheridan, Merritt, Crook and Mackenzie. For his volunteer part in the desperate fight on Sappa Creek, Kansas, in April, 1875, he was offered a commission in the Fifth Cavalry and, accepting it, marched, fought and biv-

INTRODUCTION

ouacked with that famous regiment, retiring as a colonel in September, 1911.

There is no greater living authority on the Plains Indians, none who fought them harder and, when they were vanquished, did more to civilize and lead them into the best ways of the white man. Thirty years ago this autumn, when I reported to Wheeler as his second lieutenant in the Fifth Cavalry, he was one whose character and achievements stood out among those of many gallant officers whose memories are still cherished by those of us who once followed the guidons of that splendid regiment. His story as told in these pages is the simple narrative of a fine soldier who knew the people and the scenes of which he writes. It is perhaps our last glimpse of the stirring drama which won the West, in which Time's shadowy curtain is for a moment drawn aside by one who himself played a man's part on that stage.

J. G. HARBORD,
Major General, U. S. A.

Headquarters, Camp Travis,
Office of the Camp Commander,
Camp Travis, Texas.

MANY YEARS AGO

To the people of the United States and to their Government the Indian has always been a problem, and the reason for this is plain.

It is impossible for the average civilized man to comprehend the Indian, because for uncounted generations that race has lived and thought in its own way—a way outgrown by our ancestors thousands of years ago. Nevertheless, rarely a man is found who, by temperament, is qualified after experience with them to understand the Indians—and measurably to take their point of view—and one who so understands them can get along easily with them and persuade them to do almost anything that he asks. Colonel Homer W. Wheeler is such a man.

It was many years ago, when Colonel Wheeler was a simple lieutenant of cavalry and old Fort Reno was an important military post, that I spent part of a summer there, renewing my acquaintance with the old Fifth Cavalry, many of whose officers and men I had known years before up in Nebraska.

During that visit to Fort Reno, the now forgotten "Ghost Dance" excitement was at its height and the Indians, trusting in the prophecy of one of their number, believed that conditions on this earth were to be changed, that the white people and all their works were to be swept away, that those of their own race who had died in past years were to revisit and live upon the earth, and that the vanished buffalo were to reappear and furnish to the Indians the same subsistence that they had given in the distant past. The Indians had faith in their prophet and were not very good-natured.

Long before this Lieutenant Wheeler, by authority of his department commander, had enlisted a troop of scouts among the Southern Cheyennes and Arapahoes, whose home was in the Indian Territory, now Oklahoma.

These scouts, having been enlisted and drilled, were now an effective force, understanding something of discipline, having an excellent military bearing, and appearing very creditably on drill. They had been taught the importance of taking care of their arms, accouterments, horses and horse equipment, and were favorably reported on by Lieutenant Wheeler's superior officers.

While I was at Fort Reno, Lieutenant Wheeler was putting up buildings for his company of scouts who did all the work of construction. They built stables for two hundred horses, saddle rooms for equipment, and a granary. It was an interesting sight to see the scouts at this work and to see their commanding officer instructing them.

I recall particularly a building which was being chinked and mudded up—the method by which log buildings were made tight for winter. Lieutenant Wheeler was in the thick of the work, showing the Indians how to apply the mud, and he and his Indians were up to their elbows in the soft gray clay which could only be applied with the hands. Lieutenant Wheeler did not order his men to do the work he had laid out for them. His attitude was that of the leading workman; and when the Indians saw that he himself was doing this manual work, each one of them was anxious to help to do it, and to try to do it as well as his leader.

With such a spirit as this in the head of the command and running down all through it, it is not surprising that this troop of Indian scouts became effective and won the highest praise for all who saw them. The interesting point about them was not that they could do the work, but that their commanding officer had put into them such a spirit that they were eager to do it and took joy and pride in the work.

Colonel Wheeler's volume contains much of the history of the early West, little details which throw light on the happenings of those times and so possesses a high value.

GEORGE BIRD GRINNELL.

A FREE-WILL OFFERING

I have read with great interest Colonel Wheeler's manuscript, about to be published, and can without hesitation recommend his book to every one who is interested in the history and development of the West. I am familiar with his work with the Cheyennes, Arapahoes and other Indians. There is no person living who understands the character and traditions of these people better. I have known Colonel Wheeler for more than forty years. We both took part in the celebrated winter campaign of 1876-77, in which he was conspicuous for his gallant and able services. His description of this campaign and the battle on Powder River with Dull Knife's and Little Wolf's band of Cheyennes November 25, 1876, is related in an interesting way and not exaggerated. His reminiscences of early western life are true in detail.

He organized, in 1877, Company 'A', Indian Scouts, numbering one hundred men. It was one of two experimental companies with the view of ascertaining whether or not the American Indian would adapt himself to military discipline. In this case the experiment was a success; Lieutenant Wheeler succeeded in his efforts to make a good company of it, as few officers in the army could have done, and was commended by the general of the army, (General Schofield) for his success. I believe Colonel Wheeler's book will take well with public libraries and historical societies. His reminiscences of early western life and the habits and traditions of the Indian are highly entertaining and interesting.

JESSE M. LEE,
Major-General, U. S. A. (retired).

Los Angeles,
California.

A TRUE FRIEND

I have known Colonel Homer W. Wheeler for nearly forty-five years. His old comrades have always held him in high esteem, and have known him as a gallant soldier, a true friend and an entertaining companion. His simple story of some of his experiences on the old frontier has all the interests of his ordinary conversation. He writes as well as he talks, and he has an art of his own. My only regret is, as I have told him, that he has not made a larger book of his experiences, as he could easily have done.

EBEN SWIFT,
Major-General, U. S. A.

Army and Navy Club,
Washington, D. C.

PREFACE

At the instance of numerous friends (both in and out of the United States Army) I have attempted to narrate here my experiences as cattleman, post trader, scout, Indian agent and army officer on the great plains of the West in the days when the buffalo, the gun-fighter and the Indian occupied the stage in the drama of frontier life.

From 1868 until the last Indian war of 1890 most of my time was spent in advancing the cause of civilization throughout what was known fifty years ago as "The Great American Desert," that portion of our country extending from eastern Kansas to western Colorado and Wyoming, during which time I was thrown into close contact with the red man. Because of this intimacy as Indian agent and also as inspector, overseeing the distribution of annuities and the issue of beef cattle, I had the opportunity to study the Indian from many different angles. I do not agree with the old saying that "the only good Indian is a dead one." On the contrary, I found the Indian to be keen, upright, truthful and loyal in peace, and anxious to follow the white man's road. All he asked was the opportunity to do so. During the years in which I was associated with the red man I also had charge of a company of Indian scouts numbering one hundred men and composed of members from many different tribes, and there I obtained an insight into the life of the American Indian which could not possibly have been gained in any other manner. But a short time before many of my scouts had been savages and warpath followers; yet they readily adapted themselves to military discipline and became splendid soldiers.

PREFACE

Had the government been more liberal with its funds and provided skilled men to teach the Indian how to farm, till the soil and raise crops, at the same time using tact, patience and kindness, within five years' time from the close of Indian hostilities these followers of the warpath could have been made self-supporting, instead of remaining wards of the government. From my own experience I am positive that I could have brought about this change had I been given the opportunity and the right men to act as teachers. It was preposterous to expect that within a few brief months (even though provided with farming implements and machinery) the untutored savage could change from his nomadic life, living by following the chase, to that of a tiller of the soil, without the necessary teachers to instruct him in the art of husbandry. Yet this is what the government actually expected of the Indian!

In this work I have endeavored to illustrate the dangers, privations and hardships which were encountered during the Indian troubles of the period from 1868 to 1890, and to present a truthful picture of life in the West as it was at that time, a life which has disappeared as completely as have the countless herds of buffalo which then dotted the western horizon. There is no longer a frontier within the limits of the United States; and where we trailed the Texas longhorn and scouted for warring Indians, waving fields of grain, orchards, wire fences, irrigating ditches and other evidences of civilization now exist, while cities and towns by the hundred have blotted out forever all traces of the old-time West. It is no small degree of satisfaction to me to realize that I took an active part in helping to bring about this new order of things and that while I was associated with the Indian I endeavored in so far as I had the power to assist him in getting started along the white man's road.

I hereby acknowledge with cordial thanks the assistance

PREFACE

rendered to me by George Bird Grinnell, General Jesse M. Lee, General Anson Mills* and General Eben Swift through extracts from their writings, touching upon some of the important happenings of the Indian wars. It is my opinion that General Lee has done more to assist the Indian toward adopting the white man's ways than any other individual with whom the red man came in contact.

I also desire to express my thanks to Mr. Earl A. Brininstool and Mr. Charles M. Lurie for their assistance in editing these memoirs and putting them into shape for publication.

HOMER W. WHEELER.

Los Angeles,
  California.

---

*Since deceased.

CONTENTS

CONTENTS—*Continued*

LIST OF ILLUSTRATIONS

BUFFALO DAYS

BUFFALO DAYS

PART ONE: CIVILIAN EXPERIENCES
IN THE WEST

CHAPTER I

EARLY LIFE, AND FIRST DAYS IN THE WEST

I WAS born in 1848, of Revolutionary stock. My ances-
tor, Elias Babcock, served in the Revolutionary War and
my grandfather, Elias Babcock, Jr., in the War of 1812.
Vermont is my native state. When I was about ten years
of age my parents removed to Winona, Minnesota. Winona
is an Indian name, and a legend runs that in the long ago
an Indian maiden by that name, one of the most beautiful
of her tribe, fled from a white man, a mighty hunter, and
flung herself from a projecting cliff into the calmly flow-
ing river below.

It was at Winona that I saw my first Indian. I observed some red men coming up the river in a canoe and ran
down toward them as they landed. When one of them
arose to leave the craft he picked up a butcher knife and I,
thinking that he meant to scalp me, took to my heels and
never stopped running until I reached home.

In the early 'forties, my great-uncle, David Olmstead,
moved the Sioux and other Indian tribes out of Iowa to the

northern part of the state of Minnesota. He used to enter-
tain me with stories relating his experiences with the Indians. These thrilling tales made a great impression with
me and gave me an intense interest in the red man.

The county of Olmstead, Minnesota, was named for my
uncle. My mother's brother, Lorenzo A. Babcock, was the
first attorney-general of Minnesota. His picture hangs,
with that of my great-uncle, in the state capitol. Another
brother, Brainard Babcock, was killed by the Snake Indians
near Fort Boise, Oregon Territory, in 1854. Still another
brother, General Orville E. Babcock, served on the staff of
General Grant during the Civil War, and was his secretary
during most of his administrations as president of the
United States. My father was the first representative from
Winona County when Minnesota became a state in 1858.

Because of my mother's health we returned to Vermont,
where shortly after she passed away. After her death I
went to live with my Grandmother Wheeler, who resided in
Montgomery, my old home. I attended school there for a
year or more and then entered the New Hampton Institute
at Fairfax, Vermont, which was one of the leading schools
of the state. I was to remain there during the absence of
my father, who was in the oil regions of Pennsylvania.

While I was at the institute three or four of my com-
panions and I became imbued with patriotic zeal. The Civil
War was upon us, and we went to Burlington, Vermont,
to enlist. Because of our ages, however (all being under
twenty-one), the officer would not enlist us without the
consent of our parents or guardians. Had I been allowed
to enlist at that time I would have been retired one grade
higher, that of a brigadier-general, as all veterans who
served in the war as officers or privates were elevated one
grade by act of Congress.

When the usual vacation time came I did not return to

school but obtained employment with the Vermont Central Railroad at St. Albans, loading and unloading freight. After a time I was advanced to the position of freight checker, taking the bills of lading and checking the freight in and out of the cars.

Upon the return of my father from the oil country, he established himself in business in Montgomery and requested me to resign my position with the railroad company and come into the store with him. I did so, remaining with him several months. I then entered the Eastman Business College at Poughkeepsie, New York.

I completed my course at the college in April, 1866, but instead of returning to Montgomery as my father had expected of me I went to New York City to seek employment.

When I reached New York, accompanied by my cousin, Wheeler Clark, who had attended college with me, the extent of my wealth was a solitary ten-dollar bill. My cousin was not much better off financially.

After varied experiences in New York in search of employment, and a short term of employment with a jewelry firm, I obtained a position in the quartermaster's department under General Sawtelle, my work being in the transportation office, and was finally placed in charge of Pier 43, North River.

In June, 1868, at the age of nineteen, I decided to go west and "grow up with the country." I had a friend at Fort Wallace, Kansas, who offered me a position that I accepted. I arrived there on the Fourth of July.

En route to Fort Wallace I stopped off at Lawrence, Kansas, to visit my uncle, C. W. Babcock, then surveyor-general of the state. When I resumed my journey I happened to be on the same train with General U. S. Grant, who with his staff, was en route to Denver. At my uncle's suggestion, I went into the coach occupied by the general and introduced myself to him. He received me very kindly and invited me to ride with him to the end of the road, which was then Monument Station.

We arrived there early the following morning. It was only a grading camp. A stage-coach was waiting for General Grant and his party, but there was no room in it for me. I made arrangements with a party to take me to Sheridan, a near-by canvas town of some two hundred persons, and we reached it by ten o'clock. The only frame building in the place belonged to the Southern Overland Stage Company.

There was no hotel, for every one was supposed to carry his own blankets. The grading had been completed to that point, but the rails had not yet been laid. There were two or three restaurants, dugouts with canvas roofing. After a meal, I started out to see the sights. I entered a saloon where quite a number of men were drinking, among them some colored soldiers of the Thirty-eighth Infantry, encamped there to guard the railroad workers.

Here a long-haired individual spoke to me. He was dressed in buckskin and carried two revolvers and a knife in his belt. Knowing me for a "tenderfoot" from my manner and dress, he advised me to "get out o' there," saying it was no place for a boy, as there was likely to be some shooting. Thereupon, with great confidence, I put my hand to my hip pocket where I carried a small twenty-two-caliber pistol, and remarked, "I think I can take care of myself."

The "bad man" asked to look at my gun. I handed it to him, and he looked at it for a short time, grinned and returned it to me, remarking, "Young man, if you'd shoot me with that thar gun and I ever found it out I'd kick you all over the prairie."

Soon after this conversation, shooting did commence in earnest and I did not pause to bid my long-haired acquaintance good-by, but rushed out to seek shelter in the dugout. I was not the only one hunting cover. Two or three men were wounded in the fracas, but none were killed.

I concluded that Sheridan was no place for a tenderfoot, and as I found a wagon going to Pond Creek, just beyond Fort Wallace, which was to carry some graders, I made arrangements to go with them. A short distance outside the town, the coach with General Grant and his party came along. They tried to pass us, but our driver, through pure devilment, and being half drunk, as were some of the graders, reined his mules in front of the coach, thus delaying the general and his party.* Finally tiring of this amusement, they allowed the coach to pass, the graders shouting at the top of their voices and cheering loudly for Seymour and Vallandigham. Horatio Seymour was the Democratic candidate for the presidency; he had formerly been governor of New York State. C. L. Vallandigham was a noted Copperhead during the Civil War, and had been a member of Congress from the state of Ohio.

After a while the graders became thirsty and stopped the wagon to take a drink. While doing so, they espied the head of a buffalo about twenty-five yards away. It had been lying there for some time and was well bleached out. It made a good target to shoot at. Every one had a sixshooter, so several of the men tried their marksmanship, firing at this skull. They did poor shooting. Being proud of my marksmanship, as I had had quite an amount of practise back in Vermont, I remarked, "You fellows can't shoot; let me try it." I pulled my gun and banged away. Instead

---

*Fifty-six years after this escapade I met in Los Angeles, California, Sigmund Shlesinger, one of Forsyth's scouts, who took an active part in the Beecher Island fight. He is the "little Jew" of whom Colonel Forsyth spoke in the highest terms of praise for his bravery and coolness in the battle. Mr. Shlesinger told me he was one of the party with these graders. He had read my book and called my attention to the incident.

of my hitting the mark the pistol flew out of my hand, filling it full of powder. Upon examining the gun I found that the bullet had left the chamber, passed into the barrel and burst it. In those days we had no metallic cartridges and in loading the pistol I did not put in a sufficient amount of powder to force the ball out of the barrel. This was the gun with which I was going to defend myself in the Sheridan saloon! This pistol was given to me by my uncle, Sergeant Horatio Babcock, who captured it at the battle of Wilson Creek, Missouri, August 9 and 10, 1861, where General Lyon was killed. My uncle was himself killed at the battle of City Point, Virginia, May 19, 1862. His promotion to a captaincy was received the day he was killed.

We arrived at Wallace without further incidents of interest occurring, and the graders went on to Pond Creek.

I found my cousin, V. L. Todd, and he was glad to see me. He had been a clerk during the war at General Grant's headquarters at City Point, Virginia.

The post at Wallace had been established the preceding year, 1867, by Brevet Brigadier-General H. C. Bankhead, Colonel of the Fifth Infantry, who was in command. It was situated at the headwaters of the Smoky Hill River, on the Overland Trail to California, completing a chain of four posts (Riley, Harker, Hays and Wallace) between the Missouri River and Denver, Colorado, a distance of about seven hundred miles. It was near a much traveled trail used by the red men on their trips back and forth from the Indian Territory to the north. It traversed a wonderful hunting-ground. On their annual hunting trips the Indians of the North and South met in western Kansas for trading and making treaties. This trail was used for the last time in the autumn of 1878, when the Cheyenne Indians broke away from their agency in the Indian Territory and escaped north over it, killing Lieutenant-Colonel Lewis of the Nineteenth Infantry, in a fight near Wallace.

When I went to Wallace the country was a vast wilderness. Engagements with the Indians were quite frequent. It was a common occurrence for them to run off stock, attack wagon trains, murder immigrants and run in the mail coaches. At that time the only man who really knew anything about the country was William Comstock, the post guide and interpreter. He was later killed by Indians. I accompanied Comstock on many hunting trips and thus became familiar with the surrounding country, gaining much information also about the characteristics and peculiarities of the Indians, which proved of immense value to me in later years. Had Comstock lived he would have become as renowned as did his friend, William F. Cody (Buffalo Bill).

I met both Cody and James B. Hickok (Wild Bill) at Wallace when they were in the employ of the government as scouts and kept in touch with them for several years. I saw Colonel Cody for the last time at the San Francisco Exposition in 1915.

CHAPTER II

I HAD been at Fort Wallace only a few months when some Indians came in to the post, remaining there three or four days at the government's expense. This was when I first met Lieutenant Beecher. There were about fifty Indians in this band, including a few squaws and papooses. One of the number, Julia Bent, was noted for her great beauty. Her father was an American and an old Indian trader, who built Bent's Fort, a well-known point on the old Santa Fé Trail along the Arkansas River.

While these Indians were at the post, Dick Blake, clerk in the trading store, removed his false teeth one day, in the presence of several of the red men. This caused great astonishment among them. All of the Indians insisted upon his repeating this seemingly wonderful feat.

The Indians had been out of the post but a day or so when Mr. Jones, the wood contractor, came in from his camp and reported to the commanding officer that six of his wood-cutters had been killed by the redskins. He told the following story:

He had started a new wood camp about six miles from the old one and had dug a well. When ready to place the pump, he found that he needed a monkey-wrench and returned to the old camp for it. While returning he saw about a dozen Indians coming from the direction of the camp he had recently left. As they advanced he observed

8

that they were in their war paint and carried their guns un-covered, which is not their custom when friendly. Then their weapons are sheathed in gun covers of buckskin orna-mented with beads and fringes.

Jones was riding a very good horse and his first impulse was to try to outride the savages. The animal, however, was wearied from travel and Jones was fearful of the out-come. He came to the conclusion that if the Indians were not friendly he would have to make the best of a bad situation.

As he rode up over a ridge where he could look down on his camp, he saw the bodies of his six wood-choppers lying on the ground. The Indians saw him and started for him. He motioned for them to halt, and one of the Indians then came forward for a parley. As the lone Indian came up on Jones' left, saying, "How, how, cola" (friend), the white man pulled his revolver and shot the redskin dead. He then wheeled his horse and made a run for his life, with the yelling, maddened redskins in full pursuit. Jones held his own for a time, but could feel his animal failing under him, so he headed for a dry creek bed covered with wild plum trees. He reached this cover safely, where he quickly dis-mounted and turned his Winchester on the advancing sav-ages. By running rapidly from point to point, discharging his rifle and six-shooter in rapid succession, he managed to keep the Indians at a distance, they imagining no doubt from the rapidity of the shooting that Jones was among friends. He was quite positive that he had killed two of them and wounded others.

Finally the Indians withdrew, and Jones then rode cau-tiously back to his stricken wood camp. Appearances indi-cated that the Indians had approached under the pretense of being friendly and the choppers had given them both food and water, being finally caught off their guard and massacred, for there were no indications whatever that they had made any sort of defense. Jones' escape was miraculous, as one shot grazed his temple, raising a huge welt; two or three bullets passed through his clothing and one bullet chipped a piece out of the handle of his six-shooter.

There being no cavalry at the post, the commanding officer sent out a company of infantry to bring the bodies back to the post, where we buried them. The wood-choppers at the other camp were not molested, as they observed the Indians and were prepared to give them a hot reception.

It was generally supposed that these were the same Indians who had been at Fort Wallace just a few days previous. This sad occurrence started hostilities which lasted several months.

In September, 1868, I accompanied the expedition of Colonel Henry K. Bankhead, brevet brigadier-general, from Fort Wallace to the rescue of Forsyth's and Beecher's scouts, who were besieged on the Arickaree Fork of the Republican River nine days by Cheyenne Indians.

These scouts were organized by Forsyth and Beecher at Forts Harker and Hays, Kansas, by order of General Phil Sheridan dated "Fort Harker, Kansas, August 24, 1868." Major Forsyth, brevet colonel United States Army, was aide-de-camp to General Sheridan. He had had no Indian experience. Lieutenant Frederick H. Beecher, first lieutenant Third Infantry, and second in command, had seen considerable Indian service. The first sergeant was General William H. H. McCall. He had been colonel of a Pennsylvania regiment in the Civil War, and had been breveted a brigadier-general for gallant services. The surgeon, Doctor J. H. Mooers, a native of my state, Vermont, was a practising physician at Hays City. It is my recollection that the scouts came to Wallace to cooperate with Colonel Bankhead, the commanding officer.

They remained at the post about two days and I asked Lieutenant Beecher if I might join them. He gave me permission, providing I had a horse.

The evening following the arrival of the scouts at Wallace, information was received that a mule train encamped near Sheridan had been attacked and run off by Indians. At that time, Sheridan was the terminus of the Kansas-Pacific Railroad, whence all freight for Colorado and New Mexico was shipped by mule and bull trains. The stolen mules belonged to Mr. Moore, post trader at Fort Union, New Mexico, and was composed of animals making up one of the largest trains in the freighting business on the plains. There were about forty wagons (with trails) of ten and twelve mules each, the hauling capacity of the vehicles being about twelve thousand pounds to each wagon, with its trail.

The scouts moved out at once for Sheridan. To my great disappointment, I was left behind. Upon their arriving at Sheridan it was discovered that two of the Mexican teamsters with the Moore outfit had been killed and scalped and a number of the mules driven off. After a careful examination of the ground by the scouts the conclusion was reached that the attack had been made by a war party of about twenty-five Indians. The trail was followed until dark, when the scouts camped, and the following morning continued their advance. In a few hours the trail disappeared. A consultation was held in which Sharp Grover, the guide, Beecher and McCall took part. They agreed that the Indians had seen them and had scattered on the trail to throw pursuers off the scent.

The general direction of the trail was to the north, toward the Republican River. It was thereupon decided to push on to the river and search for the trail in every direction, they arriving there on the fifth day out of Wallace. There they found a wickiup which had evidently been occupied by two dismounted Indians the previous night. They took the trail of the two warriors and followed it a short distance, finding a place where three Indians had been encamped within twenty-four hours. Following this trail, they ran into a larger one made by a small war party. On the advice of Sharp Grover these Indians were not pursued.

The scouts struck smaller trails from this time on, which gradually assumed the proportions of those of a larger war party and were easily followed. This trail led up the forks of the Republican River, whence it crossed to the north bank of the stream, gradually increasing in size until it assumed the proportions of a well beaten road, over which had been driven many ponies and loaded travois, showing that a large Indian village had passed.

Arriving at the Arickaree Fork of the Republican, the scouts found the trail led up-stream on the south bank. Camp was made at dark and the pursuit resumed at daybreak. Thus far not an Indian had been seen. In the afternoon comparatively fresh pony droppings were seen, but still no Indians.

About four o'clock on the afternoon of September sixteenth, as the scouts followed a tortuous trail, winding in and out among wild plum thickets and alders, they came into a small well-grassed valley, where the land sloped gently down to the stream, while on the opposite bank the land was comparatively level for about three-fourths of a mile, terminating in a line of low hills or bluffs, forty or fifty feet high, which shut out the view of the plains from that direction.

As the grazing was good at this point the scouts decided to go into camp. Their horses were badly in need of both feed and rest, and the command felt confident that before the close of another day they would encounter Indians. On the bank of the stream the scouts were opposite a flat plateau which was formed into a small island by the overflow of the

From painting by E. W. Denning.

INDIANS ON THE MOVE
A dog travois goes rabbit crazy

stream in flood season. At this time of the year, however, but a few inches of water flowed in the bed of the stream, which divided at the upper end of the island and meandered slowly by on each side, joining the main stream a few hundred yards below. The width of the island was perhaps twenty yards. A solitary cottonwood tree was growing at the lower end, and the island itself was covered with a growth of stunted bushes.

Sentries were posted and there was no alarm during the night, but just before daybreak Forsyth, who had kept vigilant watch during most of the night, happened to be standing by one of the sentries and the two men saw, silhouetted against the sky-line, the feathered head-dress of an Indian. The crack of the sentry's rifle was echoed by a whoop from a small party of Indians, who dashed out toward the horse herd, rattling bells, dry hides and buffalo skins and beating Indian drums, accompanied by yells such as only an Indian can give. It was evidently the intention of the Indians to stampede the horses, thus dismounting the scouts. They succeeded in running off two horses and two pack-mules.

At the first shot every man sprang to action. A sharp exchange of shots, and the little band of horse thieves were driven away, losing one of their number. At the suggestion of Sharp Grover the command was ordered to lead their horses to the island just in front of them (which the Indians had failed to occupy) and tie the animals to the bushes. The men then began to entrench themselves.

The scouts had nothing with which to dig but their hands, cups, plates and knives, so they were some time getting under shelter. At first all they accomplished was scooping out the sand and making a place large enough for a man to lie in. During this time nearly all the casualties occurred. The horses were all killed within the first hour. Lieutenant Beecher and Doctor Mooers were the first to fall, seriously wounded, both dying later. The doctor was shot in the head and Beecher in the side. Forsyth was seriously wounded, twice in the leg and once in the head, but never lost his courage for an instant, thereby serving as an example to the others. A man named Farley and his young son, a mere boy, took an active part in the combat. They were the two best shots in the command and were entrenched on a point of the island about seventy yards from the others, in a commanding position. Both were wounded early in the engagement, the father seriously, through the thigh, and the son in the shoulder. Both continued to fight, however, without mentioning their injuries, as long as there was an Indian to shoot at, although several times the Indians tried to drive them from their cover. It was said that they killed the chief, Roman Nose, and the head medicine man in one of the charges.*

Medicine men, however, rarely go into battle, but remain near by "making medicine" to encourage the others. The elder Farley submitted to the amputation of his limb upon the arrival of the relief party but died from the operation, his age being against his recovery.

The first night of the battle two of the scouts, Jack Stillwell and "Avalanche" Dave Trudeau (the latter so-called because he christened the army ambulance an "avalanche") volunteered to try to slip through the Indian lines and go for relief. They moved out about midnight but succeeded in getting only a short distance, where they remained in hiding the next day at the head of a gulch. The Indians were so near that their conversation was easily heard. The two scouts were obliged to eat very sparingly, as they carried with them only a few strips of horse meat, but luckily

---

*It was not positively known for some time after the battle that Roman Nose was the head chief in the Beecher Island fight, although it was supposed that a great chief had been killed.

they had full canteens of water. In reality, these two couriers, suffered very little from want of food, but had to remain in such a cramped position, for fear of discovery, that it was almost unendurable. It seems strange and almost incredible that the Indians did not discover them. A special providence must have protected them. They took great precautions not to be seen when they left the island, crawling many yards on their hands and knees, then taking off their boots and walking backward in stocking feet to the point where they remained in hiding at daybreak. It was expected that if their trail were discovered it would be taken for that of moccasined feet. The two men also wore their blankets Indian fashion.

The second night they made much better progress but again sought cover at dawn, hiding under the bank of a small stream. When darkness had fallen they moved out again, walking all night and a portion of the next day, stopping occasionally for a brief rest. By this time they were out on the open prairie and so far away from the hostiles that there was little danger.

The couriers, Stillwell and Trudeau, reached the stage road station at Cheyenne Wells west of Wallace, a little before sundown, remaining there until the stage-coach from Denver came along en route east. Meantime, they obtained food and rest. The following night they reached Wallace on the stage about eleven o'clock. Their feet were in a terrible condition. Walking in their stocking feet they had stepped on prickly pear thorns, which had entered the flesh, causing wounds which had commenced to suppurate, so they were obliged to discard their boots and tear strips off their blankets with which to bind up their feet.

The post commander, Colonel Henry C. Bankhead, and some of the other officers happened to be in the post trader's store when the stage arrived from the west with the two scouts. I was the assistant postmaster and had to go through the way mail sacks and distribute the mail, which explains my presence in the store at that time of the night.

The colonel at once made preparations to go to Forsyth's rescue. He despatched his orderly for the officers and when they arrived at the adjutant's office he gave them instructions. A clerk in the commissary department, Richard Blake, and I were the only ones present who had ever been in that part of the country where Forsyth was besieged. I had been there with William Comstock, the post scout, on a hunting trip, so Blake and I were taken along by Colonel Bankhead, to guide the troops, if needed.

In the meantime the commanding officer had despatched a courier to overtake Colonel L. H. Carpenter, commanding Troop H, Tenth Cavalry (colored) and some scouts, who had left the post early that same morning to establish a camp on the Denver road at the point where it was crossed by Sand Creek.

The courier overtook Carpenter, having ridden all night, and delivered his despatch, which was in part:

Headquarters, Fort Wallace, Kansas,
September 22, 1868, 11 P. M.

Brevet Lieutenant-Colonel L. H. Carpenter,
On Scout.
Colonel:

The commanding officer directs you to proceed at once to a point on the Dry Fork of the Republican, about seventy-five or eighty miles north, northwest from this point, thirty or forty miles west by a little south from the forks of the Republican, with all possible despatch.

Two scouts from Colonel Forsyth's command arrived here this evening and bring word that he (Forsyth) was attacked on the morning of Thursday last by an overpowering force of Indians (seven hundred) who killed all the animals, broke Colonel Forsyth's leg with a rifle ball and severely wounded him in the groin, wounded Surgeon Mooers in the head and wounded Lieutenant Beecher in several places.

Two men of the command were killed and eighteen or twenty wounded.

(Signed)   Hugh Johnson,
First Lieutenant Fifth Infantry,
Acting Post Adjutant.

Colonel Carpenter immediately upon receiving this information moved out, arriving at the scene of action on the eighth day of the siege.

Blake and I, with Colonel Bankhead's command, started before daybreak, the soldiers riding in the six-mule wagons. Stillwell and Trudeau accompanied us but owing to the condition of their feet rode in the ambulance. We reached the battleground a few hours after Colonel Carpenter. Two more scouts, Jack Donovan and A. J. Pliley, had been despatched by Forsyth from the island on the third night of the siege and, being unobserved by the Indians, had made their way to Fort Wallace. When they arrived there they found that Colonel Bankhead had already gone, whereupon Donovan started back the next day. Pliley was so used up that he was unable to make the return trip, and remained at the fort. Fortunately for Carpenter, Donovan had struck Carpenter's trail and followed it to the island. We, with Bankhead, had to march about one hundred and twenty-five miles; Carpenter a shorter distance. Both deserve great credit for their prompt action.

The killed and wounded numbered about twenty. Forsyth reported thirty-five Indians killed and believed that many more had been carried away, dead or wounded, on their horses, to which they were tied.* Those of the scouts

---

*It was the custom of the Indians when hunting buffalo or going into a fight to ride bareback. They would place a lariat around the pony, toward the withers, pressing their knees up under the rope to ride more securely. If wounded or killed in a fight they would thus be carried off the field, instead of falling into the hands of the enemy. Indians have a horror of being left on a battle-field wounded or dead, for fear of being scalped, which they believe prevents their entrance to the "happy hunting-grounds."

who had been killed, four in number, were buried before we arrived. This was necessary, as the bodies had commenced to decompose.

As soon as possible the survivors were taken back to Fort Wallace. The seriously wounded rode in the ambulance. It took us four days to return to the post, while but a few hours over two days had been consumed in reaching the battle-field. Our progress was slow because there were no roads, and the jolting of the ambulance over the prairie made hard traveling for the wounded. Every care was taken for their comfort, however. Forsyth was breveted a brigadier-general in the army for his gallant conduct in this combat. He never fully recovered from the wounds he received. One of the bullets grazed his forehead, slightly fracturing the skull, resulting in frequent severe headaches. He died October 27, 1915.

Jack Stillwell, one of the scouts who started for relief with Trudeau the first night of the siege, was barely twenty-one years of age, intelligent and ambitious. He afterward studied law and grew up with the great West. I had the pleasure of meeting and shaking hands with him at Reno City, Oklahoma, in 1890. He was a territorial judge at the time. He died several years ago. Trudeau was the last man one would expect to volunteer for such a hazardous undertaking. He had been the butt of every one's jokes in the command, but after his daring trip was looked upon with great respect by all who were informed regarding it. After the scouts were disbanded he was employed in the quartermaster's corral at Wallace for many months, but finally went to Arizona, where I lost track of him. He was a much older man than Stillwell.

A few months after the Beecher Island fight Captain Butler of the Fifth Infantry, with his company was sent out to recover the bodies of those that had been buried at the scene of the battle. He found only the bodies of Farley and a scout named Culver. The graves of Lieutenant Beecher and Doctor Mooers were empty. Captain Butler surprised an Indian village near the scene of the fight and gave them battle. He had a howitzer along. The Indians had little use for a gun of such proportions and scampered out of range. Captain Butler brought back to the post the bodies of Farley and Culver, which were buried there.

I remember Lieutenant Frederick H. Beecher, Third Infantry, very well. He was a nephew of the Reverend Henry Ward Beecher, the noted Brooklyn divine, and was wounded in the battle of Gettysburg so severely that he was lame for the remainder of his life. He had charge of the scouts in western Kansas and had a roving commission. Beecher, with the scouts Comstock and Sharp Grover, brought quite a band of Indians into Wallace shortly after my arrival at that post. A goodly number of the warriors came into the post trader's store for a friendly pow-wow and to trade. We purchased buffalo robes of them for twelve or fifteen pint cups of sugar. On the occasion of which I speak, Beecher and the two scouts were with the Indians in the store, all squatted on the floor smoking the peace pipe, which was passed around, each one taking a few whiffs. Grover, who was about half Indian, was doing the interpreting. Beecher asked an Indian for a pair of moccasins, saying that he was lame and his feet hurt him. He showed where he was wounded. He got the moccasins and in return gave the Indian some tobacco.

NOTE: The foregoing account of the Beecher Island fight was written, for the most part, before I had read any other description of the battle by those who had participated therein. No two stories seem to agree wholly. I believe my version of the fight to be as accurate as any account in print, as I gained my information from Sharp Grover, the scout, and Trudeau. Since this note was published first, I have met Scout Sigmund Shlesinger. On reading my account of the fight, he suggested one or two corrections which have been made.

CHAPTER III

A S I now look back I think the most hazardous trip of my plains career was carrying despatches from Colonel Bankhead at Fort Wallace to Colonel Bradley, who was encamped on the Frenchman's Fork of the Republican River, a distance of one hundred miles, and through a hostile country of which I had been over but a portion.

The message was to notify the colonel that Indians were raiding the Kansas settlements. I was accompanied by but one companion, Johnny Langford, a half-breed Cherokee Indian, and when we started there was no certainty of our reaching our destination nor of our ultimate return. However, we were both possessed with a desire for a real, hazardous adventure, and furthermore, had been promised one hundred dollars each by Colonel Bankhead to make the trip.

During the first night we ran into a small band of Indians, no doubt belonging to one of the raiding parties. We discovered them through the noise they were creating, for they were evidently celebrating the success of some recent deviltry. As we had "lost no Indians," we went around this camp.

We made the trip in about twenty hours. Upon our reaching Colonel Bradley's command, he asked us how soon we could return to Wallace with a message for Colonel Bankhead. We informed him that we were very tired and that our horses must have some rest, as they had been ridden very hard and would need to recuperate several hours before they would be in condition for the return trip.

The colonel said: "I am very anxious to have you return as quickly as possible, as these despatches are very important and may be the means of saving the lives of a great many settlers. Of course, you must have some rest. Now if you will be ready to return in four or five hours I will give you fresh mounts and one hundred dollars each."

We replied, "All right," and after we had rested several hours and had a good meal were ready to move on. This, by the way, was the first time in my life that I was ever possessed of such a sum of money at any one time.

We reached Wallace in about twenty-four hours, although on the return my horse became exhausted and I had to abandon him near Lake Creek. We made the remaining distance, about sixteen miles, relieving each other by alternately riding the other horse. We were fortunate in not encountering any Indians on the return.

In a day or so I returned to the spot where I had left my played-out mount but found him dead. The saddle equipment had been carried away, and my horse partly cut up and the meat taken. From the pony tracks in the vicinity we were positive it was the work of Indians.

Soon after Langford and I had made this trip from Wallace to Colonel Bradley's command, Langford was made an assistant wagon-master at the post. One day, while on his way to a sub-station with some stores, he had trouble with one of his teamsters named Roche and killed him. In the fracas Langford was shot through the shoulder. On his return to Wallace the commanding officer thoroughly investigated the shooting, finally exonerating Langford, as it appeared he had shot Roche in self-defense, Roche firing the first shot and wounding Langford.

Several months later Langford was hanged by a drunken

mob led by Roche's brother. Langford was out at Rose Creek Ranch cooking for the hay outfit and was sleeping on the roof of the ranch house. When the mob went to get him (it being in the night) a man named McClure, owner of the ranch, called Langford down-stairs but did not inform him that the mob was there. Had he done so there would be a different story to relate. They never would have taken him alive, and the chances were greatly in his favor of either escaping or driving the mob away, as mobs are usually cowardly.

They rushed Langford into a wagon and took him to a lone tree near the stage station, to hang him. He told the men very plainly what he thought of them. Not wishing to die with his boots on, he took them off and struck the driver of the wagon over the head with one of them, then tried to jump from the wagon but failed. Arriving at the lone tree, Langford told them he was not afraid to die and that if there was any such thing as coming back to earth and haunting them he would do it, and make their lives a hell on earth. He then climbed the tree without assistance, attached the rope to one of the limbs, gave an Indian war whoop and jumped. I do not vouch for this tale but a man whom I have reason to believe was a member of the mob told me the story. I do know that two of the gang had no peace of mind as long as I knew them. Whether it was a guilty conscience or Langford carrying out his threat—who knows?

Six men connected with the Rose Creek Ranch—Comstock, Dixon, Sharp Grover, Langford and two others, were killed, the two latter by Indians, while working in the ranch garden. I was the seventh man to take possession of this ranch. Many predicted that I would be the next man to die with my boots on, but up to the present time their prophecy has not been fulfilled.

Shortly after returning from the rescue of Colonel Forsyth's command we started out on another scout, Colonel Henry C. Bankhead commanding. The command was composed of three companies of the Fifth Infantry and three troops of the Tenth Cavalry (colored). Our transportation numbered thirty-five six-mule wagons. The infantry rode in the wagons as they usually did in those days, so they could make better time after Indians.

Arriving at Lake Station, Colorado, we went into camp. During the night a very severe snowstorm came up, the wind blowing from the north, and a number of the tents were blown down. We had to remain two or three days until the storm ceased. It was hard on the men but much worse on the animals as they had no shelter, being tied to the wagons.

Upon breaking camp, we expected to reach the headwaters of the Republican River in three or four days' march. We were in a new country; the scouts knew nothing about that section and we had no maps to guide us. The country had never been mapped. The command suffered for want of water. The cooks found sufficient for cooking purposes by melting the snow, but the poor animals were obliged to go waterless. While in camp they had drunk very little water because of the extreme cold and when the weather warmed up they became very thirsty. On the morning of the third day after leaving camp, the scouts found a water hole at the head of a sandy gulch. Doubtless the mules also smelled the water, as they pricked up their long ears and began to travel faster, finally beginning to trot and then breaking into a gallop. The drivers were having trouble managing them and it looked very much as if there would be a stampede, but the teamsters finally had their mules under control, aided by the men in the wagons, although two or three wagons had been turned over and a few of the tongues broken.

Upon reaching the water, the mules were unhitched and led down in small bunches to drink, as the water hole was very small, but four or five feet in diameter and about a foot deep. It flowed but a few yards and then disappeared in the sand. The men had considerable trouble leading the animals to the water and had to pull some of them away by main strength after they had drunk as much as was thought best. As it was, a few suffered from colic.

I was riding an Indian pony named "Squaw," which had been captured from the Indians on Sand Creek, Colorado, by Major Graham of the Tenth Cavalry. This animal did not appear to be as thirsty as the others, which I accounted for in this way: While grazing, the pony would lap up the snow with the grass and therefore get considerable moisture with it. The other animals did not do this. Many of the horses tried to eat the snow, which no doubt increased their thirst. Wild horses and those on the ranges seemed to be able to go without water much longer than those that depended upon being fed and watered regularly. Range horses will paw the snow away and find food underneath; others will not, but in time necessity teaches them this.

At this water hole there had been quite a large Indian encampment. This must have been about the time of the Forsyth fight on the Arickaree, and no doubt these same Indians were engaged in that affair, for the place where the fight occurred was not very far away.

On the next day's march we came to a stream which we thought was the Republican. We followed it down for a few miles, when, to our great surprise, we found we were on the Forsyth battleground. Upon this occasion we found the heads of the scouts' dead horses all placed in a peculiar position, undoubtedly the work of the Indians engaged in the Forsyth fight. These heads had been placed in a hollow square, all facing to the north. In the center of this square had been left an opening about six feet wide, pointing to the south. On each side of this opening had been placed three or four of the heads, thus forming a wing about eight feet in length. The ground was well packed down around and inside of this square. Indications were that the Indians had returned after the fight, remaining there several days, dancing and celebrating.

From this point we returned to the post, after a march of five or six days. We did not discover any fresh signs of Indians on this scout, although we were gone nearly a month.

CHAPTER IV

IN CHARGE OF A BULL TRAIN

THE summer of 1869 I had charge of a bull train belonging to Newman & Jones, of Leavenworth, Kansas. They were government contractors and general freighters, hauling stores from the terminus of the Kansas Pacific Railroad. I had eighteen wagons with trails, each wagon having ten and twelve yoke of oxen attached. These large wagons with their trails each held from ten to twelve thousand pounds of freight.

In ascending steep grades and going through bad places we would cut off the trail and return for it after all the rough spots had been passed. In addition to the driver there were my assistant and a night herder, as well as a man who drove the "calf-yard."* The man who drove the lead wagon was the cook and received extra pay. There were twenty-one men in my outfit. Each driver was furnished with a gun that he carried in a loop on the near side of his wagon, where he could reach it quickly if Indians were discovered.

Going into camp, a corral was always formed. The first wagon turned to the right, the second to the left, the others bearing in toward each other, stopping in line when about twenty feet apart. The other wagons swung out well to the right and left and were so driven that the poles overlapped the rear wheels of the preceding wagon, the center wagons having to swing out quite a bit to form the circle and the

---

*Cavayard—caballado—Spanish for "horseherd."

rear wagons slightly less. The last two wagons were so driven that they were about the same distance apart as the two front ones. These openings were always connected with chains or a rope. These corrals were formed to drive the cattle into when yoking them, for protection from storms or Indian attacks. I have experienced some terrible storms in which the cattle would become terrified and many of the wagon covers would be torn to shreds.

On one of my trips from Sheridan to Denver I made the quickest time on record. I covered the distance, about two hundred and thirty miles, in eleven and one-half days, making an average of twenty miles a day. Bull trains usually average about twelve miles and mule trains eighteen miles a day. Only grazing is depended on to sustain the cattle, and in order to keep the animals in good condition longer drives can not well be made. Two drives a day were made. At daybreak the night herder drove the cattle into the corral. The bull-whackers arose at once, yoked the cattle and the train moved out. About ten o'clock the train stopped, the bulls were turned out to graze and were given water if there was any. The cook then got breakfast. Having prepared everything the night before, it was a quick job. About two or three o'clock the train moved on again and completed the day's journey.

I had to make three drives a day. We were loaded mostly with salt in barrels, consigned to Bartell & Co., to-day the leading grocers of Denver. There was a salt famine at the time and my employers had contracted to deliver the salt at a specified time. This was the reason for making a forced drive.

My arrival in Denver created considerable excitement. An account of it, with the record-breaking time we made, was published in all the territorial papers. I think the only time I ever felt right proud was on this occasion, riding a fine mule, Mexican spurs at my heels, two guns in my belt, huge sombrero on my head, leading my train through the streets. The only thing I lacked to be a typical wagon-master was long hair.

While en route on this trip I was accidentally wounded by a bullet from my own rifle. I was sleeping in one of the wagons and in making up my bed while in a cramped position I had to remove my Winchester, a sixteen-shot rifle. I leaned out of the front end of the wagon and placed the gun against the wagon-tongue, and when ready to replace the weapon I was obliged to lean well over to reach it. I carelessly grasped the gun by the muzzle, and as I raised it the hammer struck the wagon-tongue. The rifle was discharged, the bullet in its flight passing through my coat and up through the fleshy part of my arm, very close to my arm-pit, making quite a bad wound. Had the ball passed a trifle closer I probably would not be here to tell the tale. I had loaned the weapon to my assistant wagon-master to shoot some antelope and in ejecting the shell he had brought a loaded cartridge into the barrel, which he failed to remove.

The *Denver News* published quite an account of my train being attacked by Indians and of my being wounded.

On another trip I camped at Kiowa Springs, about eighty miles from Denver. As we approached the springs we saw that the ranch house had been burned. The ruins were yet smoldering. We found the bodies of a woman and child who had been killed by the Indians. My assistant recognized the woman as a Mrs. Archer. Everything indicated that they had been killed the previous night. We buried the bodies, proceeded on our way, and the following day met Mr. Archer, who had been to Denver for supplies. As I did not have the heart to notify him of his great loss, I asked my assistant to do so and allowed him to return with Mr. Archer.

Returning from Denver, we camped at Lake Station, one hundred and twenty miles distant. The first question asked us upon our arrival was, "Did you see any Indians?" A party consisting of a man, his wife, two children and four other men, was camped there. They told me that Indians had fired on them that morning and showed me three or four places where bullets had struck the wagon. The men had been working on the Union Pacific Railroad, and were on their way to get employment on the Kansas Pacific.

We did not see an Indian on the whole trip. I relate this incident to show how Indians can roam about and yet not be seen. On our return trip from Denver we were loaded with wool, hides and lumber.

CHAPTER V

IN MAY, 1870, I had been in the employ of the post trader at Fort Wallace for nearly two years and had saved a few hundred dollars. I became interested in the Rose Creek Ranch, buying the property from the widow of Frank Dixon. To-day it is one of the largest and best-known ranches in western Kansas.

Soon after I sublet the contract for supplying the troops at Wallace with fresh beef. The contractor, Chester A. Thomas, of Topeka, furnished me with one hundred and fifty beef cattle, which had been driven from the Cherokee country in southern Kansas. They were worth about six thousand dollars, and I was to pay for them as the contractor received his pay from the government. I had had the contract only a short time when a terrific thunder-storm came up, stampeding my cattle. My herder, Jack Esmond, stayed with them during the storm but was not able to keep them together. When he had returned them to the corral there were thirty-two head missing. At the time of the stampede I was hauling hay from the ranch to feed my cattle during the winter. I did not know of the loss until the following morning. We then made preparations to go after them.

Not knowing how long we should be gone, we provided ourselves with food to last a day or two, consisting of bacon, coffee, bread, sugar and salt. These extra rations were not really necessary, as in those days there was plenty of game everywhere.

It was in the fall and the nights were getting chilly, so we each took an extra blanket along, which we strapped to our saddles. We could not very well follow the trail, it being almost obliterated by the storm of rain and hail. Esmond thought he could go very near the place where the stampede had occurred. The cattle had kept together until an unusually heavy clap of thunder occurred, followed by a vivid flash of lightning, by which Esmond observed that some of the cattle were breaking away. It being impossible to hold the herd, he had kept with the larger portion.

We started out and after some hours found the trail of the lost cattle and followed it until darkness overtook us. We here made camp, starting out again at daybreak. The cattle were drifting south, as they usually do in a country which is strange to them. In an hour or so we discovered where they had lain down for a rest during the night. It also appeared that when they got up they had started back toward the post. After trailing them a few miles we found where they had rested again, and this time, when they started, it was apparently toward the south. This indicated that they were bewildered.

We continued on their trail until nearly dark, expecting to overtake them within a short time, as the trail was getting quite fresh; but just at this time another terrific hail storm broke loose. We were on the open prairie and had to dismount, having all we could do to hold our horses. Some of the hailstones were as large as robins' eggs and the ground was literally covered with them. This, of course, wiped out the trail again, so we were "up in the air." But as the storm came from the north we knew the cattle would continue traveling south, and, during the storm, would hasten the speed at which they were going. We figured that we were not many miles from the Arkansas River and that the cattle would probably go there, as they were headed in that direction. We, therefore, determined to go to the river, which we did not think the herd would try to cross, as it was quite a formidable stream.

We then planned to hunt the country over before returning home. About that time our food had nearly given out, but we found jack rabbits and an antelope or two that had been killed by the hail, so we were all right as long as there was meat in the larder.

At this time the noted Seventh Cavalry, General Custer's regiment, was encamped about one hundred miles north of us, and their horses stampeded in the same storm. Their animals were on the lariat when the storm burst upon them, and one or two men were killed and several injured while trying to prevent the stampede. The injuries were inflicted by flying picket pins. Some of their horses were picked up and brought into Wallace.

We proceeded to the Arkansas River but saw no signs of our cattle. We discovered, however, that a large herd had passed up the river within the last day or so, and it occurred to me that my steers might have mixed with this herd. I, therefore, decided to follow it. We had gone but a short distance when I observed a stake about four feet high driven into the ground alongside the road. To this a paper was attached which set forth that some Indians had tried to run off the horses of the party writing the note, and warned any who should read the note to beware of the redskins. It was signed "Hardesty."

We were quite positive that the party ahead of us had placed the notice, and that another herd of cattle or horses was following. My herder, Esmond, had been a soldier in a Colorado volunteer regiment during the Civil War, serving a great deal of his time in the Arkansas River country. He had been up and down the river several times, escorting wagon trains and scouting, so he was quite familiar with the country. He said we were in what was known as the "Big Bend" of the Arkansas, and that there was a big alkali bottom known as the "Twenty-mile Bottom" between us and Bent's old fort, where he had been stationed, and that we had to pass it. It was considered dangerous to go through it by day because of the rattlesnakes, buffalo gnats, centipedes and tarantulas, so travelers passed through it at night.

We decided to pursue this course. Before arriving at the bottom we saw a smoke a little way up the river, of which we were suspicious, and Esmond said he would go ahead and investigate it. I took the horses down to a dry gulch where they could not be seen, and he went forward on foot, taking to the willows and brush to screen his movements. While he was away, I unsaddled to give the horses a brief rest. My animal lay down and rolled and when he got to his feet I observed that he had received a severe puncture in his side from the sharp willow points. The wound bled freely although it was not dangerous. Esmond soon returned and reported that the smoke was from a campfire, evidently made by the Hardesty outfit, so we continued on our way rejoicing.

We soon came to the Twenty-mile Bottom. As we had a long night ride ahead of us and our horses were tired and hungry, we stopped a while to allow them to graze and then moved out again. Soon after midnight I found that I could not stand the strain longer and exclaimed, "Rattlesnakes and tarantulas be damned!" I was tired and sleepy, too, and said I was going to stop and take a nap. Esmond said he could stand it if I could, so we unsaddled, lariated our horses and went to sleep. We knew there was no danger from Indians, as they do their deviltry just before dark or at daylight.

Along toward dawn we heard some one helloing. It proved to be Mr. Hardesty, the owner of the cattle herd. He was driving two or three head of stock out of the willows. He told me that no strays had come into his herd and invited us to make ourselves at home; that the grub wagon was on ahead and when we overtook it to ask the cook for something to eat.

When I first arose I shook one of my blankets and a rattler nearly four feet in length, having five buttons, dropped out. It had apparently crawled into the blankets to keep warm.

At that time we were about eighty miles across country from Fort Wallace. As we were riding government horses and they were getting rather worn, I concluded to ride to Fort Lyon, Colorado, about thirty miles away, to see if I could get some fresh mounts. If I succeeded, I planned to return and look around again before going home. Hardesty's cook gave us something to eat and we started out. When night came on we were at old Fort Lyon, formerly one of Colonel Bent's Indian trading stations. In 1859, Bent leased Bent's new fort to the government, and the place was at once garrisoned. The post was at first called Fort Fauntleroy, after the colonel of the old First Dragoons, but the name was soon changed to Fort Wise, in honor of the governor of Virginia. When the Civil War began, Governor Wise joined the Confederates and Fort Wise had to be renamed, this time in honor of General Lyon, killed at Wilson's Creek, Missouri, the first Union general to fall in the war. In 1866 the river began cutting away the bank and threatened to destroy Fort Lyon, and the place was abandoned and New Fort Lyon was built twenty miles farther up the river, two miles below the mouth of the Purgatoire. (To this day, Americans often pronounce this name "Picketwire.")

We had been unsaddled but a short time when we heard some children across the river.   This was a great surprise as we had no idea any one was near there.   Esmond said that he was going to cross the river and see if he could get some coffee.   Just below us he pointed out a swimming-hole where the men used to bathe and in which a man from his troop had been drowned.   He said there had formerly been a ford near by and this we searched for, but did not find.   It had been so many years previously that it had been washed out.   We decided to cross anyhow, but found the water much deeper than we had expected.   We removed our clothing, rolled our shirts and trousers in a bundle and started to ford the stream.   As the water grew deeper we had to hold our bundles high above our heads.   Esmond was a little ahead of me, carefully feeling his way, when suddenly he disappeared, bundle and all!   He soon came to the surface and struck out for shore, landing safely.   I then waded a little farther up-stream and found the water not quite so deep, but still it was up to my armpits.

After a great deal of trouble in making our way through a network of wild grapevines we came to a camp.   A woman and her children were there, picking grapes and making wine.   Her husband had gone to Las Animas for barrels to hold the wine.   She made some coffee and gave us something to eat, also some wine to drink, and it certainly made us feel "away up in the pictures."   We remained there a while, after which she showed us a crossing less dangerous than the one we had just come over.   She then warned us to look out for horse-thieves, as there were some in that country.

We returned to where we had left our horses, finding a good ford, but at some little distance from where we had bivouacked.   We wanted to move our camp, as was customary when in the Indian country or when horse-thieves were around, so that in case of an attack or an attempt to steal our horses the thieves could not locate us. It had commenced raining and we moved out a mile or so to an old cemetery, where we could get some shelter by the side of a high wall that was around the burial place. Here we bivouacked in one corner, which protected us quite a little from the storm, and we put in a very good night. Five years after this incident Fort Lyon, Colorado, was my first army station (in 1875), and while I was there I was detailed to exhume the remains in this same cemetery and remove them to the national cemetery at Fort Leavenworth, Kansas.

The following morning I started for Fort Lyon to see about getting fresh mounts. Arriving there, I reported to the commanding officer, Colonel Richard I. Dodge, then major of the Third Infantry. He had served in the Civil War and had a great deal of Indian experience. I explained to the colonel about losing my cattle and asked him for remounts. He said he had no horses but would let me have some mules, stating, however, that I must return them to the post, for if I went to Wallace with the animals it would be the last that he would ever see of them. I had to decline the mules, however, not knowing when I might be able to return them.

In a day or so I started for Wallace, changing my mind about hunting any longer for the lost cattle. The first day we returned to the place where the woman and children were making wine. We were received by the entire family with genuine western hospitality. A day or so after leaving camp my animal played out, so one of us had to walk. Esmond did most of this, as my feet were in a terrible condition from wearing rubbers. When we reached a point about twenty miles from my ranch we discovered a cattle trail crossing the road, going toward the railroad. I was quite sure these

SITTING BULL
The Sioux Leader

WASHAKIE
Chief of the Shoshones

CHIEF GALL
A Leader in the Custer Battle. (Photo by D. F. Barry.)

BLACK COAL
War Chief of the Arapahoes

SHARP NOSE
Head Chief of the Arapahoes

were my lost cattle, but we could not follow the trail owing to the condition of our animals, so we went in to the post. Not having been able during the two or three preceding days to ride my exhausted horse, I thought I would try to ride him into the post, as I did not want the quartermaster to know the condition he was in.

The following morning I went to the commanding officer and told him about discovering the cattle trail, and asked him to let me have another mount.   He declined, stating that I had killed one of the horses I had been riding.   The animal had died in the post corral during the night but this was the first I had heard of it.   Had I known the horse had died that night I scarcely think I should have gone to the commanding officer, much less ask him for another mount.   However, he was a very kind man and knew I could ill afford to lose the cattle, so he relented and let me have two mules.   With these I started out again.   We found the trail and followed it with some difficulty.   Presently we discovered where the cattle had been herded in a deep ravine on Eagle Tail.   Apparently they had not been there for several days, so we concluded they had been driven away, and that it would be a waste of time to hunt further for them.

Accordingly, we proceeded to Cheyenne Wells.   At that time the Kansas-Pacific was building its road into Denver. We inquired at Cheyenne Wells if any one had picked up some stray cattle or knew of any being found.   One man told us he had heard of some lost cattle being found.   He thought they had been driven to Kit Carson.   I asked why he thought so and he said a man lived there who had told him he would pay a good price for all the stray cattle brought in.   I told this man if he would help me find my cattle I would pay him well for his time and trouble.   He agreed to accompany us; so we started for Kit Carson.   I inquired who this man was that had made such an offer, and my informant stated it was a butcher of the town who supplied meat to the grading camps. When within three or four miles of the place we met this butcher. I asked him if he had seen or heard of my stray cattle in his country and gave him the brands. He replied that he had not. We had not proceeded very far before I saw a small herd of cattle grazing, and as we approached them I recognized a dun cow and a steer. I asked the herder to whom the animals belonged and he said, "A butcher in town." I told him they were stolen cattle and belonged to me and that I wanted them. He refused to give them up so I just took them. The herder made a break to pull a gun but Esmond was too quick for him. He had the herder covered in an instant and ordered him to put up his gun or there would be a killing right there.

Meantime the butcher came up and demanded to know the cause of the trouble. I told him the cattle were mine and that he had lied to me about them. I demanded them and after some plain talk he acknowledged the cattle had been picked up and that he had paid the man who had brought them in, believing they belonged to a herd on the Arkansas. He stated further that he had notified the owner but had not heard from him, and also that he had intended to advertise and register the brands according to the Colorado law, but that through neglect had failed to do so. He then said I could have the cattle by paying what they had cost him, which, including care, amounted to about one hundred and fifty dollars. I told the butcher it was a well-known fact that he was paying men to bring in cattle. He denied this, of course, whereupon the man who had accompanied me from Kit Carson told the butcher he was a liar, that he had made such offers to him. After some hot words we parted company and I drove the cattle to a corral in town.

There was where I made a mistake. I should have

started home with them for I could have rushed them out of the territory before the butcher could have prevented me. The next morning I went to the corral to get my cattle but found an officer at the gate, who told me I could not take them until I had proved my property and that, furthermore, I would have to pay all expenses pertaining to the care of them. I then engaged a lawyer and got out a writ of replevin, to do which I had to go into a justice's court. The butcher swore he had paid a man three dollars a day for herding the cattle. Incidentally, I heard that the herder was the justice's boy, and had received only one dollar and twenty-five cents a day for his services. This fact I proved by bringing the boy into his father's court as a witness. I also proved that the butcher had not complied with the territorial laws in regard to stray stock. I showed the fellow up as he deserved to have been shown, and the court declared that the cattle were mine but required me to give bond in case anything should arise in the premises, and furthermore, required me to pay the butcher one hundred and twenty-five dollars and the court costs! I protested, but it was useless. By the time I had recovered my cattle they had cost me nearly two hundred dollars. Naturally I have always felt that that justice was no friend of mine. A few months after this incident the butcher's partner was hung by some cattlemen for killing cattle that did not belong to him.

When I came into the army service in 1875 my first station was Fort Lyon, Colorado. Happening into the post-office at Las Animas one day to get some stamps, I recognized my "friend" the butcher. He was the post-master, and owner of the store, one of the largest in town! I do not think he recognized me, so concluded it was just as well not to renew the acquaintance, as he had "reformed" and become a member of good society.

CHAPTER VI

PERILS OF THE PRAIRIE

WHILE herding my beef cattle I was called in to the post to attend to some business connected with my beef contract, remaining away much longer than I intended. On my return, my cattle were not in sight. As they had been in the country but a few days, this worried me considerably. I did not know in which direction they had gone, so commenced to hunt for their trail. While I was thus occupied, a soldier rode up somewhat excited and informed me that the post herd which he had in charge were missing and that he had been looking for them for some time. The post herd was composed of the milch cows which I had loaned the officers and some of the companies. I told the soldier if I found the cows I would drive them in, and requested that he do likewise if he came across my steers.

About a mile from the post I found the trail of my cattle and followed it as rapidly as possible. It was rather slow work at first, for there were a great many cattle tracks around the post. I shortly found a well-defined trail, so made better progress. I finally overtook the cattle seven or eight miles from the post. They were traveling south. They had gone over the bluffs on to some table-land. On returning with the cattle, I saw four or five mounted men come out of the head of a deep ravine. They hesitated some minutes, seeming to be consulting one another. Presently others joined them, until there were about twenty riders congregated together. I could not make up my mind whether they were friends or foes.   It appeared to me, however, that they were foes, as frequently small bands of Indians roamed through the country,   They finally began to advance on me at a rapid gait, some of them forming a semicircle on each side of the main group.   Evidently the movement was to surround me so that I could not escape them.   It looked at that distance as if some of them carried lances, which fact convinced me that they were Indians beyond question.   I was very badly frightened and did not know what to do under the circumstances.   My first impulse was to make a run for my life, but my horse was not swift and, moreover, was considerably jaded, so I concluded I would have to make a fight and sell my life as dearly as possible.   I thought of killing my horse or one of the beeves and using the carcass as a breastwork, but finally determined to charge the group when they got a little nearer.

I dropped back into the herd, to get as much protection as possible in case they fired on me while approaching.   I thought if I made a charge, shooting right and left, it might astonish them so that I would be enabled to break through their line.   I had read in fiction that men had often saved themselves from death at the hands of Indians by doing some daring act.   Why not I, in this case?   If my horse were shot under me I could use him as a barrier.   I had heard men say that in a fight with Indians they would save the last cartridge to use on themselves rather than fall into savage hands; but my idea was to use your last shot on your foe and no doubt you might kill an Indian.   There was always a bare chance of an escape, but if unsuccessful one could fight with any instrument and continue fighting until the Indians killed you.   I had two Colt revolvers of heavy caliber and some extra ammunition; was a fair shot and could manipulate my guns with either hand.   I pulled my pistols and was all ready to make the effort of my life.

Before moving out of the herd to make the charge I thought best to take one more good look at the advancing horsemen. It was a good thing I did so, for I then saw they were soldiers, and who should ride up but Captain Satterlee Plummer of the Seventh Cavalry. His first greeting was, "Young man, it is a mighty good thing for you that you did not make a run for it, as I should have thought you were a cattle thief and killed you sure." Some of the men were at "advance carbines," which had given me the impression they carried lances; others wore no hats, which had also puzzled me and given me the impression they were Indians. The captain told me the soldier who had been looking for the milch cows had reported that both herds had run off and that he had seen some horsemen who looked very much like Indians. The commanding officer had, therefore, ordered Captain Plummer out with his troop, the men with him being all that were in barracks at the time.

He offered to assist me in driving the cattle to the post but I thanked him and told him it was not necessary. After he left me, however, I commenced to lose my courage and had a case of "nerves." I did not recover from my fright for a long while.

We had another danger to encounter besides Indians, cattle and horse thieves and gun men, and that was rabies, mostly confined to mad skunks and occasionally a coyote or a prairie wolf. I knew at least five hunters who had been bitten by skunks in camp. All were bitten while asleep.

Joseph Farrell, who had been one of my herders, died from hydrophobia. He was one of the finest specimens of manhood I ever saw. One time I saw a hunter who had been brought into the post suffering from skunk-bite. I did not see him in his convulsions, but was told by those who witnessed it that it was a terrible spectacle.

The post surgeon told me of a soldier who had come

under his observation at Fort Hays, Kansas, who had been bitten by a prairie wolf. When the man was brought into the hospital there were no indications of any bad effect from the bite, but he was given the usual treatment as a precautionary measure and was kept in the hospital for fear he might develop some symptoms.

One Sunday morning at inspection the commanding officer asked the surgeon why he did not return the man for duty. He was told that excitement might do the man considerable harm, and it was thought best that he should be kept under the immediate supervision of the surgeon. The colonel, who had the reputation of being a martinet, laughed and said, "Mark him for duty; there is no danger." The surgeon replied, "Before returning him for duty, I wish you would give me a written order, so that if anything should arise I would be relieved of all responsibility in the matter." However, the order was not given. Commanding officers, because of lack of technical education in medical matters, are somewhat cautious of giving instructions regarding the treatment of patients in the hospital, although it is their duty to give orders regarding the general discipline of the hospital.

Later the doctor was ordered to a post near by on court-martial duty. He was absent only a few days but on his return found that the soldier had gone on duty. At the next inspection he saw the man in ranks and noted an unusual look in his eyes. He thereupon told the troop commander that the man should be returned to the hospital at once, which was done. In a very short time he went into convulsions and died.

During the winter of 1867, at Fort Larned, Kansas, a two-company post, an officer and two men of the Third Infantry were bitten by a coyote infected with rabies. The first man to get bitten was walking Post Number One at the guard-house; the second man was bitten while crossing the parade; and the officer was attacked and received a bite in the foot while sitting on his porch steps playing with a child. The maddened animal then jumped through an open window into the hospital where it was killed. The first victim died. The second soldier and the officer recovered. It was thought probable that the virus was expended upon the trousers leg of the man on guard, which doubtless saved the lives of the others.

On November 14, 1914, I was a guest at the Hotel Sutter, San Francisco. A Major Thompson, a retired army officer, was staying at the hotel. One day we were discussing old times, and he mentioned that he had belonged to the Third Infantry and was stationed at one time at Fort Larned. I happened to mention the episode of the mad coyote and the two soldiers and the officer who had been bitten there. To my great surprise he said, "I am the officer who was bitten." He promised to give me a typewritten account of the occurrence, but was taken ill soon after and died. He was a veteran of the Civil War. I had known most of the officers of the Third Infantry, but had never met the major until 1914. He was buried in the National Cemetery at the Presidio, San Francisco, California.

It was in December, 1870, that I received my appointment as post trader at Fort Wallace, and had been east to replenish my stock of merchandise. While returning from the trip we were snowed in for several days at Monument Station on the Kansas-Pacific Railroad. Had there not been plenty of buffalo meat awaiting shipment, some of us might have gone hungry.

I had been telling some of my western experiences, which seemed to interest the passengers. In one of my narratives I told of an old frontiersman of whom I had been very fond but who had been killed by Indians only a few months before, about twenty-five miles north of the station. He had been wounded in the Mexican War, was a free-state man in the Kansas troubles, served in the Civil War and had had several encounters with border ruffians and Indians.

In the midst of our conversation I happened to look out of the window and observed a couple of wagons crossing the prairie toward the station. It was a cold cheerless morning, and a man was walking beside one of the wagons, evidently to keep warm. As they drew closer I noticed that this man had a peculiarity in his walk that seemed familiar. I thereupon remarked that he walked like my friend Douglas, one leg being shorter than the other, and said that had I not known my old friend was dead I should have sworn it was he.

When the wagons drove up to the station I was dazed and mystified, for I recognized the man as my supposed dead friend Douglas. I rushed out to see him and from our greeting one would have thought it was father and son who had been reunited after a long separation. As a matter of fact, he had always called me his "boy."

Douglas informed me that he had left the buffalo range the year before as the animals were getting rather scarce and there was no money in buffalo hides. He had removed to Texas and tried raising cotton, but the weevil damaged his crop and he did not want "any more Texas," so had come back to Kansas and was going to renew hunting as a livelihood.

About three months after this conversation Douglas was bitten by a skunk while sleeping and died from hydrophobia. The report that he had been killed by Indians grew out of the finding of an abandoned camp with a wagon and some cooking utensils, which it was supposed belonged to Douglas, who had been hunting in that part of the country.

After a man had undergone the hardships and exposures which my dear old friend experienced, it seemed rather hard for him to die as the result of a bite from a miserable skunk.

CHAPTER VII

MY SECOND CATTLE VENTURE

WHEN I obtained the contract to furnish the troops at Wallace with fresh beef I commenced buying broken-down stock from the immigrants and from Texas herds passing through the country on their way to Colorado and other territories. I usually got them at a very reasonable price as there was no other place within many miles where they could be otherwise disposed of. The stock I got from immigrants was very good, some of the milch cows being of fine breed. I used to lend them to the officers and different companies of soldiers. During the year I accumulated nearly one hundred head of stock. They wintered so well, as did also the buffalo and wild horses ranging in the country, thriving on the succulent buffalo grass, that I became convinced western Kansas was destined to be a fine grazing country. I interested my uncle and he furnished me with the funds to go into the cattle business. It was the first herd driven into Wallace County, and mine was the only herd in western Kansas for a number of years. The next herd came into the country in 1875 and was owned by Fred Harvey. That was about the time he established the Harvey eating houses on the Kansas-Pacific and Santa Fé Railroads, which are now so popular with the traveling public.

I had much to contend with to keep my cattle on the range. It was not home to them, so they were inclined to stray, and when once they got away they were likely to keep

46

traveling until they were rounded up.   There was not another herd or ranch within a hundred miles of me.   There
were, however, immense herds of buffalo ranging in the
country and at times they would stampede my stock.   Then,
too, the Indians killed my cattle and ran off my riding stock.
Horse and cattle thieves annoyed me considerably.   In addition, there were the cold storms to combat.   All these
troubles kept me very busy.   It was hard to get herders at
times owing to the condition of the country, so I was compelled to go out and hunt stray stock alone.   On these occasions I would scout the surrounding country for miles and
be gone several days at a time.   I have encountered storms
so severe as to render it uncertain that I would return home
safe if at all.   Many times I vowed that if I ever reached the
post safe I would never go out again; but on my return I
would forget all my sufferings and ere long start out again.
It was by this kind of work that I made the cattle business a
success.   Had there been other stockmen in the country
conditions would have been much easier, as we could have
worked together and I would not have had to combat many
of the difficulties alone.

It was in 1872 that my uncle, C. W. Babcock, of Lawrence, Kansas, surveyor-general of that state, furnished me
with capital of seven thousand, five hundred dollars with
which to enter the cattle-raising business in western Kansas.
I was to have the general management, paying all the running expenses of the herd, for one-half the increase.   The
contract was for five years.   The cattle were to be purchased
in Abilene, Kansas, where immense herds were driven every
year for the market from the Lone Star State.

Through a very exciting episode I came very near not
going into the cattle business.   The money was turned over
to me in Kansas City.   Instead of leaving the money in a
bank, which I could have done, I thought best to draw it

out and take it with me to Abilene and there deposit it. It was mostly in bills of large denomination so did not make a very bulky package.. I placed it in the inside pocket of my coat, not a very safe place, but my coat could be securely buttoned, the package could not easily be seen, and I thought I would take the chance of carrying it safely.

I drew the money from the bank one morning and went out to attend to some business. I then returned to my hotel for some luncheon and immediately thereafter went to the union depot and purchased my ticket for Abilene. While waiting for the train I thought of my money and placed my hand where the package should have been, but it was gone! I was mortified, chagrined and decidedly frightened. Several courses of action immediately rushed through my mind, but the question that bothered me most was, "What will my uncle think and say?" Naturally, I considered that the only thing I could do, under the circumstances, was to tell him of my loss and agree to repay him some day. However, I soon came to my senses. I did not want to report my loss to the police as it would only create excitement and be noised around, so I went to the driver of the hotel bus and asked him if he had seen or heard anything of a stray pocketbook. He said he had not and asked me how much money there was in it. When I told him he remarked, "Young man, it seems to me you are taking the matter of losing so much money rather quietly." I replied, "Well, what else can I do?" I told him I did not care to advertise my loss all over the country.

"Maybe you left it in your room at the hotel," he suggested. "Jump in, and I'll drive you there right away."

I offered to pay him for the trip but he would accept nothing. I told the hotel clerk of my loss. He called the maid who had charge of the room I had occupied but she had seen no pocketbook.

I then went to Peak & Marsh, wholesale dry-goods merchants, whom I had visited before going to the hotel to dinner.   I told Mr. Marsh of my loss.   He was a very excitable man who had known me for some time and had taken great interest in me.   He felt my loss keenly, asking if I had taken off my coat anywhere and laid it down.   It then came into my mind that I had removed my coat in the store while washing, and had laid it down on a pile of cloth on the counter.   I hastened to that particular counter and there was the lost pocketbook lying serenely between two bolts of cloth!   Needless to say, I felt better right away.   I purchased a money belt at once and went on my way rejoicing.

At Abilene I put up at the Drovers' Cottage, where a number of cattlemen were stopping.   One of them was Colonel King, the largest land owner and cattle raiser in Texas.   His widow, known as the "cattle queen of Texas," died in April, 1925.   She owned immense herds of cattle, sheep and horses.   Her land holdings are said to have been larger than the state of Rhode Island or Delaware.   I marched from Brownsville, Texas, to Fort Sam Houston (San Antonio) in 1898, and three days were occupied in passing through her lands.

I found the prices of cattle ranged from ten to fourteen dollars per head.   I bargained for six hundred and twenty-seven cows at thirteen dollars and a quarter per head, and eighty-seven long yearlings (cattle less than two years old) at seven dollars per head, also a yoke of cattle for the grub wagon.   The total amount was eight thousand three hundred and eighty-eight dollars.   Paying cash to the extent of my means, I drew on my uncle for the balance.   The cattle were to be delivered at Brookville, Kansas, on the Union Pacific Railroad.   I selected cows with big frames, good color and as short horns as possible, out of over two

thousand head.   After being cut away from the main
herd, they did not resemble the same cattle.   I intended to
turn blooded bulls into the herd to improve the progeny.   At
Brookville I was offered one thousand five hundred dollars
for my bargain over what the cattle had cost me.

I left Brookville for Wallace, two hundred and seventy-
five miles distant, by the old Smoky Hill trail.   I chose this
route because of water and grass.   My outfit was composed of three green hands who had come out to join me
at Abilene and learn the cattle business.   Two of them were
from New York City and they were thinking of investing
money if they found, after a little experience, that they liked
ranching.   I also had two professional cowboys, Asa Lathrop and Joe Edwards, and a cook who was one of my clerks
in the store and wanted to make the trip.   Billy Sullivan
was a good cook and I had him buy plenty of potatoes,
onions, flour, bacon, coffee and dried fruit, but no butter.
Bacon grease and flour gravy go pretty well on bread.
Some of the boys said they never did like butter.

There was a reason for this.   One day on the drive one
of the young men came to me and wanted some butter.   I
said, "The idea of cowboys eating butter!   I never heard
of such a thing.   They don't even like milk.   The next
thing I know, you boys will be wanting napkins and finger-
bowls."

However, I finally relented and told them they might buy
a couple of pounds at the first opportunity.   None of the
eastern youths was familiar with the saddle or knew anything about handling stock.   The young fellow who carried the butter was riding Kate, the mule.   Like all boys
just learning the cattle business, these youngsters thought it
necessary to wear spurs, the larger the rowels the better,
and the more they jingled in walking, the more pleased they
were.   Allen Clark was the young man carrying the butter.

He accidentally stuck his spurs into old Kate, which she re-
sented, and commenced to pitch with much enthusiasm.
Over her head went the rider, butter and all.   Instead of
dropping the package as he should have done when the mule
began to pitch, the greenhorn placed it between himself and
his overcoat which was tied to the saddle-horn.   When he
was picked up, dazed-like, he was asked what he had done
with the butter.   Upon investigation he discovered that
most of it was on his trousers.   The other boys howled with
delight but Clark managed to scrape some of the grease off,
exclaiming, "There is your damned old butter!   I never did
care for it, anyway." Between laughs the boys inquired why
he hadn't stuck to the mule, whereupon he earnestly replied:
"How could I, with all that grease between my legs?"

The cook, Billy Sullivan, never had driven bulls and
walking alongside them did not meet with his approval, so he
made reins out of some rope, attached them to the horns of
the oxen and guided them, sitting on his "throne" in the cook
wagon, a perfect picture of contentment.   One night we
arrived in camp after dark and Billy had to make some
biscuits for supper.   He made a mistake, and got hold of
the pail of wagon dope instead of the lard can.   We won-
dered what was the matter with the bread that it had such
a peculiar color but did not discover the mistake until next
morning.   I think the axle grease lubricated the boys'
tongues for they seemed to talk more than usual that night.

Before leaving Brookville I rebranded my cattle "W"
on the loin.   There was no regular chute that I could run
them through to brand them, but the Kansas Pacific Railroad
officials kindly allowed me to use their stock-yards, so I ran
the cattle on to their scales to brand them.

I started out of Brookville in good shape, calculating to
make drives of ten or twelve miles per day, so as to get my
herd on the grazing grounds in good condition for the win-

ter. I think it was on the third day's drive that I was
stopped by some armed ranchers and told that I could not
pass through their county, on account of the Texas cattle
fever.   I was therefore obliged to leave the regular trail and
go around quite a distance, making a difference of two or
three days' longer drive.   I was also having considerable
trouble with my city cowboys, they having had no experience.
They were willing enough but just didn't know what to do.
It made considerably more work for me as well as for my
two experienced hands, who were most competent men.

There had been a number of herds over the trail, so
whenever I could do so I would round up the cattle at night
on the old bed-grounds.   In such places they were more
quiet and not so restless as they would have been on a new
bed-ground.   About one o'clock in the morning they would
want to get up and graze, and it required quite a little skill
at such times to get them to lie down once more and remain
quiet until daybreak.   When my green hands were on herd
during those hours the cattle were pretty sure to get away,
or nearly so.   In fact, we all had to get up and help drive
them back on the bed-grounds.   Asa and Joe, the experienced cowpunchers, finally volunteered to take that watch
and remain on herd until morning.

One night when they were on herd we came very near
having a stampede caused by a herd of buffalo.   As they
were coming on the cattle jumped as one, jarring the ground
terrifically; it was almost equal to a clap of thunder.   We
all jumped up but Asa and Joe were "on to their job."   It
was wonderful how quickly they stopped the stampede.   I
do not believe the herd moved more than two hundred yards.

When cattle begin to get restless at night at first one or
two will arise and try to leave the herd to graze.   The
riders therefore have to continue jogging around the herd
to drive the strays back.   If they did not the entire herd

would be up and drifting in a very short time.   Singing to the cattle has a great charm for them.   It seems to act like a lullaby.   It is beneficial to the herder as well as the cattle because it keeps him from getting sleepy.

When we had reached a point within a few days' drive of Wallace one of the green hands, while on herd, let some fifty or sixty head stray away.   I did not discover it until we commenced to round up the herd for the night.   It was a great piece of carelessness although the country was quite unbroken.   I have always thought he got off his horse and went to sleep.   We succeeded in finding a few of them that night, but I could not tell just how many were gone without making a count, and that would have required some time and made considerable extra work, so I decided to send the main herd on and remain behind with one of the men, "Velocipede Charley," so called because he was always talking about riding his velocipede and of his great doings on it in New York.   Asa was responsible for the nickname.

Our plan was to scout the country and see if we could locate the lost cattle.   I expected to overtake the herd within a few hours so did not make preparation to remain away any length of time.   We hunted the country pretty thoroughly, without success, and then went over to a creek south of the Smoky; I think it was Walnut Creek.   However, we had no better success there, so remained that night. (That country was unsettled at the time.)   We did not get back to our camp on the Smoky until dark.   We were pretty hungry, not having eaten anything since morning and then only sparingly.   I remembered reading of some young hunters who were lost on the great plains of Texas, and, being without food, had gathered buffalo bones, placed them on a fire, cracked them and eaten the marrow.   We concluded to try it.   Billy had left the remainder of a hindquarter of buffalo in camp but the meat on it had been

about used up.   There were some onions and potato peel-
ings.   We found a couple of tomato cans and decided to
make a sort of stew.   It was mostly water with a flavoring
of onion and potato.   However, with that and the marrow
we managed to make out a fair sort of supper—but how
sick we were afterward! I really think we must have had
ptomaine poisoning.

The following day we found a few head of cattle on the
Smoky. While we were on Walnut Creek a herd had passed.
It was not very far ahead of us, so we overtook it that
night and found that a few more of our strays had come into
this herd.   We remained with the good people in charge
of that herd until we reached Wallace.   This was done to
save our horses, as they were pretty well fagged out.   My
cattle had arrived safely and I at once rounded them up and
counted them.   I found that I was short about a dozen. All
of them may not have been lost at the same time, as cattle
will be overlooked occasionally in heavy underbrush where
they go to get rid of mosquitoes and buffalo gnats.   I made
my mistake when I started out from Brookville without more
efficient men.   I should have had at least two more good
cowboys; so in trying to save a few dollars I lost out by it.
As a matter of fact, however, I do not blame the young man
who allowed the cattle to escape, as I myself let the cattle get
off the bed-ground one night.   I used to take the first herd
tour for the night, and on this occasion went to sleep in
spite of all I could do.   When I awakened, the cattle were
mostly up and leaving their bed-ground.   I tried to drive
them back but could not do it, and rather than awaken the
men I let them go.   It required some little time the next
morning to gather them up and get on the road.   There
was some excuse for my sleeping on herd, however, as there
was scarcely a night that I did not get up several times to
see if everything was all right.   The least little noise would

awaken me.   Had I called my men that night we should soon have rounded them up again, but I took the chance, as there was plenty of grass and water.   In the other case there was not.

In a few days I commenced to rebrand my cattle, throwing each one and placing the initial "H" on the fore shoulder, "W" on the side and "W" on the hip, in block letters. My uncle purchased thirty bulls from various ranchers around Lawrence, Kansas.   We got them very cheap as the farmers wanted to change them for new ones.   It is not best to let the same bulls run in a herd too long.   They were a fine lot.   Their first progeny (steers) were shipped to Kansas City at the age of three years and were purchased for the foreign market.   They were about the first lot of grass-fed cattle shipped overseas.

CHAPTER VIII

THE ROUND-UP

A GENERAL round-up takes place during the spring and autumn. This is the time when every man has to work. It is exciting, but save for the lack of sleep it is not exhausting, although to sit in the saddle from twelve to fifteen hours a day is certainly tiresome.

Each cowboy has his own "string" of eight or nine ponies, one to be used for the morning work and one for the afternoon. Each animal, therefore, would get a three days' rest before being used again. Separate ponies were also kept for night herding. The spring and early round-ups were especially to get the cattle back on the ranges, count them and brand the calves. There is much hard work and some risk in a round-up and also much fun. The meeting place was appointed where all the cattlemen gathered to make their plans and appoint a foreman or captain of the round-up. His authority was law. Each outfit was notified what section of the country it should cover. Usually every stockman had his own wagon. Some of the smaller outfits combined and in that way effected quite a saving. Each cattleman had his own range, where he endeavored to retain his cattle by line riders. There was an unwritten law that no cattleman should interfere with another's range. The cattle wandered off, to a great extent, but still kept on their ranges, which might cover several square miles.

The grand round-ups usually commenced at the source of some valley or stream. All the different outfits gathered there with their grub wagons, each carrying food and bedding. Each wagon was drawn by two or four horses and was driven by the cook. The men were called about three o'clock in the morning by the cook crying, "Come and get it." All hands turned out immediately. Dressing was a simple affair, after which each man rolled and corded his bedding. If he didn't the cook would leave it behind and he would be without it for the rest of the trip. When dressed, each man went to the fire, where he picked out a tin cup, tin plate, knife and fork and helped himself to the coffee and what food there was, squatting or standing as best suited him. Dawn was probably breaking by this time and the night wranglers were bringing in the pony herd.

The men ran ropes from the wagons at right angles to one another and into this rope corral the horses were driven. Usually a skilled roper would catch the ponies, for, if a man was unskilled and roped the wrong horse, or roped one in the wrong place, there was a chance that the whole herd would stampede.

Every man saddled and bridled his own animal and sometimes there was tall bucking, to the merriment of the crowd. It was bad taste to "go to leather"—that is, for a rider to grab the saddlehorn to steady himself under such conditions. As soon as the men were all saddled up the whole outfit started on the long circuit.

Usually, the foreman who had charge of a wagon was put in charge of several men by the round-up captain. He might keep his men together until they had gone twelve or fifteen miles from camp and then direct them in couples to take in certain sections of country. They would gather all the cattle they could find and gradually drive them to the meeting-place. Accompanying each wagon were usually eight or ten riders, while the extra horses were driven by two of the men who were known as "wranglers." These had charge of the pony herd day and night.   These men were fine horsemen, accustomed to riding half-broken animals at any speed over any sort of country, either by day or night.   They wore flannel shirts with loose handkerchiefs knotted around their necks, broad hats, and boots with jingling spurs.   Leather "chaps" protected their legs in riding through brushy country or cactus patches.

A morning ride might last six or eight hours, sometimes longer.   Each man had to take his turn at night guarding. The captain of the round-up assigned the guards, or notified the foreman of a wagon to do it.   Guards stood for two hours, the night herders usually being on duty from eight o'clock in the evening until four in the morning, when the night herders were relieved by the day herders.

There was a great deal of rough play, and as the men all carried revolvers—for usually there was a "bad man" among them—there was now and then a shooting affair.   A man who was a coward or who shirked his work, had a hard time. No man could afford to let himself be bullied or treated as a butt; on the other hand, if any one was looking for a fight he was certain to be accommodated.

The round-up having begun, the outfits proceeded downstream, driving in the cattle from both sides of the valley until they reached a home station.   All the cattle, consisting of several thousand, were rounded up many times.   Then each owner cut out his own brand.   There might be several cuttings-out by cattlemen who had adjoining ranches.   These herds were held by several cowpunchers, while only a few of the herders who worked for the owners were allowed to do the cutting out.   These were special men, well up in reading brands and with keen eyes, for in the springtime the hair on the cattle is yet long and it requires good eyesight to make out the different brands.   However, these men become so skilful at the business that they know the cattle belonging to their outfit by their looks. If a cow has a calf that has become separated from its mother she is allowed to remain in the herd until she has located her offspring. When the cattle are being gathered it quite often happens that cows will hide their calves in secluded places, leaving one of their number to guard them while the mothers go for water.

One of the greatest losses of the cattleman was occasioned by wolves. Large rewards were offered for the scalps of wolves, coyotes or mountain lions. In large herds one occasionally saw animals minus their tails. This was done by the wolves in trying to pull down the animal, as when hungry these fierce brutes will resort to any method to kill a calf or young steer.

On the owner's range he was allowed to cut out the mavericks and unbranded yearlings. The outfits took turns in furnishing meat for the different organizations. The beef killed was usually the mavericks. The word "maverick" originated from a man by that name who was in Texas, during the Civil War, where there were thousands of cattle without owners and therefore unbranded. Samuel A. Maverick, of San Antonio, was one of the first men to go into the business of gathering these loose cattle and branding them. He was formerly from South Carolina, a runaway boy. He had joined an expedition of about twenty men which invaded Mexico at the town of Mier, prior to the Mexican War and was captured there. The Mexicans killed many of them, choosing those to be shot by lot. Ten white beans and ten black ones would be placed in a sack. The unfortunate men who drew the black beans were immediately shot.

Samuel Maverick began locating land soon after the war and became the largest land owner in Texas, if not in the United States. He owned more cattle on the free public range than any other man in the Lone Star State. In 1861 nearly all the men went into the war. Maverick's cattle ran wild on the range and when the war closed there were tens of thousands of cattle that had been bred in the four years.

Maverick was the greatest claimant of these wild cattle and marked them with his brand wherever caught. Other owners and even men who had never owned cattle would brand with their own marks such cattle as they caught unbranded. It thus became the custom among cattlemen using a free range to stamp as their own any unbranded cattle they found during the round-up. To this day these stray cattle are known as "mavericks."

The men occupied in cutting out the cattle worked each animal carefully to the edge of the herd and there, with a sudden dash, drove it out at a run. Many times an animal was anxious to break back and rejoin the herd.

The writer while in the Indian Territory at a round-up saw a peculiar feat. A steer had been acting badly, seemingly bound to return to the herd after having been cut out. Cattle dislike being alone and it is no easy matter to hold the first four or five that are cut out. After a few are together they are contented. This particular steer while trying to rejoin the herd was roped by a skilled puncher. His lariat caught the animal around the horns. The cowboy's horse stopped suddenly, the rope tightened and over the steer went, turning a complete somersault. At first it was thought the animal's neck had been broken. The puncher slackened his rope, whereupon the steer arose, shook its head and quietly went back to the "cut." That particular animal gave no further trouble.

When the owner of a ranch had cut out all his cattle he began to brand, or possibly he waited until the round-up was entirely over. The branding was the hardest part of the work, for the branding-irons have to be kept on the fire until they are red-hot. The calves were roped and thrown and

SERGEANT MEAT, WIFE AND DAUGHTER

the hot irons were placed on them until the hair was burned through. It was necessary for the brander to be very careful not to burn too deeply or a running sore might develop. The largest cattle were usually driven through a chute and as they passed through the iron would be placed against them. This is an easier method than to throw the animal; the latter method is hard on the horse as well as the man. If the animal is thrown, however, the branding is usually a better job.

To throw an animal, one of the men roped it around the horns, another man by the hind legs, this latter being known as "heeling." The ropers then pulled in opposite directions, which straightened out the animal. Another man seized it by the tail and pulled it over on its side, when the brand was applied.

Some very laughable things occur during this work. The writer was responsible for one which was extremely funny for the audience but not for the victim. I was obliged to rebrand some of my cattle. I went down to the butcher corral while my men were at work (at least, supposed to be) but when I arrived they were all sitting on the fence. I told them I was not paying them to hold down the fence boards. They told me a mad cow had driven them out of the corral. I laughed and said, "Let me have a rope and I'll show you how to do it; there is no danger." There were two or more snubbing-posts in the corral, and the cow was frothing at the mouth, pawing and acting in a fighting mood. My idea was to rope the cow and if she came for me I would jump behind one of the posts or climb the fence. It was a high board fence and rather hard to get over. Taking the rope, I entered the corral, made a cast and by good luck roped her around the horns the first throw. Before I could pass the rope around the snubbing post, however, she came for me full speed, "head down and tail a-rising!"   There was a hog pen in one corner of the corral, and I made for that.   I didn't pause to put my hands on the fence but took a header over the top board, landing in a mess of filth.   When I staggered to my feet I was a sight! Luckily, no bones were broken.   The men were laughing fit to kill.   They afterward told me that while I was in the air the cow struck the fence full tilt.   The laugh was on me and I had to go to the house and change my clothes.   I sent the men a keg of beer and didn't go to the corral again that day

In driving cattle into a corral there were often some that managed to escape from day to day, remaining out to the very last and being very hard to run in.   I had one of the most knowing cow ponies I ever saw, which I rode for years.   One season we had about cleaned up our work, making our last drive into the yard, and one of the steers had broken away several times.   I was bound to drive it in, as I wanted to rebrand it.   I took after the steer as fast as I could ride and had him near the entrance of the corral, when he turned quickly.   "Monk," my pony, turned fully as quickly.   The cinch broke and off I went, saddle and all rolling against the fence.   "Monk" never stopped but just kept after the steer, turned him and ran him into the corral, stopping at the entrance and looking around as much as to say, "I didn't need your assistance."

Another time we were letting a bull out of the chute after branding him.   I had purchased several bulls from a passing herd on its way to Colorado and was branding the bunch. Fred Slagle, the post blacksmith, was assisting me.   His business was to let the bull out of the chute.   As one animal left the pen he took after Fred.   The latter, not having time to jump the fence, was in a serious predicament.   The bull was right at his heels when Fred's dog grabbed the animal by the nose, which saved the "Dutchman."   I never could get Slagle to help me again

CHAPTER IX

THE commanding officer of Fort Wallace, Kansas, Major Lon Morris, Third Infantry, had some eastern friends visiting him who had never seen a real live buffalo. The major wanted to give them an opportunity and asked me to go out with the party. I was familiar with the country and could find the game if there were any buffalo in the vicinity.

We started out one beautiful December morning in 1872, the members of the party riding in an ambulance and I riding my celebrated pony "Nibs." The plan was that if we found any buffalo, I was to try to kill one from horseback, so they could witness a mounted buffalo hunt. We were out some hours without success but saw quite a number of antelope and jack-rabbits. I got a couple of the latter.

When the party returned to the post I went to my cattle ranch near by to see how my men and herd were doing. Riding up, I did not see many of the cattle and found the ranch deserted. From appearances, I knew the men must have been away for a day or two, so came to the conclusion that they must be out hunting cattle which had strayed away. I had had nothing to eat since morning and made coffee and fried some bacon.

While I was engaged in preparing my meal, my men came up with a bunch of cattle. They had been out three days gathering them, but thought they had not found all of them. They informed me that a severe storm had come up, a strong wind blowing from the north, and that some of the

63

cattle had drifted with it.   Cattle will usually do this if the weather is cold, in order to keep warm.   After a storm they will work their way back to their own range, providing they have been on it for some time.   It is a home to them.   But mine were in a country strange to them and many herds of buffalo were passing back and forth.   As I was new in the business, this information made me anxious about them. So I told the men I would go in to the post, get another horse and some warm clothing, return that night or early in the morning and we would then round up the cattle and see how many were missing.   However, I concluded to scout the country a bit before going in to the post, hoping to find some of them.   While I was absorbed in this pursuit, before I realized it night came on, catching me about fifteen miles from the post.

Eagle Tail, a small railroad station, was not very far away, so I decided to ride in there and get some food for myself and horse before going in to the post, about ten miles, but my friends prevailed upon me to remain over night at Eagle Tail.   I was so exercised over the loss of my cattle that I accepted the invitation, instead of returning to the post.

Early the next morning I started out, continuing my hunt for the cattle.   During the day I saw quite a number of small herds of buffalo and had considerable trouble in distinguishing whether they were buffalo or cattle, so had to investigate a number of herds.   This caused me considerable extra riding.   If I had carried a pair of field-glasses all this would have been avoided.   All cattlemen should carry them; it would save them lots of horseflesh.

I had been out most of the day when I discovered, quite a distance away, some objects which did not act like buffalo, so I had to go and see what they were and found them to be quite a band of wild horses.   Thus I was again disappointed in my search.

It was now time for me to think of returning either to the ranch or the post, the former being nearer. I supposed I was between the railroad and the old Fort Lyon wagon road and that all I had to do was to ride eastward, and in time I would strike either of the places, but I expected to be out most of the night. I commenced to bear toward the wagon road, thinking to come to it very soon. Failing to do this, it dawned upon me that I might have crossed the road. That seemed impossible, however, for my horse certainly would have noticed it. I also suspected that I might have crossed the road when after the wild horses.

It was getting late and my pony was more or less weary. I was sleepy and tired myself and decided to go into camp for a while. I unsaddled, but not having a lariat I lengthened my bridle rein by detaching one end from the bit. This I fastened to my wrist, rolled up in my saddle blanket and went to sleep.

I was awakened several times in the night by the pony pulling on the rein to get more grazing ground. Toward morning, being rather cold, I saddled up and moved on. There being no moon or stars I could not use the faithful old North Star as a guide, but contented myself by riding in the general direction I thought the ranch should be.

When daylight appeared the country seemed unfamiliar, and I began to get a bit alarmed. It was quite cloudy, the sun appearing only at intervals, and I made very little headway. Soon I concluded I was lost. Several times I gave my horse his head and he would start in a new direction. I would let him go along for a while, then, concluding he was headed wrong, would start him in another direction. I afterward learned the horse was right and if he had had his own way I should have reached home that day. At the time I did not know a horse's intelligence.

I rode all that day, grazing my horse several times, and

when night came I camped as on the previous night but changed my tactics somewhat. It grew very cold in the night, so I crawled up between Nibs' legs, as he lay stretched out full length on the ground, and in that way received considerable warmth from his body. Moreover, my horse seemed to enjoy it about as much as I did. Once while I was sweetly sleeping I was rudely awakened by Nibs trying to roll over, to get a new position, I presume, or he may have thought it time to get up and move on, which I presently did.

I was not particularly hungry at any time but worried some, wondering what I should do if a storm came up. Of course, if there had been any fuel I could have started a fire in some gulch where the wind could not strike me and probably could have weathered quite a severe storm. However, I was keeping up my courage pretty well and was not feeling very greatly fatigued; in fact, I felt pretty strong and was thinking very little about food. I knew if I got very hungry I could kill a jack-rabbit.

Finally I came to a snow belt—there was quite a little snow on the ground— and there I found a wagon track and the carcass of an old buffalo bull that had been recently killed. Here was my chance to have a feast. The saddle (hindquarter) and tongue of the buffalo had been removed, I experienced considerable difficulty in carving the animal, having only my pocket knife and the hide being very tough, but finally I succeeded in getting a few pounds, and having no salt nor any matches with which to start a fire I took my steak straight. I might have made a fire by means of my cartridges but having only a few (I had expended quite a number while out with Major Morris' party) I did not know what use I might have for the few in my belt, feeling that I might need them worse if it grew much colder. Moreover, I realized that I might at any time run across hostile Indians and in that case would doubtless need my ammunition for business.

Not having salt, the meat nauseated me, so I could not eat much of it, and what little I did eat I could not chew but was obliged to cut it into small pellets, homeopathic doses. I then strapped a quantity of it to my saddle and went on my way, feeling much better.

I was quite sure that the wagon track which I had discovered had been made by one of my own wagons, for only a few days before I had sent a wagon to the Arkansas River with provisions for a cattle man whose herd was wintering there, being on the way from Texas to Idaho. The owner of this herd, while on his way to the railroad for these provisions, was overtaken by a severe snowstorm which lasted several days. He was all right as long as he stayed with his wagon but as soon as the storm had subsided he had started for the railroad station on foot, his horses having broken away from the wagon, and before he reached the railroad another storm overtook him. He managed to weather this and reach the track, but was badly frozen. He then hailed two trains but they passed, not seeing his signals. Being determined that the next train should see him he crawled on the track, feeling that he would rather stand the chances of being run over than freeze to death. Luckily, the engineer of the next train (a freight) saw him lying on the track and brought his engine to a standstill when it was almost upon the man. He was brought to the post hospital at Wallace, and was found to be so badly frozen that his legs were amputated above the knees.

Riding along, this experience was not pleasant to think about, as a storm was liable to come up at any time at that season of the year. Following the back track for some distance, I soon came out of the snow belt and at this point lost the wagon road, but a short distance farther along I found it again and followed it until I came to yet another track leading into it. This threw me into a quandary and I was quite at a loss to know which to follow. However, I thought of a story which my Uncle Olmstead had told me years before; that when he was on his way from Vermont west he came to two roads diverging, and not knowing which to take, solved the problem by standing up his cane and letting it fall. He then pursued his journey in the direction indicated by the falling cane, which led him to Galena, Iowa.

I adopted this method, using my Winchester in lieu of a cane, and started on in the direction my gun had indicated. Ere long I came to the terminus of the road where there had been an old wood-choppers' camp, and I remembered that this was the place where Mr. Jones' choppers had been killed by the Indians two or three years previously. It was evident that I had gone wrong again, but I did not mind a little thing like that. At least I knew where I was, some thirty-five miles from the post.

It was nice and warm here, so I tied my horse to a block of wood, which he could drag about while grazing, and proceeded to take a nap. I must have slept three or four hours for on awakening I discovered it was nearly sundown. Having had a good rest we moved out once more and being very greatly refreshed were able to make good time, and I expected to get to the post early the following morning. I traveled well into the night, when, feeling that my horse was probably getting tired, I thought I would give him a rest. Turning off the road a piece to a ravine, I unsaddled and went to sleep. It grew very cold and this must have awakened me. I was chilled clear through and could scarcely get upon my feet. Frankly, I was somewhat distressed about my condition.

It then occurred to me that if I rolled down the bank into the ravine below it would set my blood to circulating and

warm me up.   I did not know how much of a roll it was,
and furthermore, didn't care.   So I crawled to the edge of
the bank and over I went!   I never stopped until I reached
the bottom of the ravine.   I was somewhat dazed and
bruised, my clothing was tattered and torn, but I was "still
in the ring" and never warmer in my life.   If I had had
Nibs as a bunkie it would not have been necessary for me
to have made the perilous descent.

It was not yet daylight but I thought I had better proceed on my journey.   I crossed the trail, which was rather
dim, without knowing it, but I very soon discovered my
error, and turning to the right went back and very soon
found the road.   I proceeded a mile or more, when upon
passing through a gulch where the snow had drifted in, I
discovered some tracks.   Wondering whose they were, I
dismounted to investigate, and found they were my own,
which had been made while leading my horse through the
snow a few hours before!   So here I was, again going
back on my own trail.   Had I not discovered my tracks in
the snow I might have been going yet.   It seems that after I
had found the road I turned again to the right, when I should
have gone to the left.   This was not strange, in view of
the condition I was in.

I soon reached Henshaw's ranch on the Smoky Hill
River, some ten miles from the post, where I had had my
summer camp and my cattle before taking them to the ranch.
Here I saw a small herd of buffalo, with a two-year-old
heifer from my herd among them, and I reasoned thus,
"Here I have been out hunting cattle for five days and
this is the only animal I have seen.   I will certainly ac-
complish a little something by taking this animal to the post."
As I approached the herd, off they went like the wind, the
heifer following but not being able to keep up.   I soon came
alongside of her and tried to turn her, but she insisted on

following the buffaloes. In a desperate effort to get by, she tried to hook my horse but only struck my stirrup leathers. Finding that I could not turn her, I decided to try to "crease" her, so banged away, and over she went, as dead as a door-nail. I had shot her about an inch too low. Upon examining the brand I found that it was my own, "H. W. W." Had I not tried to "crease" her, she probably would have joined the buffalo herd, and that would have been the last of her.

Upon my arrival at the post I sent the butcher out after the carcass, but he could not find it. I then went directly to the cook house to get some refreshments and found my cook just preparing the midday meal. She told me she was going to have bean soup, but that it was not quite ready. Knowing that I was very fond of it, she asked me if I would wait. I remarked that although I had had nothing to eat for several days, an hour or so would make no difference although I must admit that the time seemed a little long. Owing no doubt to the condition of my stomach, I did not eat very much, which was probably the best thing for me. As a result of the trip, I found that I had lost a few pounds in weight, but after a good rest I felt all right.

When I walked into the store it created quite a little excitement, as my employees thought I had been hurt or was lost. They supposed I was at the ranch until that morning when one of the men came in, informing them that I had left for the post four days before. The commanding officer had made preparations to send men out to scour the country for me, but had very little hopes of finding me in that vast wilderness.

This experience was a good object lesson for me, although rather a severe one. I at once provided myself with a compass, matchsafe, salt bag and pair of field-glasses, and from that time I rarely went out without them. The compass came in handy on several occasions.   My horse had stood the trip as well as I.   I had purchased him from a man in the employ of Professor Marsh, of Yale College, who at the time was in that part of Kansas gathering fossils. Nibs was captured from a herd of wild horses, the professor assisting in the capture.

CHAPTER X

A LOST OUTFIT—CAPTURE OF A HORSE THIEF

ON one of my trips, hunting cattle, I found an abandoned wagon, two sets of Concord harness, a sack and a half of flour, some yeast powders and other provisions, a camp cooking outfit, steel traps, a reloading outfit and several blankets that evidently had been blown out of the wagon and were partly covered with snow; a home-made shirt with some initials worked in it, and one of Dickens' novels. On the fly-leaf of the book was a post-office address but no name. The address was that of a small town in Colorado.

Near the outfit were a few new railroad ties from which chips had been cut, with an ax alongside. It looked very much as if the party or parties had lost their horses and had taken the bridles and gone to look for them. A sudden storm may have come up, and possibly they were unable to find their way back. Indians could not have been connected with the incident or they certainly would have taken the provisions and blankets. I had two or three cowboys with me and we examined the surrounding country thoroughly but could find no trace of the owners, so we took the property to my ranch.

I made every effort to locate the owners by writing to the postmaster of the Colorado town, and by advertising in a Kansas City paper, but never received any response.

On another trip we discovered the skeleton of an Indian lying on a sort of shelf on a chalky bluff. It had evidently been there a great many years, and judging from the size of the bones the savage must have been a giant.

An incident relating to horse stealing occurred during the winter of 1872-73. Lieutenant Quentin Campbell, Fifth Infantry, the post quartermaster, loaned a horse to F. C. Gay, our station agent, and while the animal was in Gay's possession it was stolen. The whole community sympathized with them, especially with the lieutenant, who had no right to lend a citizen a government animal.

It was the consensus of opinion that measures must be taken to stop horse stealing, and, as the county was not organized, the people had to take the matter into their own hands. It was determined that if the thief were caught he should suffer the death penalty, as an object lesson to all evil-doers.

I presume I must have talked more than I should about the theft, and this latter placed me in a rather embarrassing position. A few nights after the theft of the horse I was awakened by a knock at my bedroom window. I heard several voices and inquired who was there. The answer came, "It is Gay; I want to see you on business." I arose and let him in, inquiring what was up. He said the horse had been recaptured near Lake Station and that the thief was outside with the balance of the posse.

I thereupon let the men all enter. They were mostly railroad men and among them was a soldier named Riley, who was a member of the party of troops that guarded Lake Station. He had been sent down as a guard over the prisoner.

To my great surprise and decided embarrassment I recognized the culprit as a man whom I had one time employed on my ranch. I always had considered him honest, so I said, "What are you doing here? This looks quite serious. Your circumstances are not such that you were obliged to resort to horse stealing."

"Well," replied the prisoner, "they have caught me with the goods. I would not have taken the horse if Mr. Gay had treated me on the square. I did it to get even with him. I now see my mistake. I saw it after I had taken the horse, but I did not have the courage to bring the animal back. This is my first offense, and I'm sorry I did it, but I suppose it is too late to make amends for it now."

I called Mr. Gay, his assistant and the telegraph operator into the next room.

"What do you propose to do with him, turn him over to the military authorities?" I queried.

"No," was the reply. "We didn't bring him here for that purpose. Our intentions were to hang him."

"Then why didn't you do it at the station, where you had a convenient telegraph pole?" I suggested.

"We wanted your assistance," was the answer. "You are more interested in this business than anybody else and are one of the prominent men here."

It was an awkward situation. However, I told the posse that I was now looking at the matter in a different light.

"I know this man," said I. "I don't think he is a bad fellow at heart. He probably thought he had a grievance, and let it prey on his mind until he committed the act. He now sees his mistake. I am in favor of turning him over to the military authorities for punishment and letting the law take its course."

I called two or three more men into the council and found that their opinions differed widely. One man intimated that I had no "sand."

In the meantime, I was called aside by one of my men who had been in the stock business in New Mexico. He had made two or three starts and each time had been ruined by losing his stock through cattle rustlers and Indians. He was loading his revolver.

"Homer," said he, "don't have anything to do with this affair. Riley and I will take him out. No doubt he will try to escape, and it will be our business to prevent it—see?"

After further council the matter was put to a vote by secret ballot, whether the thief should be strung up at once or turned over to the military authorities. With one or two exceptions the men voted to let the military authorities settle the matter. This was accordingly done and the man was placed in the guard-house.

The thief's grievance against Mr. Gay was all imagination. His grievance should have been against me, if any one. The man had turned his own horses into a pen where Gay had some hay stacked. The animals had trampled it down, destroying much of it, and I determined the sum which the man should pay.

The next morning the thief was allowed to come to my store under guard and deposit some money. He said he was afraid the other prisoners in the guard-house would take it away from him. He also told me that when he found the posse intended bringing him over to me "it was all up for him," as he knew I had no use for horse thieves. However, he had overheard enough of our conversation to know that I was not in favor of hanging him, and then the world began to look brighter.

He was tried in the United States court at Topeka and sentenced to three years' imprisonment. He had been in confinement about a year when the chaplain of the prison took great interest in his welfare and sent Mr. Gay a petition blank, asking him to circulate it for signatures to have the man pardoned. The petition was circulated and the man was freed. He returned to Wallace and Mr. Gay gave him a job on the section. In a few months he was made a section boss and put in charge of one of the sections of the Kansas-Pacific Railroad.

CHAPTER XI

IN FEBRUARY, 1875, I went with a scouting party commanded by Lieutenant Henkle, Fifth Infantry. We captured two Indians who were concerned in the massacre of part of the Germaine* family in 1874, and who, no doubt, belonged to the band that had killed a friend of mine, a hunter named Brown, whose death caused this scouting expedition.

The detachment consisted of some men from the Fifth Infantry, a number of whom were bandsmen. They came from Fort Hays, Kansas, to go on this scout, as there were not sufficient men at Wallace to send out. The garrison at Hays was also depleted, most of the men being with General Miles' expedition in the Indian Territory. We also had Lieutenant Hewitt of the Nineteenth Infantry and some men belonging to that regiment. Three civilians, including myself, accompanied the command, which consisted of thirty-five men.

While we were out in the open country a big blizzard struck us, so that we were obliged to seek the nearest shelter, which was some miles away. After some difficulty and suffering we finally reached a fork of Plum Creek, where we took shelter. Wood was not plentiful. Some of the men were frost-bitten, two or three quite badly. The Nineteenth

---

*In a letter to my friend, E. A. Brininstool, Mrs. Catherine German Swerdfeger, eldest of the sisters captured by these Indians, now living at Atascadero, California, states that the family name was *German*, not *Germaine*.

Infantry had just come up from the south, and were not prepared for such cold weather, and besides, did not know how
to take care of themselves.   I am quite sure that some of
them would have been frozen to death had it not been for
the assistance tendered by the civilians.

On the morning of the third day it was snowing very
hard, although the weather had moderated a bit; so we
broke camp.   While doing so, we discovered a herd of buffalo at hand.   We thought at first that the storm was driving them but soon discovered that Indians were after them.
We spotted the Indians about the time they discovered us.
It was a question which was the more surprised.   As near as
we could tell there were about a dozen Indians.   I parleyed
with three of them, making signs for them to come in, throwing my gun down on first one, then another, as each tried to
edge away.   Finally one escaped, but I brought in the other
two.   The one who escaped would have been killed if the
lieutenant had not cried, "Don't shoot!" for one of the hunters had drawn a bead on the Indian with a Sharps rifle.

I discovered several weeks later that the Indians were
camped very near us.   Had we known that we were in such
close proximity to them we might have captured or killed
most of the band, and vice versa.   We were in no condition
to follow the Indians, and I advised the officer in command not to follow them mounted.   Had we done so, no
doubt our little band would have become separated because
of poor horsemanship, and the chances are we should all
have been killed.   Neither were we in condition to follow
them on foot, so it was decided that we had better make for
the post with our prisoners, a very wise conclusion.   We
did not arrive there until quite late at night and were in
pretty bad shape.

Several of the Indians followed us and continued with
us for some hours.   When the redskins were first dis-

covered, Allen Clark, one of my herders, jumped into the wagon to get some extra ammunition.   He had to open an original box to get it.   He grabbed an ax to remove the cover, which was fastened with screws.   Another of the party, who had an eye to business, cried out in his excitement, "Don't smash that cover, get the screw-driver and take it off!"   Usually a screw-driver comes with each box of ammunition.   There was none with this one.   Perhaps it is needless to say that the box was opened all right.

On the Friday or Saturday preceding Brown's death I saw the Indians who I think killed him.   I was on Lake Creek hunting cattle, and through my field-glasses saw some Indians going north.   The following Monday, Brown's body was found lying near his wagon; he had been shot through the head.   All the camp equipage had been taken and his horses run off.   Brown's body was found some distance north of Lake Creek, where I had seen the Indians two days previous, and the direction they were taking would have brought them to the place where the man had been killed.

We were hunting cattle several weeks later and came across an old Indian camp in a ravine about half a mile from our own camp where we captured the two Indians.   We also discovered the tracks of two horses whose hoofprints showed that they were animals of unusual size and were shod with heel and toe calks.   We were sure they were Brown's horses, for the post blacksmith had shod them two or three days before his death.   The Indians captured at this camp were Cheyennes, father and son.   A boy, Red Eagle, was about fifteen years of age.   He was one of my scouts in 1888, at which time I learned that he was one of the Indians we had captured in 1875.   I had been in command of the scouts but a short time when Whirlwind, the celebrated chief of the Cheyennes, asked that several scouts be allowed to go with him on a visit to Anadarko agency. I gave permission to three or four of those who had just re-enlisted to accompany Whirlwind. They had been gone but a day or so when Red Eagle asked permission to go and visit a sick sister. I thought this might be an excuse to get away and join Whirlwind's party, yet I did not want to refuse him if he were telling the truth, so I questioned him closely.

He informed me that some Indians who had just come in from the place where his sister was encamped had told him she was very ill. Red Eagle was very fond of her, as she was his only living relative. He told me that he and his father had been captured several years before and had been sent to Dry Tortugas, Florida; that en route his father had tried to escape by jumping off the train, and was killed. He told me the circumstances surrounding his capture, and it tallied with that of the Indians as I have given it here.

I gave Red Eagle a ten days' pass as requested. In two or three days he returned, stating that he had found his sister not so ill as had been reported. I was then convinced that he had told me the truth, and that he was the Indian boy I had captured thirteen years previously.

CHAPTER XII

HUNTING THE BUFFALO

MILLIONS of buffalo were slaughtered for the hides and meat, principally for the hide. Some of the expert hunters made considerable money at that occupation. I knew one hunter whom we called "Kentuck," he presumably being a native of Kentucky. I never knew his real name and it was not considered polite, in those days, to ask a man what state he hailed from.

"Kentuck," in less than one year, made about ten thousand dollars hunting buffalo. He had a camp on Punished Woman's Fork, a stream south of Wallace, where he killed three thousand seven hundred buffalo. It was known as "the slaughter pen." This killing was done when thousands of the animals were going north. In order that the buffalo might not scent him, the hunter would slip quietly up on the windward side of a herd while they were grazing. They were hunted so much that after a while they seemed to anticipate this, and at the first crack of a rifle off they would go like the wind, although the shooter would usually get two or three before they withdrew from range.

The large outfits employed the aid of horses in removing the hide. The skinner would slit the hide from the head down between the legs to the tail and also skin the legs and loosen the hide around the head. A rope was then attached to the skin near the head, and the skin pulled off by the horse. The hides were then taken to camp and pegged out until they were perfectly dry, when they became as hard as flint. The average prices paid by the hide buyers were two dollars for cowskins, three dollars for bull and seventy-five cents for calf hides. Buffalo hides did not make good leather, as they were too spongy. Very few were made into robes.

Unlike the Indian woman, the white man did not know how to treat the hides properly to make good robes. The squaws would peg out the skin, stretching it as much as possible, clean off all the fat and meat with an instrument made of one of the large horns of the elk and used like an adze. The skin was then stretched upright in a frame and scraped down until it was the desired thickness. It was then worked with the hands until the robe was soft and pliable.

Some of the habits of the buffalo herds are clearly fixed in my memory. The bulls were always found on the outer edge, supposedly acting as protectors to the cows and calves. For ten to twenty miles one would often see solid herds of the animals. Keeping on steadily through them, one would come to the main herd, consisting of the cows and calves. The old bulls were driven out of the herd by the younger ones. They became poor in flesh and mangy, the fur being useless for robes. Until the hunters commenced to kill them off, their only enemies were the wolves and coyotes. A medium-sized herd, at that time, dotted the prairie for hundreds of miles, and to guess at the number in a herd was like trying to compute the grains of wheat in a granary.

When these immense herds were stampeded nothing could stop them. The stupidity of the buffalo was remarkable. When one of their number was killed the rest of the herd, smelling the blood, would become excited, but instead of stampeding would gather around the dead buffalo, pawing, bellowing and hooking it viciously. Taking advantage of this well-known habit of the creature, the hunter would kill one animal and then wipe out almost the entire herd.

Buffalo hunting was dangerous sport. Although at times it looked like murder, if you took a buffalo in his native element he had plenty of courage and would fight tenaciously for his life if given an opportunity. Like all other animals, the buffalo scented danger at a distance and tried to escape by running away, but if he did not escape he would make a stand and fight to the last, for which every one must respect him. If you rode up alongside him as he ran and gave him a ball from your rifle he would turn and charge your horse, and then be off again.

There were other dangers to be taken into consideration in hunting the buffalo, chief of which was the possibility of one's horse stumbling or stepping into a prairie dog's hole and breaking a leg, throwing the rider, who might receive a broken limb or possibly meet death. I have seen it all. I have seen men who have shot themselves as well as the horse under them in their excitement and carelessness. So when one started out after buffalo in those glorious days he ran many risks.

In the autumn of 1873 I went out on a hunt with Captain John L. Irwin, Sixth Cavalry, and some English cavalry officers, taking a detachment of men with us. I was riding a horse which the captain had given me. The animal was blind in one eye, and I found that in running buffalo he would invariably bear toward the blind eye, so that when we got after a herd this had to be taken into consideration. I used a three-banded, long-barreled rifle known as a "needle gun." In hunting buffalo I rode up to them and alongside to the right, the gun resting on my bridle arm, so that when I got opposite the shoulder of the animal I could fire, and I usually got him.

We located a small herd of five or six and started for them. The captain cried out, "Try to get the bunch!" so off we went. I tried to get on the right side of the herd but miscalculated, and I was carried around so the herd was on my right. So I had to bring my gun over to my right side to shoot. I could not take aim, but fired and broke the back of a buffalo. A sergeant was coming up on my left. I did not see him when I fired, but as I brought my gun back to reload I observed him. I yelled, "Look out!" but instead of holding up or turning his horse to the left he attempted to pass me, thinking, as he told me later, that he could do so. He was on the "blind side" and my horse did not see him quickly enough, so all I could do was to settle back in my saddle and pull on the reins as hard as possible in an effort to avert a catastrophe. It was too late, however, and I ran into him, knocking his horse over. The animal took a terrible fall and I thought I had killed the sergeant. When we got to him he was insensible, but he soon recovered. It was discovered that he had sustained a broken shoulder and was badly bruised otherwise. I was not to blame, as the blind horse was the cause of the accident.

The Englishmen thought my shot was wonderful. It was never explained to them that the shot was accidental, but, on the other hand, they were told some remarkable stories about my marksmanship. They thought I was a wonder. The soldiers used to take great delight in "stuffing the tenderfeet," as they called the newcomers.

Another time I went on a hunt with Mr. Treadway, of the *Denver News,* and Mr. Fisher, of the firm of Daniels, Fisher & Co., Denver. Lieutenant Tom Wallace, Third

Infantry, accompanied us. I furnished the mounts for the party, and as the lieutenant was a good horseman I let him ride one of my best animals. It was considered one of the fastest horses in that part of the country.

We came across an old buffalo bull, but a lively one, and ran him into a gulch, wounded, where he put up a good fight. The plan was to let the Denver people do the killing, as they had never been on a buffalo hunt, although they had seen thousands of the monarchs of the prairie. Our guests were not having very good success in knocking the old bull out, so the lieutenant rode up to help them. He rode within a few yards of the enraged bull, when the animal charged the lieutenant's horse. The officer had partly turned the horse around to get out of the buffalo's way but was not quick enough, and the bull struck the horse in the fleshy part of one of its hindquarters. The horn penetrated clear to the bone, making an ugly triangular wound. Had the horse been gored anywhere else it would have been its death wound. It was the first time this horse had engaged in a buffalo hunt, and of course did not realize the danger. I had no means of stopping the flow of blood, but I packed the wound with dirt, and on my arrival at the post I threw the horse, cleansed the wound, and sewed it up. In a few weeks the horse recovered, but there remained an ugly scar.

On another of my hunting excursions with some of my friends I had Edward Lane and Joe Farrell with me, both of whom I have mentioned heretofore. We came across a small herd of buffalo composed mostly of cows and calves. Lane and Farrell rode alongside them, singling out two cows with calves. They killed the cows, and when the animals dropped the calves remained with their mothers. The little creatures were about six weeks

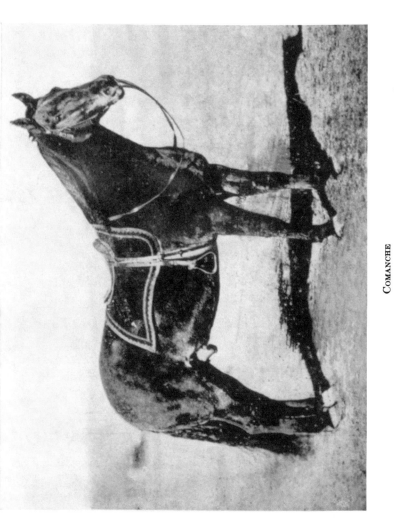

COMANCHE

The horse ridden by Captain Myles W. Keogh in the battle of the Little Big Horn, June 25, 1876.

old, and the next day we loaded them into my wagon and started for the ranch. They were too young to graze, so we fed them on condensed milk. When we first arrived at the ranch they were very hungry; and I had a cow, whose calf had been killed by wolves, driven into the corral with the buffalo calves. She was very much afraid of them, but the calves made a rush for her, bunting her into one corner of the corral where they succeeded in nursing her. In a day or so she became reconciled to them, and grew very fond of her unnatural babies. The cow soon commenced to lose flesh, the nursing of the two calves being too much on her; so I had her driven in to the post, in order that she might feed on the refuse from the quartermaster's stables. That night she returned to her adopted children, jumping off a bank six feet high in order to get into the corral where the calves were.

I decided to drive them all in to the post, so they could feed off the manure heap. It was pretty good picking for them and they thrived very well. I kept them over two years. They were beauties and I tried to sell them to the Barnum & Bailey Circus. They offered me two hundred dollars for them if I would deliver them at Kansas City, which I declined to do, as the shipping charges alone would have been nearly that sum. I was rather disappointed with their offer, as I had an idea they were worth at least a thousand dollars. Shortly afterward a herd of cattle was passing through on its way to Colorado, and I traded the young buffaloes for some lame cows. I disposed of them for the reason that they were getting very large.

It was considered unsafe to cross the buffalo with domestic cattle, because of the belief that the cow could not deliver her calf, owing to the peculiar construction of the frame (hump) of the buffalo. I believe that theory was afterward exploded by "Buffalo" Jones in Oklahoma. I understand, too, that at one time Miller Brothers, on their 101 Ranch in Oklahoma, were crossing buffalo with cattle and having very good success, calling the new progeny "cattalo." It was thought that by crossing the breed it would develop a much hardier cattle.

On one of my hunts I came very near losing my life. I had wounded what was called a "spike"—a bull, which is a two-year-old, with short sharp horns. I had put one bullet into him but not in a vital spot, so tried another shot. About the time I was ready to shoot my horse stepped into a prairie dog hole, and over he went! I instinctively threw myself away from the horse, so he did not fall on me. The "spike" was nearly all in, and stopped near where I parted company with my horse. He saw me and came for me. I held on to my gun, and as luck would have it there was a shot in the chamber, so I blazed away, hitting the bull in the breast. He dropped dead within five yards of me. When I fell off my horse my gun plowed along the ground, and some dirt entered the muzzle. When I fired, the barrel was split about six inches from the muzzle. I was able to file off the barrel, which made it more like a carbine and improved the gun very materially for mounted hunting.

The most successful mounted hunting of buffalo I ever did occurred once when I was haying at my ranch. One day while I was running the mowing machine, quite a herd of buffalo passed, going south. This was the first of the animals we had seen for several days. I had about a dozen men in my employ and thought this was a good chance to get some fresh meat for them. I unhitched my team from the mower and took the harness off "Hano," my private horse, one of the best trained animals for buffalo hunting in the country.

I had my gun with me, for I kept one on the mowing machine for emergencies. I told the man who was operating the horse rake to come out with the wagon to bring the meat into camp. He inquired if I were not counting my chickens before they were hatched, but I replied, "Never you mind; do as I tell you. If I don't get a buffalo, it won't be your fault." Then I jumped on Hano bareback, and off I went to overtake the herd.

The animals had not been frightened, and when I reached the table-land were grazing quietly along. I rode out of the head of a gulch and succeeded in getting quite close before they saw me. I killed seven of them in ten shots, some of them dropping so close together that it looked as if one could jump across one carcass to the next. I don't think I ran them over half a mile, and could have killed more had I wished. I ran alongside some of them so close that when I fired the hair was singed. After each shot Hano would swerve a little and carry me along to the side of another. It was murder, but I wanted meat. Most of my shots struck just back of the left shoulder. Other shots were used to finish those that were wounded and could not escape. I saved the saddles, loins, tongues and brains, and there was no meat wasted, as I sent some of it in to the post.

On one occasion I was out with a scouting party of two troops of the Tenth Cavalry. We were encamped for the night near some water holes and the sun was just going down, when our attention was called to a sound which resembled the rustling of leaves in a forest. It seemed to be coming nearer, then increased to a rumbling, and we thought the wind was rising. Some said a storm was coming, but we thought that strange, as it was a clear beautiful evening.

Suddenly the ground seemed to tremble, and almost instantly we heard the thundrous tread of thousands of hoofs. "Buffalo stampede!" yelled several of the men. They were headed straight for our camp, thousands of them.

Tremendous excitement reigned immediately. It looked very much as if the buffaloes were going to run over us. The commanding officer ordered his men to fire upon them, with a view of turning the herd. At the report of the guns the herd seemed to hesitate, but only for a few seconds, as others behind were pushing the leaders along. It looked pretty serious, but at last they commenced to open out to the right and left of our camp. Our horses were on their lines in the rear of the camp, and our wagons which held the forage were lined up on our right. The buffalo cleared our camp a hundred yards or more on our left, but on our right we did not fare so well, for they struck two of our three wagons which were loaded with forage, toppling two of them over and breaking them up badly. The mules were attached to the wagons, and off they went. We never did get them all back. It was a very narrow escape. Had they struck us squarely we doubtless would have been knocked out as badly as if a cyclone had passed through our midst.

CHAPTER XIII

MY MINING EXPERIENCE

A T a government sale I had purchased a condemned horse and mule and a lot of harness, which cost me about a hundred dollars. I had a wagon, worth about sixty dollars, that I had purchased from Joe North some little time before his sudden death. With this outfit I made up a very good work team.

Then I traded the outfit to a party from Denver for a house and lot. There was a small cottage on the lot, which was renting for twelve dollars a month. The owner and his partner wanted to go hunting buffalo, which, at that time, was very profitable. There was a mortgage on the place for six hundred dollars. I gave the owner my team complete, about two hundred dollars' worth of merchandise, including guns, ammunition and groceries, and three hundred dollars in cash. I afterward sold the property for two thousand five hundred dollars to a party to whom I owed some money. I was not obliged to dispose of it and was confident it would be of considerable value some day because of its location, but I wanted to get out of debt.

Some years later I was in Denver, sitting on the porch of the Tabor Hotel, talking with some gentlemen. I pointed to a lot diagonally across the street and asked them what it was worth. They told me it had just been sold for fifteen thousand dollars to a syndicate which intended to erect one of the largest office buildings in the

city. I told them that at one time I owned the property,
and sold it for twenty-five hundred dollars.

In the spring of 1873, owing to the scarcity of the
animals, buffalo hunting was practically discontinued.
Undoubtedly most of the herds had been killed off. When
the buffalo disappeared the hunters did likewise. My
business was mostly with them, as the troops at Wallace
had been reduced to one company of infantry.

I had on hand a number of horses, mules and wagons,
which I had accumulated in trading with the hunters and
immigrants passing through the country and from which
I was deriving no income. I was obliged to dispose of
them elsewhere, as there was no demand for them at
Wallace.

The San Juan mining country was just then receiving
considerable notice in the papers and many people were
going there. I thought it might be a good country in
which to dispose of my outfit. So I decided to load my
wagons with the surplus goods that I had in the store and
start for the San Juan country, via Las Animas and Pueblo, Colorado. I had eight four-horse-and-mule teams,
and one wagon with two horses that I drove. It was a
valuable train. One pair of horses weighed thirty-two
hundred pounds. I bought this team from a party from
Missouri, who had gone to Colorado to make their home
but did not like the country and were on their way back
to "good ol' Mizzoury," as they expressed it. One pair
of mules weighed nearly as much as the horses. I traded with the Southern Overland Stage Company for them.
They were too large for the stage business and had run
away on one or two occasions.

I stopped at Las Animas a day or so while waiting
for a shipment of goods that I had purchased in the
East. Las Animas was the terminus of a branch road

of the Kansas-Pacific running from Kit Carson. While there I discharged one of my teamsters, as I was about to move out. Daniel Daney, an old schoolmate of mine, who had charge of the corral where my stock was quartered, said he would like to go with me. I said, "All right, jump on." He had heard one of the men call me "Homer" and asked me if I formerly lived in Winona, Minnesota, and attended Mrs. Henry's school. I answered, "Yes." He then told me his name, and I recognized him as one of my old schoolmates. He had been a lieutenant in the Twentieth Infantry, and in the consolidation and reorganization of the army (in 1869, I believe), he was an extra officer—took a year's pay and went out of the service.

On the way to Pueblo we passed through the Purgatory and Rocky Ford country, where the celebrated melons, known all over the country, are now raised in such abundance. Little did I dream then that that country of sagebrush and sand would one day be one of the garden spots of the United States. Irrigation has made that soil to blossom like the rose.

From Pueblo to old Fort Garland, on the Rio Grande River, I went over the Moscow Pass, taking the first wagons that went through the pass. The road had not been completed, but by good management we got through by doubling teams in many steep places. On one mountainside we snubbed our wagons down by ropes. We took all the animals off the vehicles, save the wheel teams, attached a rope to the axle, and thus lowered the wagons. Some of my teamsters had freighted in the mountains and were skilled in mountain work. My experience here was very useful to me in handling transportation after I entered the army service. The builder of the road was very anxious to get wagons started going over his toll road and told me if I would go his route he would not make any charge. I thus saved a few dollars, which paid me very well. Moreover, it was a shorter route.

From Garland we went up the Rio Grande to Loma, a little hamlet opposite Del Norte. Here I leased a store and opened up for business. There was a scarcity of flour, which made prices pretty high, so I sent my wagons to Canyon City for thirty-five thousand pounds of the "Rough and Ready" brand. This I shipped from Denver. When my teams returned the price of flour had declined materially, but I made good freight money. Flour came in from Taos, New Mexico, the wheat having been threshed out by driving sheep and goats over the ground, and then cleaned by the wind. For that reason the housewives preferred my flour. There was no demand for mules or horses, so I sent my outfit back to Wallace. Later, I sold the pair of very large horses and mules to a man who had the contract to plow the fireguard for the Union Pacific Railroad.

I spent the Fourth of July in Loma. We had a lively celebration, the miners coming forty and fifty miles to help us celebrate. A number of Mexicans were among the party. We had all kinds of games—climbing a greased pole to secure the prize, a five dollar gold piece which was placed on top of the pole; catching pigs that had been shaved and greased, the party catching the pig getting the animal, grease and all. The Mexicans took a hand in this and thought it great sport. To wind up the festivities, we had a Mexican burro, with a five-dollar prize for whoever could ride it. It was a lively little animal, and succeeded in throwing two or three riders. About this time we were all feeling "pretty good." I made a bet that I could ride the beast if they would hold him until I was on his back and not turn him loose until I gave the word. I got on him facing his tail, then secured a twist on one of his ears with my left hand and seized his tail with my right. Then I locked my legs around his body as well as I could and told them to let him go. I had seen this trick done at a circus. We certainly had a monkey-and-parrot time of it. When the beast found he could not get me off he lay down and tried to roll me off. I opened my legs but kept hold of his ear and tail; then the little animal got to his feet and tried to rub me off against the porch of a gun shop. Not succeeding, he bolted inside the store and tipped over one of the show-cases, doing considerable damage. That ended the circus. I was declared the winner and the "champion burro rider of the Rio Grande." But my five-dollar gold piece had to go toward paying for the damage done in the gun shop.

Loma did not turn out to be a good business place, so I moved over to Del Norte after a few months. I closed out my business at a loss, selling a bill of goods to the cashier of one of the banking houses who was interested in a store in one of the mining camps. He told me to step into the bank and he would pay me. The bill amounted to nearly a thousand dollars. I told him that I was not quite ready to leave the country and did not want to carry the money on my person, but would call for it when I wanted it. In the meantime the firm failed and I lost my money. Some two years later I saw in one of the San Juan papers that this same cashier was the recorder of one of the mining districts. I wrote him for my money. He answered that he would pay his share of the bill by installments but was not able to pay the full amount, and that his partner was living in Europe. I accepted this proposition, feeling that "half a loaf was better than none," and finally got from the cashier what had been promised, but the remainder was a total loss.

While here I traded some goods and part cash for two

lots costing me one hundred and fifty dollars. Shortly
after I had made the purchase an owner of a burro corral wanted to buy the lots for the purpose of using them
for a corral. I told him he might have them for three
hundred dollars. I went to a Mr. Van Guesin, who lived
in a pretty house adjoining my lots, and told him that a
party wished to buy them to use for a corral but that I
didn't care to sell them for that purpose. Mr. Van Guesin
thereupon offered me three hundred and twenty-five dollars for them; which offer I accepted.

(In March, 1912, I was on the steamer *Ismailia,* going
from Alexandria, Egypt, to Greece. I met a party who
were from Colorado, and in our general conversation I
learned that they formerly lived at Del Norte. I related
the above incident to them and a lady in the party said
that Mr. Van Guesin was her uncle. This was nearly forty
years later.)

Upon my arrival at Loma, about the first man I met
was a Doctor Dorr, whom I had known at Wallace a year
before. He was prospecting western Kansas for coal and
oil. He gave the officers at Wallace a very interesting
lecture on the mineral deposits of Kansas. Doctor Dorr
said he had some good prospects in the Summit district
and wanted me to help him out. I became interested with
him and we organized the Telluric Mining District, adjoining the Summit. We had some very good prospects,
the ore assaying fifteen dollars and upward in gold, silver and iron. The doctor explained to me that the iron
ore (which ran ten per cent. in some of the assays) was
a valuable flux in the fusion of the ore.

On one of our leads we erected a good log cabin.
The doctor and my man, Daney, were to open up the mine
during the winter. I made arrangements with Mark Bidell,
a merchant of Del Norte, to let them have a reasonable

amount of stores, and I left the country, via Denver, where I bought a mining outfit, including a forge, steel for drills, etc., (they were to sharpen their own drills), and shipped the outfit to them. The purchase amounted to about one hundred and fifty dollars. The next news I had from them was that water was running into the mine and they needed a' pump, and as they knew I was not able to put one in the plant they would shut down for the winter, the doctor intending to practise his profession, while Daney would endeavor to get a school to teach. I later received a letter from Bidell, stating that the doctor and Daney were doing nothing but were both drinking freely. He advised me to shut off some of their privileges. They had hired a little cabin and were doing their own cooking. I accordingly countermanded my order to Bidell for goods, giving them only a month's supply. Probably I would not have done this had I not met with some business reverses and been obliged to retrench. I had left seven or eight good burros with them. When I was ready to leave the country I had some trouble in finding my two horses. I had turned them out above the cabin. I knew they could not get out of the canyon without passing where we had been at work.

While looking for them I heard loud yelling up the mountainside. It was the doctor. I hastened there and he had a big ball of mud in his hand, declaring excitedly, "We have struck it bigger than a wolf." He started in to tell me what the ball was composed of, but in an angry voice I exclaimed, "Damn your strike! I want to find my horses and get out of the country." He retorted, "Damn you and your horses! Here we have the world by the breeches and you do not appreciate it!" I found my horses, and the next day started for home.

I made a trip to the little mining camp of Howardsville

some time before I left for home, about one hundred and thirty miles from Del Norte. I think it was on the Animas River or one of its tributaries. The camp was composed of about a dozen log cabins and was located at the mouth of Cunningham Gulch, named for the man who discovered the pass.

The Little Giant Mine was near by. It was owned by a New York syndicate and was in litigation at the time. The court was in session in a log cabin and there was considerable excitement. The judge, fearing trouble, had sworn in several miners as marshals to protect the court. I here met some miners who were very anxious for me to purchase a half interest in the North Star Mine, which they had located and were developing. A Frenchman named Gupell owned a half interest. He furnished the men with a grub stake and also the money for the food, for a one-half interest in all they discovered; they were to do the work.

Mr. Gupell was a small ranchman, and not able to furnish the necessary money to develop the mine. He was willing to sell his half for one thousand dollars. I went to the mine and found they had done quite a little work and had considerable ore on the dump. They selected several pieces of ore which they thought was about the average. I was to take it to Del Norte and have it assayed. If the result pleased me I was to purchase Mr. Gupell's interest. We were to pack the ore in sacks to Antelope Park, where my wagons could reach it, and I was to haul it to Canyon City, about two hundred miles, to be milled. It was thought that the ore would pay for the developing of the mine. Three miners were to do the work. They were the prospectors who located the mine.

On my way out I stopped to see Mr. Gupell. I made an agreement with him that in the assaying of the ore, if it met with my expectations, I would give him one thousand dollars for his half interest. He was to take in part payment a pair of horses, wagon, harness, and merchandise out of my store; with some cash. I had the assay made, which ran $167.50 to the ton. I consulted the assayer, who was a friend of mine, and my friend Bidell. They said the assay was good but that there were many mines in that district which were assaying much higher, and the chances were that I could buy a half interest in several mines for that money. Thereupon I decided not to make the purchase.

Now for the aftermath: Before I left the country that mine was purchased for thirty thousand dollars by Mr. Van Guesin, who was the agent for Jay Cooke & Company, bankers, of New York city. A year or so after that I read the official report of E. H. Ruffner, engineer's office of the Department of Missouri. He mentioned several mines in the San Juan district, and the North Star Mine was given as the richest one in the entire group!

On my return to Del Norte and after coming out of Cunningham Gulch, where snow and ice remained the year around, I got off the trail in a blinding blizzard. After floundering around in the snow, my horse at times clear up to his belly, I got back on the trail, and as I got down to the snow line the storm subsided. I soon reached Pole Creek, where I had to remain all night, because of high water caused by melting of the snow during the day time. In the night the water ran out, so by morning I could ford the stream safely. Knowing that I would have to do this, I had provided myself with all the comforts of camp, extra blanket, knife and fork, sack of ground coffee, bread and a piece of bacon; also a feed for my horse. I made him comfortable, fixed my coffee and then was ready to retire. I built two fires, spreading my blankets between them, and I with my saddle for a pillow was soon fast asleep. My boots were wet through from tramping in the snow, so I made sure to put them carefully near the fire to dry them. When I arose and attempted to draw them on they were still quite damp, and my horse was not in sight or hearing. He had pulled up his picket-pin and no doubt had started back on the trail.

As the horse had to be found immediately, I left my boots drying near the fire and from an old grain sack manufactured a pair of "California moccasins," then started out to locate the animal. Just before I got to the snow line I found him grazing. I went back to camp, where I found my boots *very* much dried—nearly burned up, in fact, and I was obliged to return to Del Norte wearing the California moccasins.

CHAPTER XIV

IN APRIL, 1875, I sent a party of five men, thoroughly armed, in charge of H. A. Clark (now a prominent citizen of Wallace, Kansas), to gather up cattle that were supposed to have drifted down on Punished Woman's Fork, some forty miles from Wallace.

A few days later I received a despatch from Clark dated at a station on the Santa Fé Railroad, saying his party had been corralled by Indians on Punished Woman's Fork, but he had succeeded in driving them off and they had started in a northerly direction.

I showed the despatch to Major Hambright, Fifth Infantry, the commanding officer at Fort Wallace, who telegraphed to General Pope, the department commander at Fort Leavenworth, Kansas, as there were no cavalry stationed at Fort Wallace. The general ordered a detachment of Troop H, Sixth Cavalry, in command of Lieutenant Austin Henely from Fort Lyon, Colorado, to Wallace, a distance of one hundred and twenty-five miles. They marched to Kit Carson, Colorado, sixty miles, and there entrained for Wallace. They arrived on the eighteenth. We all moved out on the morning of the nineteenth with forty men and two six-mule wagons for transporting forage and rations. The post surgeon, Doctor Atkins, and Lieutenant C. C. Hewitt, Nineteenth Infantry, accompanied the expedition.

The commanding officer and Lieutenant Henely thought

we ought to go direct to the place where my men were corralled.   I suggested that we might be able to cut their trail, as when the Indians were last seen they were going north, and if they had done so would doubtless take the old Indian trail east of Wallace some thirty-five miles.   It would not take much longer to try out their trail, and if we did not succeed in striking it we then could go on to Punished Woman's Fork.

These officers had just come into the country and had had no Indian experience, so they readily fell in with my suggestion.   About noon we struck a fresh Indian trail of some twelve or fifteen lodges, just where I thought we would, and as our transportation was cumbersome the lieutenant cached one of his wagons in a deep ravine, attaching the extra mules to the other wagon.   We took nothing with us but what was absolutely necessary and were quickly ready for a forced march.   We traveled rapidly until dark and then bivouacked.   It rained on us nearly all night; we had no tentage and the men had only their overcoats to protect them from the storm.

We could make no coffee as there was no wood in the country, and even if there had been it would not have been advisable to build a fire, as it might have been seen by the enemy.   The night passed as pleasantly as could have been expected under the circumstances.   We moved out early next morning, found that the trail had been almost obliterated, and experienced considerable trouble in following it.

We reached the Union Pacific Railroad about noon. There the Indians seemed to have scattered, I think intentionally.   Not that they knew we were on their trail, but they do not like to be seen when passing through the country, so they took this means of passing in small parties, thinking that the railroad people would be less likely to notice them. The railroad officials usually notified the troops when large bodies of Indians were crossing the railroad and doubtless the Indians were aware of this.

After crossing the railway we were unable to find a sign of the trail for some time. When a trail is lost the order of procedure is for the men to circle around and see whether they can pick it up. Each time the circle is made a little larger, until the trail is found. Finally, Private James T. Ayers reported that he had found a single pony track about half a mile to our right. This single track was followed for some miles, when it was lost completely. There were a great many wild horses in that part of the country at the time. We were on their range and could not follow the Indian trail longer.

Not discouraged, we continued north, knowing the Indians would come together sooner or later on some one of the many small streams in that country. That night we camped at the headwaters of the Solomon River. Here we held a council of war and I suggested a plan which was finally adopted. We moved out the next morning at daylight and about nine o'clock met some hunters whom I knew. They told us that the Indians we were after were on the north fork of Sappa Creek and that they had robbed their (the hunters') camp the previous day while the men were absent. The latter thought the redskins might be about seventeen miles from us, as they did not believe the Indians would travel much farther. There were plenty of buffalo, and they would stop to have a hunt.

I prevailed upon the hunters to turn back and show us where the savages were at the time they robbed the camp. We marched about six miles and camped in a deep ravine until sundown, when we continued on to within five miles of Sappa Creek. Here we halted and went into camp.

As stated we had calculated that the Indians would not go much farther than this creek, for they must have had good luck hunting and were bound to go into camp at the first opportunity and have a feast. I proposed to the hunters that we start after dark and try to locate the Indian camp. Acting upon this suggestion, the lieutenant loaned us black horses to ride, as they could not be plainly distinguished in the night time.

Nothing occurred to attract our attention until we arrived on the next stream, the north fork of Sappa. Here the hunters thought they could distinguish the Indian camp in the bottom. They wanted to return and inform the lieutenant that we had found the camp, but my eyes were not so good as theirs. I could not see anything resembling an Indian camp and told them it was nothing but some white banks or alkali spots. I wanted them to go with me to investigate, but they refused.

Finally, I told them if they would remain behind I would go forward on foot and ascertain whether they were correct. I thought best to go on foot, lest my horse should whinny if taken away from the others, which would have alarmed the Indians and our game would have decamped.

I followed on down the gully several hundred yards, then crawled on my hands and knees for some distance, finally coming in sight of the objects the hunters had seen. As I expected, it proved to be only white alkaline banks. I went back tired and disgusted. We then followed down the stream some distance, when the hunters again thought they had found another camp, which proved to be two old buffalo bulls.

The men said they would go no farther, as it was clear that the Indians were not on that stream. I asked them how far it was to timber and they said about twelve miles. I told them the chances were that the Indians had struck for shelter, as it was cold and disagreeable, and I suggested that we ride on and ascertain; but they refused, so I started off alone. After riding some distance I discovered that they were following me and felt better, even though they were a few hundred yards behind.

These men were not cowards. One of them, "Hank" Campbell, had been in an Indian fight with me on a previous occasion, when we captured the Indians who proved to be part of the band that killed three members of the Germaine family on the Smoky. The hunters thought the Indians were not on that creek and it was stubbornness on my part that prompted me to go on farther; so I rode cautiously on, keeping my eyes open as I went down the stream. It was still dark, as the moon had not yet risen. The stream was crooked and boggy; I was weary and had about made up my mind that I had taken too big a contract. Presently my courage rose, for I had discovered fresh horse droppings although they might have been made by wild horses which roamed in that country.

In the meantime the moon arose and I had less trouble in finding my way. At last I rode up on a ridge and carefully looked over the top. Here I saw some horses grazing in the bend of the river. At first I thought they were wild horses but soon found I was mistaken, for they had seen me and did not seem frightened.

I remained there until the hunters came up, when I told them to look over the ridge and see whether they could locate anything. One of them exclaimed, "Holy Smoke! There they are!" and started to ride away. I grabbed his bridle rein and told him to keep quiet; that there was no danger, as the horses were not frightened and the Indians must be in camp below them. The thing to do was to ride slowly and cautiously away for a short distance, so as not to alarm the ponies, and then speed back and inform the lieutenant of our discovery.

This we did, arriving in camp about two o'clock. The

lieutenant was called and the men were ordered to saddle up at once without any unnecessary noise. Within a half-hour we were on the march. I struck out in a northeasterly direction. The hunters started northwest and the lieutenant followed them, but soon discovered I was not with them. He sent his trumpeter to me to tell me the hunters thought I was going too far toward the east. I told him to tell the lieutenant that I was the man who had found the horses and knew I was not mistaken in the direction. The officer soon joined me and said the hunters had been in that country for some time and knew it better than I did. I remarked, "Very well, sir; you take their advice, and I will ride home."

He said, "Mr. Wheeler, I have acted on your judgment so far and it has not failed me yet. I will not go back on you. Lead on."

Upon reaching the divide I told him to keep just at the head of the breaks running down into the stream, and I would go nearer the stream and keep down it, where I could see everything and when I discovered the camp I would not be long in letting them know it. Within an hour or so after leaving him I discovered the herd again in the same place where we had left them, but could not locate the Indian camp. I turned back and reported to the lieutenant, who then made his plan of attack.

I then left him, followed the stream down and discovered the camp a few hundred yards below the horses. By this time the ponies had been rounded up and it was near daybreak. Three or four of the tepees were old and nearly the color of dead grass. I did not see them until quite near. No one was stirring in the camp; not even the dogs had given the alarm as they usually do when prowlers are around.

Hearing a slight noise, I looked around and saw, not

more than two hundred yards away, an Indian herder running for dear life to notify the camp of the approach of enemies. The Indians were instantly stirring and I saw them pour from their tepees as I started to warn the lieutenant.

We had some difficulty in crossing the stream, as it was boggy. None of the men followed us. The sergeant said it was impossible for the men to cross there. The lieutenant remarked, "We have crossed; now every man of you must cross." The troopers then rode in without further hesitation, and after much floundering all crossed safely, although one man lost his carbine and another his pistol.

We moved up and ordered the Indians to surrender, making signs which they well understood. One warrior said in pretty good English, "Go 'way, John; bring back our ponies." They then fired on us and the fun commenced.

I must have been greatly excited, for I remember little of what was going on during the next few minutes. When I recovered my senses I was lying on the ground, pumping lead into the Indians. It was a hand-to-hand conflict. Two of our men, Sergeant Rapier and Private Robert Themis, were killed within a few feet of the Indians. Themis was our cook and was supposed to remain with the wagon; in fact, was told to do so. Poor fellow, he lost his life by not obeying instructions.

One of the Indians reached over the bank and secured one of the trooper's guns, and used it against us. The lieutenant had some trouble in getting his men to lie down. They fought like madmen. Their whole desire seemed to be to charge the Indians and drive them out. Finally, we got down to business, and whenever an Indian showed his head we would shoot at it. It seemed as if we never would drive them out. Some of them hid behind the creek bank and the men could only see them when they raised their heads to shoot.

I went around to the rear, unnoticed by them, but to do this had to crawl some distance on my hands and knees through the grass. From my new position I could see the Indians lying along the bank, and I soon drove them from this position. As soon as they had discovered me they all commenced firing on me and made it mighty uncomfortable, and I was not slow to leave my dangerous position. I had to run the gauntlet for some fifty yards in order to reach a place of safety. I ran in a zigzag manner, falling down two or three times, which no doubt saved me, as the bullets whistled around me as thick as bees when swarming— at least, I imagined so.

While I was in that position, a large Indian dog came running toward me. I was somewhat frightened and was about to shoot it. When about five yards from me the animal turned and ran in a different direction, evidently having just discovered me. I felt much relieved. I joined one of the detachments to the left and volunteered to lead a charge.

When we arrived at the rifle pits a big Indian jumped out of one of the holes and fired at us, the ball passing through my cartridge box. A young soldier, a mere boy, and I ran after him. The soldier was several feet in advance of me, firing at the Indian with his six-shooter. He emptied it as the Indian dropped down behind a little ridge and took dead aim at the soldier. Throwing up my gun, I "beat the Indian to it," and shot him through the head, killing him instantly. This was the first intimation the soldier had that I was near him. He grasped my hand, with tears in his eyes, and thanked me for saving his life. This was the last Indian in the fight and was no doubt one of the chiefs. He had a three-banded Springfield rifle, which was half cocked, and a cartridge was in the chamber. I shot so quickly that the Indian did not have time to pull the trigger.

The soldier and I divided his ornaments. I got the war bonnet, afterward presenting it to General Pope at Fort Leavenworth, Kansas, after coming into the army service. (There are twelve feathers in the tail of an eagle, and as many as sixty or seventy are used in making war bonnets. They readily bring in trade one or two ponies, but some Indians will not part with them for any price, feeling that good luck would desert them if they did so.)

It was near noon when we finished destroying the camp, and we moved at once for Fort Wallace, as we were sure there were other Indians in the country. About eleven o'clock that night it commenced to rain and snow very hard, and the men had so much trouble in driving the captured stock that we had to halt until daylight, and during the night lost most of them. I was completely tired out, not having had any sleep for thirty hours, so I wrapped my saddle blanket around me, leaned against a wagon wheel and went to sleep. When I was awakened I found that Lieutenant Henely had thrown his cape over me and had himself been without any covering during the storm. We moved out as soon as it was light enough to see. It commenced to snow about one o'clock and continued until we reached Sheridan station, where we went into camp.

Lieutenant Hewitt and I went to the section house to sleep. Early the next morning Doctor Atkins came to our door and knocked. He informed us that it had turned very cold during the night and they had suffered a great deal. When the lieutenant got the men together there were several missing, and he was afraid they had wandered off and perhaps frozen to death, and he desired the doctor to wire the post for succor. I asked the doctor to delay wiring until I could see the lieutenant. I told Henely that we had done so well I did not like to have him ask for assistance if we could avoid it, that we had better make a thorough search for the missing men and could then wire if they were not found.

Doctor Atkins suggested that the men might be covered with snow. He found a pole and commenced to poke it into some of the drifts where he thought they might be. Finally, he heard a faint voice crying out, "Stop that! You are hurting me; get off my feet!"

"Here they are!" shouted the doctor. All hands immediately went to work and dug out the missing men. They all said that they had not suffered but had put in a comfortable night. It seems that they had located under a little bank to break the wind and the snow had blown over them, acting as a comforter, and they had slept "like a bug in a rug."

Too much can not be said in praise of Lieutenant Henely's gallantry and management of the fight. It showed that he was a commander of men. His coolness while under fire was very noticeable. He had served a short time in the Civil War and had been appointed to West Point from the ranks. Shortly after the Sappa Creek fight he was ordered to Arizona with his regiment, the Sixth Cavalry, and was there with Lieutenant Rucker in charge of Apache scouts. They were both drowned forty miles south of Fort Bowie while crossing a swollen stream during a storm. I was very sorry to learn that the lieutenant's career was so suddenly cut off. Had he lived and been given the opportunity he would have made an enviable record in the service. He was a natural-born soldier. Lieutenant Hewitt deserved mention, he having taken an active part in the fight and having assisted in rounding up the ponies. About one hundred and fifty animals were captured, including a Mexican burro which belonged to me. There were six or seven very fine mules in the bunch.

Doctor Atkins, a contract surgeon, also deserved great

CRAZY HORSE, A LEADING CHIEF IN THE BATTLE OF THE
LITTLE BIG HORN, JUNE 25, 1876

praise for his actions, not only during the fight, but on the entire trip. He risked his life in going where the men were killed and bringing their bodies away under fire from the Indians.

These officers should have been breveted for their actions in this fight. However, department commanders had become tired of recommending officers for brevet, because Congress failed to act upon their recommendations, so merely mentioned them in orders, thanking them for their service, as was done in this instance. I presume these orders were filed away in the archives at Washington, but in those days the War Department was not as particular about an officer's record as it has been for the last few years.

The enlisted men could not have done better. They all showed great courage; in fact, they were over-zealous and risked their lives when there was no necessity. Sergeant Kitchen, senior non-commissioned officer, afterward reenlisted in the Fifth Cavalry and was first sergeant of Troop I for several years. Later, he was made quartermaster sergeant in the quartermaster department, where he served faithfully for years, and is now retired. Corporal James T. Ayers, who was of great service in trailing the Indians, reenlisted in the Fifth Cavalry. In 1895 he was a general service man at General Miles' headquarters, Chicago, where I saw him at that time.

Shortly after our return from the fight my men located the ponies we had lost during the storm and were driving them in to the post. Mrs. Robinson, wife of an officer, sent one of her boys into the store to tell me the men were coming in with the ponies. I rushed out and told them to return them to camp. They told me they thought they would bring them in, as they might get some ponies by so doing. I told them that they were strays and did not belong to the government. In the meantime, Sergeant Kitchen came up with a guard and said the commanding officer had sent him for the ponies. I told him they were mine and that the men were taking them out to the ranch. He said, "Oh, no. I recognize that pony over there; it is one that you rode on our return from the fight." This pony evidently belonged to one of the squaws. The ears had been pierced and blue ribbons were tied therein.

Therefore, to my regret, I had to turn the ponies over to Sergeant Kitchen. He said he was sorry to take them but "orders were orders." Later on I went to the quartermaster's corral and cut out five or six mules and four ponies (I didn't have time to take any more). I kept the mules and gave the ponies to my men. These ponies were afterward sold at auction by the government. I think that the Indians we wiped out were some that escaped from General Nelson A. Miles in his winter campaign of 1874.

In a day or so, I went on another scout to the Punished Woman's Fork. We saw no Indians but I found that the Indians we had fought had killed at least one hundred head of my cattle. On their trail we found several cows with my brand that they had killed, just cutting out the tongues and unborn calves. The latter, as well as the tongues, are a great delicacy with the Indians. I also found in one place the skeletons of thirty-two head of cattle. This was on Punished Woman's Fork near where my men were corralled. It is probably needless to add that the government never paid me for the cattle. I presume my papers in the premises are carefully filed away "for future action." These were only a few of my many experiences. I not only had Indians to contend with but was bothered by cattle and horse thieves.

I received my commission in the army for my services in this fight.   General Pope recommended it.   I knew nothing about his recommendation until I received my appointment.   I was opening the mail and found an envelope addressed to Second Lieutenant Homer W. Wheeler.   Enclosed was my appointment, to my great surprise.   The same mail brought me a letter from Major McKee Dunn, who was on General Pope's staff, congratulating me on my appointment.   I hesitated some little time before accepting it, but finally closed out my business satisfactorily and entered the service in October, 1875, and have never regretted it.

I have been asked on several occasions whether graduates of West Point did not think they were a little better than those officers who were appointed from civil life and from the ranks, and treated them accordingly.   I have also several times seen such a question asked in the newspapers. If there is such a feeling, I have never seen it shown.   General Royal, a veteran of the Mexican and Civil Wars (well known by older officers), while on one of his tours of inspection, asked me that question.   I told him that these officers had always treated me with the greatest consideration, and he said that such was his own experience.   If there are any persons who now have that impression, I should like to disillusion their minds of that idea.   My dearest and best friends were West Pointers, and many of high rank.

Henely wrote an official report of the Sappa Creek fight, in which he said:

"Mr. Homer W. Wheeler, post trader at Fort Wallace, left his business and volunteered to accompany the detachment as a guide.   His knowledge of the country and of Indian habits was of the utmost service.   He risked his life to find the Indian camp—was the first to discover it in the morning—and, although not expected to take part in the fight, was always on the skirmish line, and showed the greatest courage and activity. The three hunters, Henry Campbell, Charles Schroeder and Samuel F. Scrack, who, with Mr. Wheeler, found the camp, performed important services. They participated in a portion of the fight and drove in the herd of ponies which otherwise would not have been captured. When these men turned back with me, I promised them they would be suitably rewarded if they found the camp. I respectfully request that their services, as well as those of Mr. Wheeler, be substantially acknowledged."

PART TWO: MY ARMY CAREER

CHAPTER XV

I JOINED my troop at Fort Lyon, Colorado, in December, 1875, and performed the duties incident to that time. After the Custer massacre, June 25, 1876, my troop (L) and Troop H, Fifth Cavalry, were ordered sent to the old Red Cloud agency (now Fort Robinson), Nebraska. We remained there but a few days, when we were ordered to march to Camp Sheridan (Spotted Tail agency). It having been reported by courier that the camp was surrounded by Indians, and that the commanding officer, Captain Mears, Ninth Infantry, would like to have more troops, we made a rapid march, covering the distance (fifty miles) in about eight hours. We found the garrison (two companies) prepared to make a gallant defense. They had piled cordwood around the post—quite a common mode of defense in those days—as it made a good breastwork in case of an attack. We remained there only a short time and then returned to Fort Robinson.

It was at Camp Sheridan that I first met General Jesse M. Lee, then a first lieutenant of the Ninth Infantry. General Lee is yet living at the Presidio of San Francisco, California, and we have always been great friends. We were both very much interested in the welfare of the red man and worked together on several occasions in the Indian Territory (now Oklahoma). He was the Indian agent at Spotted Tail agency and had great influence over those Indians. It was generally conceded at the time of the 1876 Indian troubles that he kept those Indians from joining the hostiles.

On the occasion of the trip to Red Cloud agency I had charge of the wagon train. There were six wagons, each drawn by six mules. With me were two non-commissioned officers, who had charge of the troop kitchen, the cooks and three or four men, about nine in all.

On the way, as we were passing over a culvert it broke down, and I had to repair it before I could get all my wagons over. This delayed me for a short time, allowing the column to get some distance ahead. While working on the bridge I noticed half a dozen horsemen coming toward me and I soon discovered that they were Indians. We had passed through the agency some little time before. I conjectured that they might have come out for some deviltry and made up my mind if they had they would not catch me napping.

It did not take me very long to repair the bridge and we then continued our march. The Indians continued to come in from different directions, stopping in little groups on the prominent high ground around me. I asked a couple of the teamsters who had been in my employ while in Kansas and had been out on Indian scouting parties, what they thought about it. They replied that it looked a little bit suspicious, so I called the non-commissioned officers and told them of my plans.

I sent one of them, with my compliments, to the commanding officer, to report that I had been delayed; that there were a number of Indians hovering around, and that, while there might be no danger of attack, I did not like the looks of things; their actions were suspicious and I did not want to take any chances. I then called the corporal's attention to a ravine ahead, through which the road passed, and instructed him to be careful in approaching it, as there might be Indians lurking there, and that if he saw anything which did not look right not to attempt to cross the gulch but hasten back to the wagons.

I at once made preparations to corral my wagons on a little eminence near the ravine, which commanded the surrounding country and was a good position from which to stand off the Indians if they made an attack. There were about a dozen Indians on the hill and I told Sergeant Clark of my troop to take three or four men and run them off. He started off, I following him as fast as the mules could go, but it was slow progress, as the wagons were heavily loaded. The sergeant ran off the Indians, and leaving his men to occupy the hill hastened back, laughing, and informed me that the Indians were some young bucks and squaws. I felt rather foolish over the scare, but one can not always tell what an Indian may do. I later learned that the young people of the tribe care for the ponies and early in the morning drive them out to the grazing grounds. They no doubt had been doing this and on their return to the village had stopped in groups and were gossiping and watching us out of curiosity.

I did not complete the corralling of my wagons but straightened them out and moved on. My courier reached the commanding officer safely and delivered my message. Thereupon, Captain Hamilton, commanding H Troop, came to my "rescue." One of my men said to me, "Lieutenant, we had a pretty close call, didn't we?"

For my own part, I would just as soon be killed as frightened to death. I think there is more truth than poetry in that expression.

On October 23, 1876, I was engaged in the affair on Chadron Creek, about forty miles from Red Cloud agency, where the villages of Red Cloud and Red Leaf were located. It was thought they were communicating with the hostiles and that some of their young men had joined them. It was also feared they might break out into hostilities. They had been ordered by the agent to move in close to the agency but failed to comply with the order, and General Crook ordered General Mackenzie to bring them in.

We left the post just after dark (when everything had quieted down) with six troops of the Fourth Cavalry and my troop (L) and H Troop, Fifth Cavalry, avoiding the agency, so the Indians would not see us, as they might notify Red Cloud that we were coming. The men were cautioned not to light matches or indulge in loud conversation. After we were well under way, Major Frank North joined us with his famous Pawnee Scouts.* Along toward morning we came to a point where the trail forked, one branch leading to Red Cloud's camp and the other to Red Leaf's.

General Mackenzie, with five troops of his regiment, and Major North and some of his scouts, set out for Red Cloud's camp, reaching there before daylight and surrounding the village. At break of day the Indians were notified that they must surrender, whereupon the women and children made for the brush to hide themselves, but were driven back. The men remained in camp but their arms

*Captain Luther H. North, now (1925) living at Columbus, Nebraska, in his seventy-eighth year, is a brother of Major Frank North, organizer and chief of the famous Pawnee Scouts, who did such valiant service as allies of the government between 1865 and 1880. At that time Luther North was his brother's first lieutenant in the Pawnee Scouts. Captain North is now writing the story of his life, including a history of the Pawnee Scouts. Unquestionably, there is no living person better qualified to write of the Pawnee Indians than Captain North, who, with his famous brother, lived many years with the Pawnees, speaking their language as fluently as English, and being thoroughly conversant with their customs, dances, religion and daily life in general. Major Frank North died March 15, 1885, of pneumonia.

were promptly taken away, making resistance futile. No doubt they had cached their best guns, for they had been ordered to turn them in some time before, the arms taken being practically useless. The women were told to go to the pony herd and select a sufficient number on which to pack their camp equipage.

General Mackenzie had some trouble in making the squaws take down their lodges, but they were told that if they did not get to work he would burn the tepees. The women, however, did nothing, and the soldiers commenced to fire the tepees, whereupon the squaws swiftly set to work.

Red Leaf's camp was captured in about the same manner as Red Cloud's, by Major Gordon of the Fifth Cavalry, and M Troop of the Fourth, and a few scouts under Luther North, brother of Major North. The only shot fired was by accident. I was very much afraid that the shot might make trouble. We captured four hundred ponies. My cattle experience came in good play. On rounding up the village, we joined General Mackenzie's column. The captive warriors numbered about one hundred and fifty, and there were about seven hundred ponies captured altogether. The women and children were not counted. The Indians claimed there were only one hundred and twenty men and about three hundred ponies captured.* They may have been right as regards the number of men captured but were mistaken as to the number of animals. My squadron was detailed to escort the captives to Camp Robinson and the other troops went into camp.

We left Robinson about nine P. M., and returned the next night about eleven o'clock, being absent from the post about twenty-five hours, a good part of which time was

*The "Record of Engagements" says four hundred men and seven hundred horses.

spent in the saddle. Taking into consideration the rounding up of the Indian ponies, our squadron must have ridden more than one hundred miles, not a bad day's work.

Shortly after the capture of the Red Cloud and Red Leaf camps a trail was discovered leading away from the agency. It was surmised that a small party may have gone out to join the hostiles. My captain, Alfred B. Taylor, was ordered to take his troop (L) and investigate this trail, to ascertain where it was leading, but was directed that, under no conditions, should he go beyond Hat Creek. If the trail led to this stream and crossed it, it was pretty good evidence that the party was on its way to join Sitting Bull. The trail might have been made by a party from the hostiles which had slipped into Red Cloud reservation for information and supplies, and then out again. It was well known that the Indians were having intercourse with each other, but the authorities had never been able to detect any of them.

Just before we moved out our surgeon (a contract doctor), who had joined us from Chicago and had seen no service of any sort, came to me in civilian clothing and asked me to give him a saber. I inquired what he was going to do with it. He said that Lieutenant McKinney had told him he ought to have one and to come to me for it. I realized that this was one of the lieutenant's jokes, so without even a smile I told the surgeon that a revolver was better than a saber and gave him one.

We discovered that the trail was a small one, there being evidently about half a dozen Indians in the party. We followed it rapidly and in a few hours' ride found that it turned back toward the agency. By this time it was almost dark and was raining a little, making it difficult to follow the trail, and we abandoned it, bivouacking for the night. We were satisfied that the party had returned to the agency.

On arriving in camp, I noticed that the doctor had lost his saddle blanket and asked him what had become of it. He had not discovered his loss, remarking, "I must have lost it away back somewhere, as my saddle has been getting very hard for some time." The poor doctor was very tired and well he might be, for he had not been on a horse in years. Furthermore, this was the longest ride he had ever taken. He was certainly game.

When the drizzling rain set in I suggested to my captain, who was not very strong, that the doctor and he sleep together, and I would give them my blanket, a heavy one which I had strapped to my saddle, to spread over them. This suggestion was acted upon, and after assisting them in preparing their bed I rolled into my saddle blanket, with my saddle for a pillow, and went to sleep. During the night I heard the doctor and the captain talking. It seems that the doctor, in his sleep, was rubbing the captain's back. This awakened the latter, who asked what the doctor was trying to do, to which the latter replied that he was dreaming, and thought he was back in Chicago scratching his wife's back. Then, with a long sigh, he added, "And I wish I was there right now."

We put in a fairly good night and returned to our camp in the morning.

CHAPTER XVI

RACING IN THE ARMY AND AMONG THE INDIANS

IN THOSE days every troop of cavalry had a horse the men thought would run, and they were always willing to back their favorite with money. We had some exciting races, and as this was about the only amusement we had we enjoyed them very much. When we raced with civilians, however, we usually found that our horse could run just fast enough to lose the race.

We had a horse in L Troop, ridden by Trumpeter Brandsome, which was supposed to be a world beater. I arranged a race with one of the officers of the Third Cavalry, his troop belonging to the regular garrison. When the race came off all the garrison were betting on this horse, of course, and those outside the post were placing their cash on mine. The race was for a stake of fifty dollars, and the distance was four hundred yards. It was to come off just back of the post, where a track had been improvised for this particular race. General Mackenzie and Major Gordon were the judges. At the appointed time the whole command turned out to witness the race. There was a crowd of several hundred, including many Indians, who were very fond of racing their ponies.

The horses got off in good shape. They were neck and neck for the first few yards, then the horses would alternately forge ahead. I had arrived at the conclusion that the Third Cavalry horse was the better of the two.

Near the finish he was a little ahead, and it appeared that he was a sure winner. Suddenly he flew the track, attempting to go to the stable, which was near by. The rider, in trying to keep the animal on the track, pulled him just enough to allow my horse to pass.

The judges decided that the Fifth Cavalry horse had won the race, although the animals had not finished between the judges. The other party claimed that it was no race on that account, and demanded that it be run over. I claimed that it was a gentlemen's race, and that my horse was the winner. Evidently the judges thought the same in making their decision. Finally, it was decided that the race should be run over on the following Sunday. Then the other party wanted to put on a new rider and run the race over another track. To this I would not consent. The judges decided that the race must come off under the same conditions as the first one.

A day or two later I went into the officers' club, where there were quite a number of officers, and of course we had to talk about the coming race. One of them wanted to bet me two hundred dollars that the Third Cavalry horse would win the race. I did not care to put up any more money, as I was convinced that the other horse was the better. After some discussion this officer remarked, "Wheeler, you are not a thoroughbred. If you were, you would take my bet. The idea of a race-horse man being afraid to bet on his own horse; I never heard of such a thing."

This nettled me somewhat and I told him to put up his money. He asked me if his word was not as good as his money, and I replied, "No, money talks with me." I was basing my action on the thought that perhaps his horse might fly the track again, which was the reason I would not consent to having the race run on another track. Final-

ly, the money was put up, the officer having to borrow
some to make up the amount.

Just before the race came off I told my rider to keep
on the track under any and all circumstances. The other
horse again tried to bolt the track in about the same place
as before, and headed for the stables. I had taken the
gambler's chance and won!

Horse racing, as well as foot racing, is one of the
standard amusements of all Indians. The Utes of the
Colorado reservations made annual visits to the Washakie
agency, for the purpose of trading and racing, mostly the
latter. They usually returned home loaded with their
winnings, buffalo robes, furs and a goodly number of
ponies. The agent, Mr. Potter, threatened to put a stop
to the Utes' visits, but I do not think he ever did. The
races were usually short distances, from one hundred to
four hundred yards, the latter being their favorite. I
have known Indians to run for miles to test the endurance
of their ponies. Their animals receive, as a rule, no special
training, and rarely are precautions taken in regard to
feeding them before the races. The riders ride bareback
and commence to whip from the start, continuing to the
end of the course with legs and arms flying; but with
the perfect seat of the rider, the harmony of motion of
horse and rider do not allow this to interfere as much
with the stride and speed as one would naturally expect.
Usually, whatever is wagered is placed in a pile at the
winning post, and very rarely is there any dispute of the
result of the race. At times, so reckless is the betting
that the bettors are reduced from comparative wealth to
abject poverty.

In the foot races of the Indians, any advantage which
a runner can obtain over another by trickery is not only
considered proper and fair but is commended.

CHAPTER XVII

WHILE at Robinson, we built temporary quarters for the officers and men of our squadron, and stables for the horses. Each organization had a kitchen, a mess hall and a store room. Details were sent into the woods to cut logs and haul them to the agency sawmill, where they were cut into lumber. For our quarters we erected huts that would accommodate twelve men. Each was fitted with two windows, single sash, with four panes of glass. We constructed fireplaces of rock and mud on the outside of each hut at the rear. By doing this, the huts were made more spacious on the inside. All the work was done by soldier labor under the supervision of the officers, the only expense to the government being for nails, strap-hinges for the doors, window sash and glass. They would have been very comfortable quarters for the winter but we did not remain there to occupy them.

One night, along toward morning, we heard a terrible screeching just across the creek, where the Fourth Cavalry was encamped.

"To arms" was sounded and repeated by all the trumpeters in the different camps. As soon as the alarm was sounded, all the men, some three thousand or more, fell in on their company parade grounds, awaiting orders. I fell in with my troop and presently Major Gordon, our squadron commander, asked me to join him. A few minutes later "recall" was sounded, and everything quieted down.

Upon investigation, we learned that a recruit, who had just joined, had nightmare. He said he was dreaming that an Indian was going to scalp him. At any rate, the alarm call was a good object lesson, and the first, in fact, that we had had.

On November 1, 1876, the following named officers and troops under General Ranald S. Mackenzie, Colonel Fourth Cavalry, moved out of Fort Robinson, Nebraska, comprising fifty-two officers and fifteen hundred men, to join the Powder River expedition at Fort Laramie, Wyoming:

OFFICERS OF THE FOURTH CAVALRY

Henry W. Lawton, First Lieutenant, Regimental Quartermaster.*

Joseph H. Dorst, Second Lieutenant, Regimental Adjutant.†

Captain Clarence B. Mauck, Troop B.
Charles M. Callahan, First Lieutenant, Troop B.
J. W. Martin, Second Lieutenant, Troop B.
Wentz E. Miller, First Lieutenant, Attached to Troop.
Captain John Lee, Commanding Troop D.
Stanton A. Mason, Second Lieutenant, Troop D.
Frank L. Shoemaker, First Lieutenant, Troop E.
Henry H. Belles, Second Lieutenant, Troop E.
Captain Wert Davis, Troop F.
Captain William C. Hemphill, Troop I.
J. Wesley Rosenquest, Second Lieutenant, Troop M.
John A. McKinney, First Lieutenant, Troop K.
Harrison G. Otis, Second Lieutenant, Troop K.

---

*Henry W. Lawton was a major-general during the Spanish-American war. He was killed in action at San Mateo, Manila Province, December 19, 1900. He was a gallant officer.

†Joseph H. Dorst retired as colonel of the Third Cavalry. His many friends believed he should have been advanced to the grade of a general officer before his retirement. He died January 11, 1916.

OFFICERS OF THE THIRD CAVALRY

Henry W. Wessels, Captain, Troop H.*
Charles Hammond, Second Lieutenant, Troop H.
Gerald Russell, Captain, Troop K.
Oscar Elting, First Lieutenant, Troop K.
George A. Dodd, Second Lieutenant, Troop K.†

OFFICERS OF THE FIFTH CAVALRY

John M. Hamilton, Captain, Troop H.
Edward W. Ward, First Lieutenant, Troop H.
Edwin P. Andrus, Second Lieutenant, Troop H.‡
Alfred B. Taylor, Captain, Troop G.
Charles Rockwell, First Lieutenant, Troop G.
Homer W. Wheeler, Second Lieutenant, Troop G.

OFFICERS OF THE FOURTH ARTILLERY

Cushing, Taylor, Bloom, Jones, Campbell, Crozier, Frank
G. Smith, Harry R. Andrews, Greenough and Howe.

OFFICERS OF THE NINTH INFANTRY

Jordan, McCaleb, Devin, Morris C. Foot, Pease, Baldwin, Rockefeller, Jesse Lee, Bowman.

OFFICERS OF THE FOURTEENTH INFANTRY

Vanderslice, Murphy, Austin, Krause, Hasson, Kimball.

The scout officers were First Lieutenant Philo Clark, Second Cavalry, Second Lieutenant Hayden Delaney, Ninth Infantry, and First Sergeant James Turpin, Troop L, Fifth Cavalry.

These scouts were the choice of the Arapahoes, Ban-

---

*Henry W. Wessels, brigadier-general, retired April 23, 1904. He was an excellent soldier.

†George A. Dodd, retired July 25, 1916, by operation of law. He was promoted brigadier-general prior to his retirement, for valuable services on the Mexican border. Since deceased.

‡Edwin P. Andrus, retired as colonel of cavalry, December 31, 1912, at his request, after forty years' service. He displayed courage and good judgment in the fight with Dull Knife's band of Cheyennes.

(I have mentioned only the officers who became generals and colonels. All the others did good service. Many of them had served in the Civil War.)

nocks, Pawnees, Sioux and a few friendly Cheyennes. Some of the Arapahoe chiefs were Sharp Nose, Black Coal, Old Eagle, Six Feathers, Little Fork, White Horse and William Friday, the interpreter.

Of the Cheyennes: Thunder Cloud, Bird, Blown Away, Old Crow, Fisher, Hard Robe.

Among the Sioux were Charging Bear, Pretty Voiced Bull, Yellow Shirt, Singing Bear, Tall Wild Cat, Black Mouse.

The original idea was to organize two companies of Indian scouts, Lieutenant Philo Clark acting as major of scouts and to command all. Had this plan been carried out I was to command one of the companies.

The battalion and squadron commanders, as I remember, were Captain J. B. Campbell, brevet major, Fourth Artillery; Captain Jordan, a brevet major, Ninth Infantry; Captain Krauss, Fourteenth Infantry. There were four artillery companies, four companies of the Ninth Infantry and two of the Fourteenth Infantry. Captain Mauck commanded five troops of the Fourth Cavalry, and Major David Gordon of the Fifth Cavalry commanded two troops of the Fifth, two of the Third, and Lieutenant McKinney's troop of the Fourth.

On our arrival at Fort Laramie we found General Crook and his staff. First Lieutenant John G. Bourke, Third Cavalry, was acting assistant adjutant-general, Walter S. Schuyler, first lieutenant Fifth Cavalry, and First Lieutenant Philo Clark, Second Cavalry, aides-de-camp. First Lieutenant Charles Rockwell, Fifth Cavalry, was commissary officer, Surgeon Joseph R. Gibson was chief medical officer.

Our command was increased on our arrival at Fort Laramie by Captain Egan's troops of the Second Cavalry. It was detailed at General Crook's headquarters. Four companies of the Ninth and Twenty-third Infantry, and two companies of Pawnee scouts, numbering sixty-five men each, in charge of Frank North and his brother. These scouts gained quite a reputation in the Summit Springs fight, Nebraska, July 11, 1869, when General Eugene A. Carr defeated the "dog soldiers" under Tall Bull.

The regimental commanders were Colonels Richard Irving Dodge and Townsend. We must have had at least three thousand men, including our Indian scouts. Some of our troops of cavalry were filled up to and over one hundred men. Troop L had one hundred and eighteen. These were new men known as "General Custer's Avengers." At least one-half our men were recruits, but very little drilled and with still less camp experience. However, it does not take long to break in new men where there are plenty of old non-commissioned officers and soldiers.

We remained at Fort Laramie three or four days, fitting out the expedition. No finer, cleaner cut expedition was ever known in our service. Each soldier was provided with heavy underclothing, fur cap, gloves, leggings and arctic overshoes. They were allowed two blankets each. "A" tents were supplied, to each of which four men were assigned, and the tents were pitched to face each other, allowing sufficient room between to place a Sibley stove and to pin the flaps of the tents together.

I wore a suit of heavy underwear; over that a suit of perforated buckskin, a blouse and cardigan jacket; leggings and moccasins (made by the Indians with the hair inside), a soldier's overcoat which was very heavily lined with overcoat material, with fur collar and wristlets, a sealskin cap and gloves. Such was the officer's apparel. The great drawback to wearing all this extra clothing was that we had to walk a great deal, which warmed us considerably, and we would get chilled when we mounted again.

The men took turns in keeping up the fires and when

wood was scarce they would gather buffalo chips and sage-brush for fuel. On this expedition I saw stacks of sage-brush and greasewood piled up that were much larger than two tents, and even this amount would not last very long as it burned quickly. As soon as the tents were up the men who had no other duty to perform would begin to make preparations for comfort during the night. They would go out and pull up grass and sage-brush, spread their blankets on this, and have a "bed of roses," so to speak.

When we moved out of Fort Laramie each troop of cavalry had three six-mule teams and each company of infantry had two. We had one hundred and sixty-eight wagons, which required about one hundred and ninety wagon-masters and drivers. We also had seven ambulances. Lieutenant Lawton, then first lieutenant of the Fourth Cavalry, was the quartermaster of the mounted troops, and Major John V. Furey was quartermaster of the expedition. In addition, we had four hundred pack-mules under Tom Moore, chief packer. Some of the noted packmasters with us were Delaney, Patrick and Daley, Dave Mears, Young and others.

After five marches we reached Fetterman, one hundred miles away, drew supplies and moved on to Cantonment Reno at the crossing of Powder River, distant about one hundred miles farther, and some four or five days' march. Part of the time we were marching in the teeth of a biting storm, and had some trouble in fording Powder River because of the running ice. Cantonment Reno had been established for the protection of supplies to be issued to expeditions like ours. The officers and men stationed there were living in dugouts. The commanding officer was Major Tom Pollock, Ninth Infantry.

At the cantonment, Tom Cosgrove, with one hundred Shoshone scouts from Fort Washakie, joined us. Lieutenant Schuyler, Fifth Cavalry, who was an aide on General Crook's staff, was put in command of them. The noted chief, Washakie, of the Shoshones, was not with his Indians. He sent word that he was suffering from rheumatism and did not like to run the risk of a winter campaign, but had sent two sons and a nephew and would come in person later on if his services were needed.

While we were at Reno, quite a number of miners from Montana came in. They were almost starved and had suffered considerably in the blizzard.

We remained at Reno only long enough to allow the storm to subside, and on Wednesday, November 22, 1876, we continued our march to Crazy Woman's Fork, a branch of Powder River, about twenty miles from Cantonment Reno.

It was General Crook's intention to push out from Crazy Woman's Fork and strike the camp of the great Sioux chief, Crazy Horse, at that time believed to be on the upper Rosebud River, Montana, near his old battle-field of the previous June. The plan was changed, however, by a trifling circumstance. Early on the morning of November twenty-third, a Cheyenne Indian known as Sitting Bear, who had been despatched from Red Cloud agency by Colonel J. W. Mason in advance of the expedition to bear an ultimatum to the hostiles and ask them to surrender without bloodshed, gave General Crook the important information that the capture of a young Cheyenne warrior had alarmed his people, and that they had started across the hills to join Crazy Horse. There was, however, so he understood, another large Cheyenne village in one of the deep canyons of the Big Horn range, near the source of the Crazy Woman, the very stream we were on. So to discover the location of this village, to surprise and destroy it became the order of the day.

CHAPTER XVIII

FIGHT WITH DULL KNIFE'S BAND

GENERAL MACKENZIE was ordered to take all the scouts and cavalry, except Troop K, Second Cavalry, and push up the Crazy Woman Fork to its head, then strike into the Big Horn Mountains and hunt for what fate might have in store for him. Ten days' rations and extra ammunition were packed on mules, and to each man was issued one hundred rounds of ammunition to be carried on the person. Our effective force was twenty-eight officers and seven hundred and ninety men, and about two hundred scouts. We left early on the morning of November 24, 1876.

About three P. M., on the third day's march, we were halted, ordered to unsaddle, feed and make coffee. That morning I had been detailed to take charge of the guard over the pack-train, which was a usual detail of twenty-four hours; but I was relieved by another officer when we bivouacked, and ordered to join my troop. At that time I did not understand why.

At this time I saw several Indian scouts riding their ponies as fast as they could make them go. I asked Frank Grouard, the chief scout, the reason for this. He told me it was an old Indian custom to do this before going into a fight, as it gave the ponies their second wind. Grouard furthermore stated that some scouts had come in reporting that an Indian village had been located some distance away, and that the command would move on it as soon as the sun went down.

This we did, marching all night, surprising the village at the head of Willow Creek, a tributary of the Powder River, at daylight on the twenty-fifth. A short time before reaching the village I dismounted to remove my overcoat. In doing this I broke the strap of my field-glasses and stooped down to pick them up, when, to my great surprise, I saw another pair of glasses at my feet! I hurriedly rolled up both pairs in my overcoat and strapped it to my saddle, but as my horse was very restless I could not fasten my coat securely and lost both pairs of glasses. I made every effort to learn if any one in the command had lost any field-glasses but no one had. I think that some Indian must have dropped them and that they had originally belonged to some officer in the Seventh Cavalry, for later, in Dull Knife's village, we found a great many articles which belonged to that regiment, showing that these Indians must have taken an active part in the Custer battle of June twenty-fifth.

When we arrived in the vicinity of the Indian village, H and L Troops of the Fifth Cavalry were ordered to charge through it. Lieutenant McKinney's troop was to support us, but instead of doing as he was ordered he went in with us and was killed, his troop being fired on from a ravine directly in its front. The lieutenant was struck by six balls, his first sergeant was seriously wounded in the head and six troopers were wounded. McKinney's troop fell back breaking through H Troop, cutting off three or four sets of fours, and the captain, Hamilton. The horse of Lieutenant McKinney's trumpeter* was shot

---

*McKinney's trumpeter's sobriquet was "Shorty." He and my striker, O'Grady, a regular "Mickey," were great friends. An officer calling on me overheard this conversation in my tent, which he tells with great gusto:

under him, falling on top of its rider, who could only partly disengage himself, for the horse was lying on its rider's leg. However, the man managed to turn into such a position that he was able to open fire upon the Indians, and helped to drive them away.

Several Indians came out of the ravine to rob the dead and wounded, but Captain Hamilton gallantly drove them back, sabering one or two. This act was never mentioned in the reports of the fight yet it was well known that he did it. Had an act of this kind been performed during the Spanish-American War, Hamilton would have been made a brigadier-general and given a medal of honor.

Here was the heaviest part of the fighting. Hamilton remained here, and L Troop, commanded by Captain Alfred Taylor, continued to charge through the village. Hamilton, with the aid of Major Davis, drove the Indians out of their strong position, twenty of the Cheyennes being killed and eight of their number falling into our hands.

After the enemy were driven out of the village I saw a dozen Indians trying to run off about fifty ponies. Some of the savages were on foot. I called for volunteers, and Sergeant John Nicholson, Trumpeter Brandsome and Farrier Miller came out and we charged them, driving the Indians off and recovering the ponies. Nicholson's horse was shot through the leg and had to be killed. Miller's horse also was wounded. All we ever got out of it was the information from my captain that to call volunteers was not the proper thing to do and that men should have been detailed for that sort of work. The Indians we

---

"Shorty, take a good big drink. It is good stuff. The left-inant told me that any time I wanted a drink, just help meself and ask me friends."

I had some brandy that cost me almost as much as it does nowadays, and I brought it out only on special occasions.

Photo by D. F. Barry.

RAIN-IN-THE-FACE
Chief in the Custer Battle

charged while recapturing the ponies went up a gulch which I am quite sure was the ravine from which McKinney was fired upon

Troop L having charged through the village and driven out the last lurking sharpshooter, we dismounted and occupied a small fringe of timber just beyond the camp. Shortly after, Captains Hamilton* and Davis came in on our left. In this fringe of timber Private McFarland, an old soldier who had recently joined L Troop, received his death wound, being shot through the left lung. He was only a few feet from me at the time. He was a gallant soldier and had served during the Civil War.

My attention was called by Sergeant Divine to an object lying in a little depression in the ground about two hundred yards in front of us. I was quite sure it was an Indian and told some of the men to fire at him. A' Pawnee scout who happened to be with us cried out, "Pawnee! Pawnee!" and firing ceased. It seems the Indian was recognized from the way he wore his hair. He had been unhorsed and was lying low between the two fires. He must have borne a charmed life.

A number of Cheyennes rode out under fire, hurled their contempt and defiance at us, and then returned to cover. There was one daring warrior who seemed to take great delight in exposing himself to our fire. He was riding a fine horse and bore on his left arm a shield of buffalo hide and upon his head a beautiful war bonnet, the tail of which swept the ground. Bullets struck all around him. I borrowed a carbine from one of my men and fired several shots at him, but my carefully aimed shots did not seem to bother him any more than the hundreds of other bullets flying all around him. He

---

*Hamilton was killed at the battle of San Juan Hill, Cuba, July 1, 1898. He was then lieutenant-colonel of the First Cavalry.

remained too long under fire, however, and finally went over, pony and all. Immediately after he fell, a warrior decorated with a profusion of feathers, mounted upon a spirited pony and bearing also upon his left arm an elaborate shield made of buffalo hide hardened in the fire, charged recklessly into the face of death, chanting loudly the war song. On he came, dismounted and bent over the body of his friend, lifted it, placed it across the withers of his pony, sprang into the saddle and turned back to ride into their lines. At one time it looked as though he would reach his goal in safety, and I think all those who were witnessing the daring feat were wishing he might escape the hundreds of flying bullets; but evidently his "medicine" was bad, as he finally toppled off his horse, which also dropped under the fire of our men. This incident was the first of the kind I had ever witnessed, but it is a well-known fact that such daring acts have been performed numerous times by the Cheyennes and the Sioux.

During a lull in the fight Bill Rowland, one of our interpreters, who had married into the Cheyenne tribe, crawled up, with some of our Cheyenne scouts, close to the enemy's position and began a parley; but the hostiles were not inclined to participate therein. However, enough of a conversation was had to let us know that Dull Knife had with him Gray Head, Turkey Leg and Little Wolf, who were the chiefs in command; in fact, three of them approached near enough to Rowland to let him know that he (Dull Knife) had lost three sons in the fight, and personally was willing to surrender but was unable to influence the other chiefs who were in the village.

These Indians called out to our Indian scouts, "Go home! You have no business here! We can whip the white soldiers alone, but can't fight you, too." General Mackenzie very wisely did not attempt to force them out of their improvised rifle pits or from behind the rocks on the hillside. Had he done so our loss of life would have been fearful.

To make sure of what we had gained, the general moved off all the herd of ponies and ordered the village to be totally destroyed. He sent back to General Crook for the infantry, with a view to having them bring their more powerful rifles to bear on the hostiles in case they did not withdraw to another position. At that time the carbine used by the cavalry was not so powerful as the rifles of the infantry, but to-day both use the same arm. I, for one, was glad the hostiles decided to withdraw.

I was now ordered by General Mackenzie to collect a number of men, take a position near the "hospital hill" and remain there until further orders. Lieutenants Lawton and Dorst told me it was the general's intention to have me make a charge on a certain position. In carrying out my instructions I crossed quite a wide plain, instead of going around it, as I should have done, but I thought I would take the risk. I started across it at a walk, but two or three bullets whistled past me. As they commenced coming faster I increased my gait, so that very soon I was lying low on my horse and giving him the spurs vigorously. He was slightly wounded.

A trooper named Kline had his horse shot from under him. I heard the bullet when it struck the horse, which swayed back and forth several times and then dropped dead. Kline commenced to remove the saddle and bridle, but I told him to hurry up and get out of there, or he, too, would be shot. He answered, "Lieutenant, I don't want to have to pay for this saddle and bridle." It is needless to say he did not have to.

An incident worth relating shows that Indian scouts were valuable allies and could be depended upon. The wounded were behind a hill know as the "hospital hill." From some rocks a little way up the mountainside the hostiles were firing upon them and on a number of lead horses, making it very uncomfortable. General Mackenzie asked Major Frank North, in my presence, at the hospital hill, if he thought he could drive the Indians away from there. North replied that he thought so, if there were only a few of them. He blew a call on his Indian whistle, which sounded to me very much like a turkey call used by hunters. In a short time half a dozen Pawnees, with a non-commissioned officer, appeared. When told what they were to do they stripped down to their "gee strings," removing their heavy boots and substituting moccasins (they were wearing uniforms) and then, tying handkerchiefs around their heads, so they might not be taken for hostiles, they quickly disappeared up the mountainside. The firing soon ceased. I was later informed that the scouts killed one or two of the hostiles and scalped them.

After the fight was over my troop was detailed for guard and I as officer of the guard. I had just established an outpost on a prominent position overlooking the field of battle when an orderly notified me that the general wished me to report to him at once. The position where I had located the outpost was on the same hill which Lieutenant Walter Schuyler, with his Shoshone scouts, had occupied early in the morning in driving off the hostiles. This was an important position overlooking part of the village, and the Indians were compelled to abandon it because of the very heavy firing from Schuyler's scouts. He was commended for the active part he took in the fight and was recommended for brevet. Finally, however, he received his appointment as brigadier-general, and is now retired.

On my reporting to the general, he ordered me at once

to make preparations to move the dead and wounded to our camp on Powder River, more than a hundred miles away. I asked the general for twenty men and as many packers as he could spare, saying that I would let him know later how many men I needed with the travois train.

The men and four packers reported to me and I sent them out to gather up all the travois and tepee poles they could find, as well as any other material that could be used. This was no easy task, as the one hundred and seventy-five lodges of the village were on fire and nearly destroyed. Nevertheless, they brought twenty or thirty travois, a few tepee poles and a few buffalo robes. All the travois had to be strengthened and new ones made, which required a great deal of labor. One officer and six privates had been killed, and twenty-six enlisted men wounded. Two of the dead were buried on the field. We needed thirty litters, as three of the men had fallen sick and could not ride their horses, and as we were short of material decided to carry four of the bodies on mules. My men had very little sleep that night, but in the morning were ready to move out with the command. We built large fires to make the wounded comfortable and to give us light to work by, and as fast as the litters were completed we placed the wounded on them in two lines, facing each other. The fires were kept burning all night between the lines. We were able to put the travois in any inclined position, so the men were very comfortable, and I never saw a more cheerful lot.

We worked all night and moved out in the morning. While we were preparing to start, General Mackenzie came around to see how we were getting along. He called my attention to some travois which the men were holding in position, waiting for the packers to attach the mules. I explained to him that I had only four packers; that it took two for each travois; that the soldiers did not know how to hitch the mules to them properly, and that if I had a sufficient number of packers I could hitch them all up at once. The general rode away, saying to one of his aides, "I think I had better let Wheeler alone; he seems to know what he is about."

This incident was related to me by Lieutenant (afterward Major-General) H. W. Lawton, regimental quartermaster Fourth Cavalry, a day or so after the affair.

I asked for a personal detail of one hundred and twenty-eight men and eight non-commissioned officers. I assigned two men to each mule that carried the bodies and four men to each travois, one to lead the mule, two to dismount and ease the travois over rough places, and the fourth to hold their horses. One non-commissioned officer looked after every five travois and two non-commissioned officers assisted me. On reaching a bad place, two men would dismount and lift the travois over it, so that the occupant would not get jolted. These two men would remain at this point until the entire travois-train had passed it; then they would hasten back to their original position. At the next bad place the men with the litter following would do the same thing, and so on throughout. Great care had to be exercised that the dead should not be disfigured by a mule running away or brushing against objects which might break a leg or arm. In fording a stream, the packers dismounted, two on each bank. The rear of the litters would be handed by two of the packers to two mounted men to be supported while crossing, and then lowered by the packers on the opposite side of the stream. These men would remain until the entire train had forded the stream.

Only one accident occurred. At the crossing of one stream a litter was dropped but the mule passed along so quickly that the occupant did not get very wet.

General Mackenzie had told me that I probably would be unable to keep up with the column and should take my time, and that he would leave two troops of the Third Cavalry as guard.   To the astonishment of the whole command we kept right up with the column.   The advice and suggestions I received from Colonel Tom Moore, the chief packer and a veteran at packing, were of great assistance to me in the organization and handling of the travois, and the packers who assisted me were excellent men.

At one point the train wound round the mountainside, and the trail was so narrow in some places that we could not pass over it without jeopardizing the lives of the wounded and the mules.   If by some accident one of the travois were to go over the embankment, it would drop several hundred feet.   We were therefore obliged to find a place where we could lower the litters down the mountainside or carry our men over the bad places.   As we had no stretchers it would have taken some time and would have been a hardship on the poor fellows to carry them, and we soon found a place where we could lower the travois by means of our lariats tied together, making a line nearly two hundred feet long. We attached two of the lines to a travois, so they could be lowered safely.   The men and mules were on hand below to receive them and the lines were soon disengaged and drawn back.   In the meantime, another travois had been made ready for the descent.   As they arrived at the station the packers attached the mules to the travois, and by the time the last litter had come down, the train was ready to move on.   One of the wounded said the slide was equal to a toboggan ride.   All were lowered without accident, in a remarkably short time.

During the march several amusing incidents occurred. While we were passing through what was known by the Indians as Race Horse Canyon a travois had fallen out for repairs. I looked back to see if it was coming and saw it approaching as fast as the mule could run. I hastened back to reprimand the corporal in charge for such gross carelessness, and as I began to upbraid him in emphatic language the wounded man cried out: "Let her go, Lieutenant. If I had sleigh bells I'd think I was taking a sleigh ride." This man was Private Holsom of H Troop, Fifth Cavalry, who was very badly wounded in the hip. The great comfort of a travois is due to the inclined position in which the patient is carried, as there is little or no jolting. The travois are much more comfortable than an ambulance.

A Shoshone Indian, one of our scouts named Amzi, was shot through the intestines and brought into the hospital about dark. We also had a private named McFarland who had been shot through the lungs. The surgeon said that neither of them could live. We placed them in the only tent with the command, which General Mackenzie had kindly sent over to us. The surgeon had told me that these men would require some stimulants and left a bottle of brandy, with instructions to give them a drink occasionally if they were suffering. I gave them each a drink at once (not forgetting to take one myself). After a while Amzi called out, "Oh, John." (It was customary for Indians to call all white men "John.")

I went over to see what Amzi wanted. He grunted "Oh, John, heap sick! wickiup overhead—whisky!"

I thereupon gave Amzi another drink. On two or three other occasions during the night he repeated his request and I gave him a drink. The next morning Amzi was missing, and I learned that he had got on his horse and gone to his Indian friends, the other scouts! On the second day after we started back he came to me with a couple of his friends who were supporting him on his horse, and said he could ride no farther. As Private McFarland was just at the point of death, I stopped the travois until he had ceased to breathe.   I then gave Amzi the travois and strapped poor McFarland's body on a mule.   One of McFarland's friends who belonged to his troop and had been taking care of him pleaded with me not to put his dead bunkie on the mule; but I told the man that Amzi was one of our scouts, and wounded, therefore I was obliged to take care of him as well as I could, and that even if Amzi had been a hostile, it would be my duty to care for him.   McFarland died on November twenty-eighth, and on the same day we had to face another rather stiff snowstorm.

We arrived safely at the field hospital, where we left the infantry command and turned the wounded over to the surgeon.   Next morning I went over to the hospital to see how the wounded were getting on, and as I entered the hospital tent I heard once more, in familiar tones:

"Oh, John!   Heap sick!   Whisky!"

Looking over in the corner, whom should I espy but Amzi!   I went over to him and explained that I had nothing more to do with his case now, as I had turned him over to the hospital authorities, and was unable to give him any more whisky.   He was much disappointed.   He made me understand that he was cold and wanted to be moved nearer the camp stove.   I spoke to the surgeon in charge, who had him removed there.

We continued our march for a day or two, and arrived at Cantonment Reno.   Amzi remained in the hospital for two or three weeks, then got on his horse and rode over to Fort Washakie agency, about two hundred miles distant! His rather miraculous recovery may be explained, in part, by the fact that he had not eaten anything for nearly twenty-four hours prior to the time he was wounded, and his intestines were thus empty, which greatly facilitated his recovery.   About two years later I was at Fort Washakie, and made inquiry about Amzi. I learned that he, thinking perhaps he bore a charmed life, had gone over to steal horses from the Crows, and was killed.

One of the men of my troop, named Wildie, was detailed as orderly for Major Gordon. He was leading the pack-mule belonging to the squadron headquarters and was not supposed to go into the engagement. However, he turned the mule loose, pack and all, and went into the fight. During the engagement he exposed himself unnecessarily to the fire of the enemy while greatly excited. His captain told him several times to lie down, or he would get shot. He remarked that no redskin bullet could hit him. No sooner were the words out of his mouth than a ball struck him. As he fell he exclaimed, "Yes, they can, too, Captain; give 'em hell!" As soon as he discovered that the wound was not serious he went to shooting again.

Lieutenant Kimball of the Fourth Infantry tells the following story on me. It may or may not be true. He said that when I met him just after the fight he was eating a big chunk of the captured dried buffalo meat and that I said to him, "Man, what on earth are you doing? That meat may be poisoned, throw it away!" He hastily did so, whereupon I immediately got off my horse, picked it up, remounted and rode off eating the meat!

As stated, after the fight we returned to Cantonment Reno. Next morning, Thanksgiving Day, we buried our dead, four in number. Two men of the Fourth Cavalry were buried on the battle-field. Lieutenant McKinney's body was sent home to his people.

It was a beautiful winter morning, when the funeral occurred, and the ceremony was very impressive. The entire command turned out, headed by Generals Crook and Mackenzie, Colonels Townsend, Dodge and Gordon, and the bodies were followed to the burial-ground and preceded by the trumpeters playing the funeral dirge. The grave was in a beautiful wooded valley where Fort Reno had been some years before. The four bodies were interred side by side; "taps" was sounded and the usual volleys were fired by the guard of honor. Rocks were piled on the graves to prevent the wolves digging up the bodies, and a great quantity of wood was placed on the stones and set on fire, obscuring the grave, so that the Indians might not locate it, for they would frequently dig up bodies and scalp them.

Dull Knife's village contained at least fifteen hundred souls and there must have been between four and five hundred fighting warriors. It was usually estimated that each lodge would average three men capable of bearing arms. Boys twelve years of age and upward were considered capable of putting up a good fight. I have heard old Indian fighters say they would sooner fight men than boys; that Indian boys had no sense, did not know what fear was and would take greater chances. A boy was not given a name nor allowed in the councils until his courage had been thoroughly tested. Therefore he was very anxious to become a warrior. It is thought by Indians of many tribes that if they are killed in battle they will be made chiefs in the life beyond death. Indians possess as much courage as any people, and when young sometimes not only scorn death, but actually court it.

I once heard a man say—he was wounded on my ranch and at the point of death—that he did not care so much about dying, but regretted that he had to be killed by a mere boy!

The destruction of the Cheyenne village was a terrible punishment to those Indians. It was no doubt the richest prize that ever fell into our hands. Two hundred and five lodges, mostly of canvas, issued by the Indian Department, and quite a number of buffalo robes and hides were de-

stroyed.   That alone should have been sufficient punishment without killing any of the Cheyennes.   Every lodge
was fully supplied with food for the winter.   There must
have been tons of dried buffalo meat, together with deer
and elk meat.   There were hundreds of bladders and
paunches of fat and marrow which had been preserved by
the squaws.   In addition, there were cooking utensils, warlike trappings and horse equipments, quite a few of which
had belonged to the Seventh Cavalry.   These were all destroyed by fire.   That these people had taken an active part
in the Custer massacre was plainly evident.   Some of the
articles found in their lodges are herewith enumerated:

A pillow case made of a silk guidon of the Seventh Cavalry; memorandum books of the first sergeants of the
Seventh Cavalry, one of which had an entry made the very
day of the fight.   It read: "Left Rosebud June 25th."   It
had the names of the men in the troop and of those who
were for guard on the morning of the fight.   This book
had been used by a Cheyenne warrior to record the picture
history of his own prowess.   On one page he was lancing a
mounted trooper wearing sergeant-major's chevrons.   The
horse was branded "U. S." on the shoulder and "6th. Cav."
on the hip.   It is thought to have represented the killing of
Sergeant-Major Kennedy, who was with Major Elliott in
the battle of the Washita, November 27, 1868.   Elliott
became separated from Custer, and with fourteen of his
men was surrounded and killed.   On another page the
Indian was killing a soldier who was running away from
Reno's barricade on the hill, amid a shower of bullets.   On
another page he was killing a teamster, and on another a
poor miner.

There were cavalry horses branded "7th U. S. Cavalry"; a buckskin jacket, supposed, from certain marks, to
have belonged to Captain Tom Custer; a pocketbook containing money (one found by Sharp Nose, an Arapahoe

chief, containing not quite fifty dollars) ; the hat of Sergeant William Albin, Troop I, Third Cavalry, killed in Crook's fight on the Rosebud, June seventeenth, and identified by the sergeant's name on the band; the scalps of two young girls, one white and the other Shoshone; a buckskin bag containing the right hands of twelve Shoshone babies; the hand and arm of a Shoshone squaw and a necklace of human fingers. This ghastly trophy of aboriginal religious art, the especial decoration of High Wolf, the chief medicine man of the Cheyennes, can be inspected at the National Museum, Washington, D. C., where it was deposited by Captain John G. Bourke (deceased).

There were also found war bonnets of eagle feathers, shields, squaw robes of tanned antelope skin, ornamented with bead work and dyed porcupine quills and elk teeth, marvels of aboriginal beauty, stone pipes, some inlaid with silver, and tobacco bags, most elaborately ornamented with bead and quill work.

In my collection of Indian curios I had several articles which came out of this Cheyenne village.

The Indians had gone into winter quarters.   There could not have been found a more ideal spot to camp for the winter. It was a stronghold in itself, well sheltered, with abundance of timber and fine running water, and, last but not least, the country was alive with game, buffalo, elk and deer.   The Indians doubtless thought they were perfectly safe from attack, as they had no runners out to give them warning if there were any enemies in the country.*

---

*This has been denied by the Indians themselves. However, they were not prepared to meet us. I think General Mackenzie reported thirty killed. I saw a dozen or more bodies. It was said that twenty-five fell into our hands, and the Indians must have carried away some of their dead. The full loss was never known. When the Cheyennes returned to the Red Cloud agency they admitted that forty were killed but never stated the number wounded. A few of the latter and some of the frost-bitten Indians were treated at the agency hospital. It was said that they killed some of their ponies, removed the entrails and placed their papooses inside the carcasses to keep them from freezing.

During the month of November we marched three hundred and eighty miles.

EXTRACT FROM REGIMENTAL HISTORY
FOURTH U. S. CAVALRY

On November 25, 1876, an expedition under General Ranald S. Mackenzie, comprising B, D, E, F, I and M Troops, Fourth Cavalry, while scouting on the Powder River, came upon Dull Knife's band of Cheyennes. The commanding officer's report is as follows:

"About twelve o'clock M, on the twenty-fourth inst., while marching in a southwesterly direction toward the Sioux pass of the Big Horn Mountains, I was met by five of the seven Indian scouts who had been sent out the evening before, who reported that they had discovered the main camp of the Cheyennes at a point in the mountains fifteen or twenty miles distant. The command was halted until near sunset, and then moved toward the village, intending to reach it at or before daylight. Owing to the nature of the country, which was very rough, and in some cases difficult to pass through with cavalry, the command did not reach the village until about half an hour after daylight. The surprise was, however, almost, if not complete. The village consisted of two hundred and five lodges and their entire contents were destroyed. About five hundred ponies were taken and twenty-five Indians killed, whose bodies fell into our hands, and from reports, which I have no reason to doubt, I believe a much larger number were killed. Our loss was one officer and five men killed and twenty-five soldiers and one Shoshone Indian wounded. Lieutenant McKinney, Fourth Cavalry, who was killed in this affair, was one of the most gallant officers and honorable men that I have ever known."

DOUBLE TROPHY ROSTER

I am indebted to Mr. George Bird Grinnell of New York City, author of *The Fighting Cheyennes,* for the fol-

---

After our fight with Dull Knife my captain, Alfred B. Taylor, was taken ill, which left me in command of the troop, L, Fifth Cavalry.

lowing extracts from this roster written soon after 1905. The original was given me by First Sergeant James Turpin, Troop G, Fifth Cavalry, who found it in Dull Knife's village the day of the fight. It was in my collection of Indian trophies when I disposed of them. I have since learned that it is now owned by Mr. J. J. White, Jr., of New York City.

DOUBLE TROPHY ROSTER

PROPERTY OF J. J. WHITE, JR., 52 BROADWAY, N. Y.

"This is a squad roster kept in 1876 by First Sergeant Brown, of G Troop, Seventh Cavalry, commanded by Lieutenant Donald McIntosh. Such memorandum books were used only in the field.

"The roster appears to have been started April 19, 1876, at which time the troop was just leaving Louisiana—where it had been stationed since the autumn of 1874—for the regimental headquarters, Fort A. Lincoln, Dakota. The earlier entrances during April tell of the incidents of the journey from the south as far as St. Paul, Minnesota, where the company took the train for Bismarck, Dakota, which was then the end of track of the N. P. R. R. The earlier pages of the book, to page twelve, inclusive, show the names of the men in the company, and the duty which they performed during the months of May and June. The black triangles under various dates in the square opposite a man's name, indicate that he was on duty, as 'S' for stables, 'P' for police, 'D. D.' for daily duty, etc. Lieutenant McIntosh's name is mentioned on page sixty-five, where, under date of May 24, 1876, seven men are named as his fatigue detail. Mention is made in the book of the date at which the company left Fort Lincoln to join General Terry's expedition, and the lengths of two or three marches are given. The latest entry in the book reads: 'McEgan lost his carbine on the march while on duty with pack train, June 24, 1876.' "

CHAPTER XIX

FOLLOWING the Dull Knife fight we remained at Fort Reno a few days, drew supplies and then started out on another expedition into the Black Hills country. We had some very cold weather on the Belle Fourche, in which a few animals were frozen to death. One of the mules insisted upon backing into the tent occupied by the surgeon, Marshal W. Wood, and me, loosening the tent cords. I got up two or three times during the night, driving the mule away and tightening the cords. It was so cold that my nose and fingers were nipped by the frost. I wanted the doctor to get up once or twice to drive the mule away, but he would not do so. I told him the tent might come down on us, whereupon he replied, "Let her come!" Shortly afterward it did come down, the mule falling over into it, frozen to death. He came within an ace of falling on the doctor, and from the state of my feelings at the time I rather wished he had. The remainder of the night we put in very uncomfortably. It must have been more than forty degrees below zero, as the bulbs in our thermometers were frozen.

Sergeant Clark, who was acting as first sergeant of my troop, reported to me that it was impossible to hold the herd with the number of men he had, as the horses were backing into the tents and pushing them over, so the men could not sleep, and he suggested that the guard be doubled. This was done, and we lost no horses. On our starting out the next morning, nearly every organization had lost a few animals, so

men were left behind to gather them up. During the march
General Mackenzie came up and asked me how many horses
I had lost the night before. I told him none and he inquired
how that had occurred. I told him that I had doubled my
guard and he remarked: "It's very strange that some of
these older officers didn't think of that. Half of my horses
are scattered over the prairie."

I didn't tell the general that Sergeant Clark should have
received credit for saving the horses from straying but ought
to have done so.

The march across the Pumpkin Buttes on Christmas Day,
1876, was one of the most disagreeable imaginable. A
furious storm was raging. We had to walk, and lead our
horses, to keep from freezing. Two of our thermometers
indicated twenty-six degrees below zero, Fahrenheit.
Neither of the instruments was of any service. Spirit thermometers in Deadwood registered that day forty degrees
below, and in Fort Saunders, Wyoming, thirty-eight degrees.
We were in direct longitude between the two points.

On New Year's Day, 1877, it was very cold, but there
was no storm with it. We walked most of the day. I
had a very unpleasant occurrence on that day. The night before, I had gone into camp in a ravine. It was a mile at
least from where the trail crossed the ravine. When I
moved out the following morning, the snow nearly a foot in
depth, instead of following down the canyon to the road I
started out leading my horse diagonally to the road, thereby
saving nearly a mile of travel. When I reached the road the
command had not arrived. My position in the column was
the third troop. In marching, each organization alternates
daily. When there is a long column, it makes quite a difference in time in getting into camp.

When the column came along the officer commanding
the troop where I should have taken my place would not let

me in. I sent a message to the officer in command. General Mackenzie did not happen to be at the head of the column and this officer made me wait and fall in at the rear. I was very wroth about it, not only for myself, but for my men. I did not get into camp until after sundown. As we were going into camp, Lieutenant Andrus of H Troop, my regiment, to whose mess I belonged, came out to look for me. He inquired what the trouble was. I told him, in very emphatic language, my grievance.

While we were talking, who should ride up alongside me but General Mackenzie! I was pretty frightened. The general remarked:

"Mr. Wheeler, when you have any grievance with your commanding officer you had better be more careful what language you use and when you use it."

He then continued: "Mr. Wheeler, I have a good place for your troop to go into camp, plenty of wood and water. You fall in in your regular place in the morning."

It was a wonder he did not place me under arrest. He had just placed two officers in arrest, and they had to march in the rear of their troops the next day. When I got my troop into camp and everything in shipshape order for the night, it was after dark. Before I could go to my dinner every one had finished eating, but my friend had the cook save me some dinner, and our good doctor, a member of the mess, had a small flask of brandy which he had been saving for emergency cases—and mine was one of them. He made me a hot brandy sling. My dinner was composed of desiccated potatoes, elk meat and bread, and, for dessert, canned pears. It seemed to me at the time that it was the best meal I had ever eaten.

While on the Belle Fourche, I was the officer of the guard and had to visit the different sentinels and picket lines during the night. It was very cold when I made my rounds.

I thought I would go on foot to save my horse, so started out. One of the squadrons was in camp quite a little distance down the river, which was frozen over, so I thought I would walk on the ice. It was a dark night—no moon—and I walked into an airhole! Down I went into the water and mud up to my armpits! It did not take me very long to get out, but before I had completed my rounds my clothing was frozen stiff. I found one sentinel who had slipped, and broken his carbine.

We were out a number of days, not discovering any fresh Indian signs, and therefore returned to Cantonment Reno. On the return a very sad accident happened. One of the Fourth Cavalry troops was watering. They had led their horses down to the water, because of the abrupt banks of the stream. A horse belonging to one of the sergeants slipped on the ice, and, falling on the sergeant, crushed the life out of him. He was a veteran of the Civil War, and could he have had his choice in the premises, would doubtless have preferred to die on the field of battle.

We were at Reno a few days and then started for Fort Laramie, where the expedition was to be broken up, the troops going to their several garrisons.

While we were at Fort Fetterman, another accident occurred. A member of the guard had placed his carbine in a wagon, and in taking it out it was discharged. The bullet in its flight passed through the back of the clerk of H Troop, Fifth Cavalry, killing him, He was sitting in a tent near by, making up the muster rolls. It was the old story, "didn't know the gun was loaded." The culprit had failed to eject the cartridge when he came off guard. He was tried by a military court-martial for neglect and gross carelessness, was sentenced to be dishonorably discharged from the United States Army and to serve a term in a military prison.

On our arrival at Laramie we received orders to proceed to our new stations, which were located all over the department. The Fourth and Third Cavalry returned to Camp Robinson. Our troops were ordered to proceed to Fort D. A. Russell, Wyoming, which was the headquarters of the Fifth Cavalry, commanded by General Wesley Merritt of Civil War fame.

We arrived there the latter part of March, 1877. We must have marched nearly fifteen hundred miles that winter. A portion of the time we had no forage and had to depend upon grazing, and quite frequently would change our horses to fresh grass two or three times a night. When there was heavy snow on the ground we would cut willow and cottonwood boughs and pull up long grass and sweet sage and put it on the picket lines for the horses to feed on. In the morning the bark would be peeled from the limbs as smoothly as if it had been done with knives.

We lost very few animals, owing to the good management of General Mackenzie, who used great judgment in marching, in selecting fine camps and in seeing personally that we took good care of our stock.

We remained at Fort Russell until the latter part of May and then we were ordered into the field. There were four troops commanded by Major Hart, which were to go into camp near the head of Tongue River, near Lake De Smet. This was on the old overland route to California.

Upon arrival at Fort Fetterman, L Troop was ordered to proceed to Fort Washakie, Wyoming, to escort Lieutenant-General Sheridan and his party across the Big Horn Mountains to Fort Custer, on a tour of inspection.

We followed the North Platte River to old Fort Casper, crossed over to the Sweetwater, camping near Independence Rock, mentioned by Major John C. Frémont in his report to the secretary of war on his trip across the continent.

He was at the Rock August   1842. It is about fifteen
hundred yards in circumference, the height at the north
end about two hundred feet; the southern end not quite so
high.   Near the middle is a depression of about sixty
feet, where the soil supports scanty growth of shrubs.
Where the surface is sufficiently smooth, the Rock is
engraved with the names of travelers.   Many names foremost in the history of the country, and some of well-known
scientists, are to be found there, with those of travelers
for pleasure, traders, curiosity seekers and missionaries to
the Indians.   Some of these names have been washed away
by the rains, but the greater number are yet legible.

Five miles above Independence Rock we came to a
place called The Devil's Gate, where the Sweetwater cuts
through the point of a granite ridge.   The length of the
passage is about three hundred yards, and the width is
thirty-five yards.   The height is about four hundred feet.
The stream in the gate was almost choked by masses of
rock which had fallen from above.   It had been said that
no one had ever been able to pass through the gate, owing
to the great number of boulders and the volume of water
rushing through it, which formed a regular torrent.   Upon
our return several months later, Colonel Tom Moore, the
chief packer, passed through it on his mule.   It was during
low water, and he had great difficulty.   It was considered
a daring exploit.

On leaving The Devil's Gate, we followed up the
Sweetwater several miles, then crossed the river, thence
over the Beaver divide to the river by that name.   We came
down what was known as the great slope of the Beaver
range, more than five miles in length and having a fall
of several thousand feet.   From the Beaver, we went over
a low divide to Twin Creek, thence to the Little Popoagie,
and from there to Lander City and Fort Washakie.

CHAPTER XX

I SERVED with the escort for the lieutenant-general of the army, going en route from Fort Washakie, Wyoming, in June, 1877, to Fort Custer, Montana, via the Big Horn Mountains, Lake De Smet and Fort C. F. Smith, for the purpose of visiting the Custer battle-field. General Sheridan's party consisted of General Sackett, inspector-general; our department commander, General Crook, and his two aides, Lieutenant Walter S. Schuyler and Lieutenant John G. Bourke, of the Fifth and Third Cavalry, respectively. Colonel "Sandy" Forsyth and General Sheridan's aide, Doctor Julius H. Patzki, medical corps, were also with the escort. In addition, there were two or three citizen friends of General Sheridan. Lieutenant Carpenter, Ninth Infantry, quite a noted botanist, also was along. Lieutenant Charles Rockwell commanded the escort, Troop L, Fifth Cavalry. Frank Grouard, the chief of scouts, and about a dozen Indians, all of whom had taken part in the Custer massacre the previous year, completed the escort.

The Indians called General Crook "Gray Fox," and had the greatest respect for him. I know of no other officer or civilian who knew the Indian character so well. Sharp Nose, a noted Arapahoe chief, told me that the general never had deceived them.

One of the Indian scouts accompanying the expedition was a Sioux who had taken an important part in the fight at Slim Buttes in September, 1876. He was credited with having shot and killed a scout, Jim White, nicknamed "Buffalo Chips," in that battle. It appeared that this Indian, with two or three other warriors and several women, had taken refuge in a sort of cave, from which position they had poured a deadly fusillade into the troops under the command of Captain Anson Mills. This particular Indian caught sight of "Chips" stealing up a near-by ridge, and killed him the first shot. He had then fought with great fury until his rifle became clogged by an empty shell, and had finally surrendered upon promise of good treatment. The Indian was accompanied on this expedition by his squaw, who had also been with him in the Slim Buttes fight. Both had been wounded in that engagement.

We had two pack-trains in charge of Tom Moore, the chief packer, who had a wide reputation as a great organizer of the United States Army pack-trains.

Upon starting out, J. K. Moore, post trader at Fort Washakie, a man well known to older officers for his generosity, gave our party some whisky "for snake bites." Mr. Moore, the packer, who was messing with us at the time, said he would see that the whisky (which was in two champagne baskets) was placed on a safe mule.

A good sized pack-train consists of forty pack-mules, twelve riding animals, and, last but not least, a bell-mare. There is a pack-master who has supervision and is responsible for the efficiency of the train; a cargador, who keeps the aparejos (saddles) in repair, and sees that they are properly fitted to each mule. The aparejos are numbered, and each mule has a corresponding number. This is essential, as the conformation of each mule differs. The cargador also regulates the weight and size of the packs, so that they will balance equally on the backs of the animals. This is very important, as a preventive of sore backs. In addition, there are a horseshoer and eight packers. Every man belonging to the train, however, has to assist with the packing. On the march, the cook leads the bell-mare. This animal is usually of an off color, so that she can be readily distinguished, and of a gentle disposition. The mules become perfectly infatuated with her and are never out of sight of her or of hearing of the bell, which is tinkling most of the time. If there is any unusual excitement or danger of a stampede, the first thing to be done to quiet them is to commence ringing the bell. They will follow the bell animal wherever she may go.

Two men are required to pack a mule. During the packing a blinder is used, a broad strap that is passed over the eyes. After packing, the strap is slipped off and away the animal goes to join the bell-mare.

When the train arrives in camp after a day's march with troops, each pack-train goes to the organization to which it has been assigned, the load is removed, and the animals are taken to the place designated for that particular organization's camp. Here the aparejos are removed, the blankets being left on until the backs of the animals dry. I know of a case where a troop of cavalry unsaddled on a very hot sunny day, removed the blankets at once, and, as a result, many of the horses' backs were so scalded that it made them sore and in a few cases the hair came off.

When removed, the aparejos are placed in the form of a square, thereby forming a corral, leaving an opening for entrance on one side. When the mules are to be fed they are driven into this corral and, if they are fed with hay, remain there all night. Strange as it may seem, each animal knows its own equipment and will take its place in front of it. As a rule, a mule will pack three hundred pounds. I have known of four hundred pounds being placed on a mule that carried the kitchen outfit, but in that instance the load grew lighter daily.

CURLEY, ONE OF CUSTER'S CROW INDIAN SCOUTS, AND REPUTED
SOLE SURVIVOR OF THE BATTLE OF THE LITTLE BIG HORN

The advantage of a pack-train is that it can go anywhere with a command and keep up with it, while wagon-trains can not. The packers are exceptionally good men at their calling, receive good pay and live well. In fact, it is considered quite a treat to be invited to dine with them. A packer never sleeps cold at night as he has the use of the blankets belonging to the train.

We left Fort Washakie the latter part of June, 1877 making a march of about thirty miles the first day. This proved to be too much for those who had not ridden a horse for a long time, so General Sheridan and some of his guests rode in an ambulance part of the way. Our first night's camp was situated near the confluence of the Big and Little Wind Rivers, which form the Big Horn, after passing through the canyon of the Big Horn Mountains, about seventy-five miles from Fort Washakie.

Before starting out, Lieutenant Rockwell told me to take charge of the troop, and he would superintend the pitching of the general's tentage on the trip. After our camp was established that night Rockwell said he would try his hand at fishing, with a view to having a fish supper. The very first pool into which he cast his fly yielded a fine grayling. Continuing, he caught six others as fast as he could cast. As soon as this was known, a number of the party hastened to get out their fishing tackle and started for the river, anticipating fine sport. But they were disappointed; none of them got a rise. Apparently, this little school of grayling was all there were in this hole. I think this was the first intimation that grayling inhabited these streams. There was quite a discussion among two or three of the party who were familiar with this variety of fish. I believe grayling are quite plentiful in the streams of Wisconsin and Michigan, as well as in parts of Montana.

The next morning we broke camp bright and early.

Below our camp the Big Wind River broke through the Big Wind River range and our trail led through the gorge, gradually ascending the mountain. When the pack-train had nearly reached the top of the ridge the trail narrowed, and just at this point the steady safe mule that was detailed to carry our antidote for rattlesnake poisoning decided to turn around. While doing so the animal was pushed over the cliff by one of the mules when trying to pass, and over it went, whisky and all, rolling down the side of the mountain some hundred feet or more, landing on a shelving of rock. This no doubt saved the mule's life, for had it continued to roll it would have taken a drop of several hundred feet into the chasm below. However, great was the fall thereof! Every bottle, save one, was broken. The mule was badly bruised, which gave considerable satisfaction to some of us who were hard hearted. Some one suggested that the mule may have wanted to view the scenery, which was undoubtedly superb. Needless to say, there were no smiling faces in our mess that night.

A day or so after this we came very near having another serious accident. The command, dismounted, was on its way down the mountainside. The trail was winding, to lessen the grade, and so steep that we were obliged to lead our horses. Colonel Forsyth was just in front of me. Suddenly, away up the mountainside, a large boulder weighing several hundred pounds was loosened and came bounding down the mountain in great leaps. In its flight it was bound to cross the winding trail which we were traveling, and I think it came into every man's mind at the same instant that some one was likely to be badly hurt or perhaps killed. All therefore held their breath, awaiting to see who the unfortunate man or horse would be. In the last bound, before it crossed our path, it struck the ground a few yards above the colonel and myself, rebounded and passed just over the back of the colonel's horse! Had he been mounted the boulder would surely have hit him, and both man and horse would doubtless have been killed.

On another occasion the colonel had a very narrow escape from drowning. Evidently he did not realize how dangerous it was to ford a mountain stream in high water, or else he did not think about it. Riding at the head of the column, he struck right out into the swollen flood, and over he went horse and all! But his life was saved by Mr. Patrick, the pack-master, who threw a line to him and pulled him ashore. His horse, which we did not find until the following morning and had given up for lost, came out on the opposite bank of the stream, several hundred yards below. The colonel must have had a charmed life. He served through the Civil War, and was with Beecher's scouts, whom Captain Bankhead's expedition rescued in 1868 on the Arickaree, after an eight days' siege by Cheyenne Indians under Roman Nose.

At the place where this near-accident occurred the water was so high that we were unable to cross that night. The next morning the stream had receded considerably, since because of the extreme cold the snow had not melted during the night. However, we had some trouble in finding a fording place, but the Indians finally found one some distance down the river. The pack-mules had no trouble in crossing, as their packs held them down, but the men had some difficulty as the water very nearly carried their horses off their feet. I was riding "Crazy Horse," and he was so small and light that I hesitated about crossing on him, for I feared the swift current might carry him down-stream. But noticing how nicely the pack-mules were crossing, their loads holding them down, I asked one of the packers who was no light weight to get on behind me, and we crossed without difficulty.

On the Fourth of July we had a pretty camp surrounded by snow-capped mountains. The general invited all of us to call on him, and we took a stroll. After walking a few hundred yards from the camp, we came upon a large snow bank, quite a little glacier, and it developed that there were deposited therein several bottles of Mumm's Extra Dry champagne, one for each of us. After the delivery of a few remarks appropriate to the occasion by the general, we drank to the Stars and Stripes, and sang with great emotion our national anthem, and wound up our celebration with three rousing cheers, the echo of which resounded back and forth several times quite distinctly.

(A few years ago I made a trip through the lakes of Killarney, Ireland, which are situated in the mountains and are well known for their wonderful echoes. Our boatman called our attention to this by shouting and suggested that members of our party do likewise. However, the echo did not begin to compare with that up in the Big Horn Mountains on that memorable Fourth of July.)

A day or so after our celebration, General Crook, Lieutenant Schuyler and Mr. Delaney went out on a hunt, taking along a pack-mule to bring back their game. While they were out a snowstorm came up, so severe that the party was unable to make their way back to camp that night but had to remain out. Their absence caused some little uneasiness in camp, but I told some members of our party that they need not worry, as it was not the first time these people had been obliged to remain away from camp; that they were skilled woodsmen and would rather enjoy their outing. They turned up all right the next morning, and Lieutenant Schuyler told me they put in a very comfortable night. Although they had no blankets, they built a good fire, leaned their backs against a big log and went to sleep. They brought in a mountain sheep and other game. The sheep's head and horns were about as pretty as any I ever saw. I would judge the prize head weighed at least fifty pounds. I saw one in Colorado, on one occasion, that weighed sixty-eight pounds.

The head of the sheep which the party captured was given to General Sheridan, who had it mounted. I afterward saw it at his quarters in Chicago, upon which occasion he called my attention, with a great deal of pride, to a bearskin rug on the floor. This also was a souvenir of our trip. The general thought he had killed it, but as a matter of fact, Frank Grouard, the chief scout, with some of the Indians wounded the animal at the head of the canyon near camp. Grouard left his Indians to watch bruin, and hastened to camp to inform the general that he had a bear corralled in a near-by gulch. The general therefore went out and shot it. It was thought that he did not know the animal had been wounded.

CHAPTER XXI

ONE day we went into camp just over the divide of the Big Horn Mountains. The ground was quite uneven, so we could not pitch our tents with any regularity. After camp had been established Captain Bourke and I were in our tent taking a siesta, when we were awakened by a jarring of the ground, followed by a dull rumbling. This created quite a commotion in camp. I thought at first a big storm was upon us, which is not very pleasant in the mountains, but we soon discovered what made the noise. There were at least a hundred mountain buffalo coming toward our camp and they were almost upon us.

Our pack-animals were grazing below the camp. Upon seeing the buffalo, the herder in charge of the animals started for the corral as fast as possible, leading the bell-mare, and with all the mules following. Mr. Moore ran to the camp for a bell, and commenced to ring it loudly. The mules responded. This quick action of the herder undoubtedly saved the mules from stampeding with the buffalo.

About a dozen of the buffalo broke through our camp, passing very near the tent occupied by Captain Bourke and myself. A big bull ran into the tent cords, breaking some of them, and pulling up the pins. Bourke, aroused from his nap, gave the bull a parting salute by running out in his pajamas and hitting the creature across the back with a tent pole. I was full of laughter, and a picture of the episode would have been humorous in the extreme. The bull, with others, ran up the side of the hill to a plateau where our horses were grazing and stampeded them. They divided into two bands, the larger one going back on the trail we had just come over. Although the side-lines were on the horses, the herders could not prevent them from stampeding. Two members of the herders followed the smaller bunch, and the remainder of the guard took after the rest. My pony was lariated near my tent and was the only horse in camp. Jumping on him bareback, away I went to assist the herders. It was a swift pony.

My pony was named "Crazy Horse" after the celebrated Sioux chief by that name who led the Indians in the Custer massacre and was afterward killed at Fort Robinson, Nebraska, while trying to escape from the guard-house. The pony was captured by Major Anson Mills, Third Cavalry, (later a general on the retired list) in the Slim Buttes affair with Sioux, September 9, 1876. It was reported at the time that the animal was Crazy Horse's war pony, which he had ridden in the massacre of General Custer's command.

When I arrived where the horse herd had been grazing, I saw some of them just disappearing down the tortuous trail we had recently come over. I made after them and soon overtook some of the stragglers that could not keep up with the others, because of their hobbles breaking and the chains swinging around their legs, hurting them. Soon I came across one of the herders who had been thrown from his horse. He had not been seriously hurt and was holding three or four horses. I told him to tie them to the sage-brush and come on, and we could pick them up on our return. This precaution was taken to prevent them from following and bruising their legs with the chains all the more.

Before proceeding, we caught a few more horses and tied them to the bushes. We soon met the other men coming back with the rest of the animals. After hard riding, with much danger to themselves, they had succeeded in heading the horses off. We recovered all but two. We did not get back to camp until after dark and were pretty well played out. I never rode harder in my life nor over more dangerous ground. Nearly all the men had been thrown and I was riding my second horse. When I reached the camp I had difficulty in dismounting, because of exhaustion. I could not throw my leg over the horse's back but just had to fall off. During the latter part of my ride all that I could do was to keep my knees stiff and ride clothespin fashion. I injured my sciatic nerve so badly that for several days I had to be helped on and off my horse, and was bothered for years with sciatic neuralgia. General Sheridan called me to his tent the next morning and thanked me for the recovery of the horses, saying that it looked very much at one time as if he would have to ride a mule. I told him the herd guard deserved all the praise as they had succeeded in heading off the horses, while I only helped drive them back to camp, whereupon he called the men to his tent and thanked them.

It seemed that the Indians, on their own initiative, caused the stampede by running into the buffalo herd. Supposing the general and his party would like to see a real buffalo chase, they drove the bunch up the canyon toward the camp, not considering that they might stampede our horses and mules

A few days out of Fort Washakie we came across a dead man, the body being badly decomposed, so much so that we could not tell by his garb whether he was a hunter or a prospector, but presumably the latter. Near by was an old camping-place, but nothing in it that gave us any clue to the man's identity. He had evidently been killed, but by whom will never be known. We buried the body.

At the Clear Fork of the Powder River, afterward Fort McKinney, Colonel Verlingain K. Hart joined us with three troops of the Fifth Cavalry. From there we took the old Bozeman trail, passing through the abandoned posts of Forts Phil Kearny and C. F. Smith. These posts, with Fort Reno at the crossing of the Powder River, were abandoned by the government in August, 1868, through a treaty with the Sioux, they agreeing to stop their hostilities provided the government would relinquish those posts and give back the country to the Sioux, which was done. It is stated that the forts were burned by the Indians on the very day they were abandoned.

These posts formed a line of forts about a hundred miles apart, extending from Fort Sydney, Nebraska, on the Union Pacific Railroad, to Fort C. F. Smith, at the crossing of the Little Big Horn River in the present state of Montana. Fort Smith was the last post on the old Bozeman Trail. At the time we passed its site there was a small ruin on the bank of the river, in fair state of preservation. Fort Phil Kearny was established by General Henry B. Carrington, lieutenant-colonel Eighteenth Infantry, in July, 1866. It was located on the banks of Big Piney Creek, a tributary of Powder River, some five miles from the Big Horn Range, with the snow-capped peaks in plain sight. The elevation was about fifty-two hundred feet.

On the present trip, when we passed the ruins of Fort Phil Kearny, quite a good portion of the flagstaff yet remained standing and part of the old stockade was also left. The post cemetery, enclosed by a brick wall, was well preserved. A couple of years later, when I passed through there, none of the cemetery wall remained. It had been removed and the bricks had been used by the settlers to build chimneys for their cabins. Apparently they had no respect for the soldiers buried there. The Indians, however, had, which shows that the savages are more humane than the whites—in this instance, at least. Afterward the soldiers' bodies were exhumed and reburied in the national cemetery near the Custer battle-field.

Before reaching the abandoned post of Fort Phil Kearny, some eight miles away, our trail leading along and over Lodge Trail Ridge into Peno Valley, our attention was attracted, in passing, to a prominent pile of rocks on which stood an Indian lodge pole with a tattered piece of cloth attached. We were told that this was the place where the Fetterman massacre occurred on December 21, 1866, about ten years prior to the Custer catastrophe.

It appeared that a wagon-train of logs for the construction of buildings at Fort Phil Kearny was attacked by the Indians. The commanding officer, Colonel Henry B. Carrington, ordered to their succor Captain William J. Fetterman, with forty-eight men of the Eighteenth Infantry, and Lieutenant George W. Grummond with twenty-seven men of the Second Cavalry. Accompanying the expedition as volunteers were Captain Frederick H. Brown, who had just received his promotion and was under orders to join his regiment, and two citizens, Wheatley and Fisher, frontiersmen and hunters. When the Indians saw the soldiers coming to the rescue of the train they withdrew, and were pursued by Fetterman and his men about five miles. Evidently the Indians were leading him on until they had drawn him into an ambush, then fell upon him in overwhelming numbers, exterminating the whole command. It was said that about three thousand Indians were engaged in the fight, led by Chief Red Cloud.

'At this pile of rocks Fetterman made his last stand, where his ammunition gave out. Here the Indians no doubt rushed in, killing all the soldiers left alive, by arrows, tomahawks and spears. Of the forty-nine men found there, only four, besides the two officers, had been killed by bullets. Brown and Fetterman lay side by side, each with a bullet wound in the left temple, their heads burned and filled with powder around the wounds. Seeing that all was lost, they had evidently stood face to face and shot each other dead with their revolvers, rather than be captured alive. The bodies of the other men were found strung along the road. The remains of Grummond were found on the trail farthest from the fort, while those of the two citizens, Wheatley and Fisher, were located behind little piles of rocks. The body of Wheatley bristled with one hundred and five arrows! Apparently they had been fighting desperately for their lives. They had been armed with modern Henry repeating rifles (just patented and put on the market that year), the magazines holding sixteen cartridges. By the side of one of the men fifty empty shells were counted, and nearly as many by the other. They must have done wonderful execution with the new repeating guns, and if their ammunition had not given out the chances are that they would have stood the Indians off, not only saving their own lives, but those of many others who were not so well armed.

This massacre was another case of disobedience of orders. Captain Fetterman had had very little Indian experience, having been in the country but a short time. He had begged for the command of the expedition, pleading seniority of rank as justification of his request, and Carrington had reluctantly acquiesced. Fetterman's orders were to relieve the wagon-train and drive away the Indians, *but not under any circumstances* to pursue them beyond

Lodge Trail Ridge. As soon as he had accomplished this, he was to return to the fort immediately. He may not have understood his orders—we are in hopes that such is the case—but the fact remains that he was again cautioned just before leaving the post. Through his zeal, excitement and over-confidence, he probably did not think about his orders until it was too late to turn back.

CHAPTER XXII

VISIT TO CUSTER BATTLE-FIELD—THE BATTLE

OUR visit to the Custer battle-field on the Little Big Horn River occurred about a year after the fight. A few days before our arrival a severe hail storm had devastated the whole valley, washing out several of the bodies which had been buried near a ravine. The men had been buried where they fell in battle and the graves were marked by stakes driven into the ground at the head and foot of each. An empty cartridge shell containing a slip of paper with the name of the fallen man was placed at the head, so that the bodies could be properly identified when exhumed.

While we were there I reburied all the bodies that had been washed out. A few months later all the bodies were reburied on a commanding position on the battle-field. General Custer was reburied at West Point, October 10, 1877. A monument was erected to their memory July 2, 1883; it is surrounded by a high iron fence to prevent vandals from chipping or disfiguring the shaft. It was officially declared a government cemetery and as such will always be cared for. The superintendent lives on the grounds in a neat little lodge.*

---

*Captain John Ryan, First Sergeant M Troop, Seventh Cavalry, states: "The battle-field was divided off into five sections. The company commanders went over the field to find the bodies of the commissioned officers. The first sergeant of each company had orders to advance with their companies over certain spaces of the field, burying what men were found and keeping account of the numbers and

General George Armstrong Custer, lieutenant-colonel Seventh Cavalry, commanded the regiment in the memorable but disastrous battle of the Little Big Horn. General Sturgis, the colonel, who lost his son in the engagement, was on other duty. General Custer attacked the villages of Crazy Horse and Sitting Bull, June 25, 1876, and lost his life, with two hundred and eight of his immediate command. The Indians were led by Crazy Horse, Rain-in-the-Face and Gall of the Sioux, and Two Moon of the Northern Cheyennes, and not by Sitting Bull, as is generally supposed. Sitting Bull, who was forty-two years old at the time, was the great medicine man of the Sioux nation, and during the battle was "making medicine" on the mesa, just in the rear of, and overlooking, the Indian village, which extended some four miles along the right bank of the Little Big Horn River, and was estimated to have contained from ten thousand to fifteen thousand men, women and children. Probably one-third of this number represented the fighting strength of the band.

General Alfred H. Terry, of Fort Fisher fame during the Civil War, had taken the field with a large command from Fort Abraham Lincoln, Dakota. He ordered General Custer to proceed with his regiment toward the valley of

who they were. I helped to bury forty-five of Custer's men; among them was General Custer. We found the body of the general on a gravel knoll. He was shot in two places, one bullet having struck him in the right side of his face, and passing through to the other side; the other on the right side of his body, passing through to the left side, and which I understood at the time one of the soldiers took from his body. The general was not scalped."

Captain John Ryan's article was written expressly for the *Billings Gazette,* and it was published June 25, 1923.

Captain Ryan served throughout the Civil War, being wounded five times while with General Meagher's Irish brigade. He served from 1866 to 1877 as an enlisted man in Troop M, Seventh Cavalry, was the first sergeant of the troop in the battle of the Little Big Horn. Sergeant Ryan was honorably discharged from the service. He returned to his old home at West Newton, Massachusetts, and became a policeman, serving with credit in that capacity until 1916, when he was retired, having been a captain of police for nine years.

the Little Big Horn, scout that country and see whether
he could locate the hostiles, who were supposed to be up
in that mountainous country. Crazy Horse and Sitting
Bull, without permission, had left their agencies with a
large following of their people.

General Custer's orders were not to bring on an engagement if he could possibly avoid it. It was General Terry's
intention, if he succeeded in locating the hostiles, to try
to get in touch with them and, if possible, prevail upon
them to return to their homes without fighting.

It may be well to explain here that it was generally
known that Custer was under a cloud; that he had incurred
the enmity of the War Department and President Grant,
and that the Secretary of War, General Belknap, had ordered
or was about to order, Custer to Washington to answer
certain charges. It was believed by many that General Custer had fully made up his mind that if the opportunity
offered of making a big showing against the hostiles he
would take advantage of it. If he succeeded he evidently
thought it would appease the minds of the "powers that be"
at Washington and thus restore himself to their good graces.
I do not think he made the attack wholly to counteract the
feeling toward him, but he did it for personal aggrandize-
ment; for if he had succeeded in his undertaking and
destroyed the hostiles he would have been lauded to the
skies, especially by the western people, who, to a great
extent, "had no use for Injuns, only dead ones."

General Custer was a man who was extremely fond of
notoriety, inclined to spectacular display, impulsive, impet-
uous and daring. There was no such word as fear in
his vocabulary. I have heard it said in his defense and
have seen it published in the papers, that he would not
have made the attack on Sitting Bull's village had he known
that it contained so many hostiles. But those who so

contend did not know the man.*   The great number of
Indians did not worry Custer; "the more, the merrier."
He was like Fetterman at Fort Phil Kearny; he thought
he could whip the whole Sioux nation with the Seventh
Cavalry.   It was well known that thousands of Indians
had left their agencies in a fighting mood and were congre-
gating somewhere in the Big Horn country for the purpose
of holding a council with all the tribes of the Northwest,
and to decide upon a general outbreak against the whites.

Custer's command consisted of the following:

Commissioned officers 31
Enlisted men 585

*He did know it was a large village. Major V. K. Hart of
Custer's regiment, who was with him when the scouts reported that
they had discovered an immense Indian village which extended well
up and down the Little Big Horn River, told me that upon receipt of
this information Custer pulled off his hat, waved it about his head
and exclaimed, "Custer's luck! The biggest Indian village ever
struck!" Immediately after this he announced his plan of attack. He
had made a similar attack in November, 1868, on the villages of Black
Kettle, Satanta, Lone Wolf and Kicking Bird of the Cheyennes, Co-
manches, Arapahoes and Kiowas on the Washita River, in what was
then the Indian Territory, now Oklahoma. This village was fully as
large as that of Sitting Bull. Custer's plan of attack in both these
fights was to divide his forces into several divisions and attack sim-
ultaneously from different points. Military men concede that Custer
made a mistake in thus attacking the Sioux on the Little Big Horn,
as he knew the Indians outnumbered him greatly.

In the battle of the Washita, Major Elliott, the second in command, with Captain Hamilton and nineteen enlisted men, was killed.
In some manner Major Elliott, with several men, was separated from
the main command. Their remains were not discovered for several
days. Friends of Elliott and Hamilton allege they were deserted by
Custer, just as they now blame Reno for not going to Custer's rescue.

In the Washita fight, Custer wiped out two of the villages, destroying the lodges by fire, together with their contents, and capturing
over seven hundred ponies. Not being able to herd these animals back
to his post, they were shot on the spot, to prevent their falling into
the hands of the Indians again.

No doubt Custer used good judgment in withdrawing from the
Washita immediately after the fight. Had he not done so the battle
of Washita might have been his last, for the Indians belonging to the
other villages farther down the stream were massing their forces as
rapidly as possible to attack him. As it was, many of them followed
him nearly to Camp Supply, whence the expedition started. Comment on these two battles must be left to the reader.

Citizens 3
White scouts 3
Colored interpreter 1
Crows 6
Half-breed guide 1
Arickarees 25

Total 655

On June twenty-fourth the Indian scouts, White-Man-Runs-Him, Hairy Moccasin, Curley and Goes-Ahead, came in with the information that they had seen on the Little Rosebud fresh signs of Indians, and that their trail was leading toward the Little Big Horn Valley.

Custer immediately saddled up and made a night march of four or five hours, then bivouacked and moved out at early dawn the following morning. He had been on the march only a few hours, when the scouts came in under great excitement with the information that from a high point overlooking the valley they had seen an immense camp of Indians on the banks of the Little Big Horn River. The column was halted, and orderlies were despatched to notify all officers to report to the general at once. He informed them that the hostile camp had been located and gave them the following instructions for the attack:

Major Reno, with three troops, A, M and G, was to proceed to a point on the river which was just above the camp, move down and attack the enemy. Captain Benteen, with three troops, H, D and K, was to move in a southerly direction, and to Reno's left, and if he saw any Indians, to attack them. Captain MacDougal, with his troop and a detachment of twelve men from each organization, and with the pack-train, was to keep in touch with the command. The extra detail was to equalize the different commands, giving each troop about fifty men. Custer, with the remaining five troops, C, E, F, I and L, would continue along and behind the high ridge they were on, so as not to be seen by the enemy, and he would attack the lower end of the village, which extended at least three or four miles down the right bank of the river.

I think Custer may have intended Major Reno and Captain Benteen to make the first attack on the hostiles. My reason for thinking so is that they had only four or five miles to go to reach the river, while Custer had to travel at least twice that distance. If Reno made the first attack, which he did, this would attract the attention of the full fighting force of the enemy, which would hasten to repel Reno, not knowing there were other white soldiers in the immediate vicinity. During that time Custer would appear on the scene and attack as contemplated, which attack, it was expected, if pressed with his usual vigor, zeal and fearlessness, would throw the hostiles into consternation.

Reno carried out his part of the program, possibly not with the intrepidity that was expected of him, but he did the best that was possible under the circumstances, and with the small number of men he commanded. He was fighting a desperate enemy; they were striving to save their women and children. Only a few days before (June seventeenth) they had had a successful encounter with General Crook's command, forty miles south on the Rosebud River, Montana. Crook's command numbered about eleven hundred men. This victory, of course, encouraged the Indians, and they fought all the better.

Since the publication of the first edition of *Buffalo Days,* I have had personal interviews with several officers and enlisted men of the Seventh Cavalry who were with Reno in the fight on the Little Big Horn River, June 25-26, 1876. I have read a number of articles pro and con and have had access to official documents that have never been published. I am now more than ever thoroughly convinced that Major Reno handled his command judiciously and skilfully and should be commended and not censured for his action in the premises in withdrawing from the timber and charging through the Indians to reach the high bluffs across the river. Had he remained in the timber many minutes longer his entire command would have been sacrificed. He showed further good judgment in refusing to charge the village swarming with thousands of warriors, with only one hundred and twelve men in his command. It would have been a repetition of Custer's massacre farther down the river.

One week after the battle the survivors sent the following petition to the president and Congress to fill the vacancies among the commissioned officers, caused by the battle, by advancing the officers of the regiment, but it was found impossible to do so.

Camp near Big Horn, on Yellowstone River,
July 4th, 1876.
To His Excellency, the President
and the Honorable Representatives of the United States:

Gentlemen:—We, the enlisted men, and survivors of the battle on the heights of the Little Big Horn river, on the 25th and 26th of June, 1876, of the 7th Regiment of Cavalry, who subscribe our names to this petition, most earnestly solicit the president and representatives of our country, that the vacancies among the commissioned officers of our regiment, made by the slaughter of our brave, heroic and lamented lieutenant-colonel, George A. Custer, and the other noble dead commissioned officers of our regiment, who, fell close beside him on the bloody field, daring the savage demons to the last, be filled by the officers of the regiment only; that Major M. A. Reno be our lieutenant-colonel, vice Custer killed; that Capt. F. W. Benteen be our major, vice Reno, promoted; the other offices to be filled by officers of the regiment by seniority. Your petitioners know this to

be contrary to the established rule of promotion, but prayer-
fully solicit a deviation from the usual rule in this case, as it
will be conferring a bravely-fought-for and justly-merited
promotion on officers who, by their bravery, coolness and
decision on the 25th and 26th of June, 1876, saved the lives
of every man now living of the 7th Cavalry who participated in the battle, one of the most bloody on record, and one
that would have ended with the life of every officer and
enlisted man on the field, only for the position taken by
Major Reno, which we held with bitter tenacity against
fearful odds to the last. To support the assertion, had our
position been taken one hundred yards back from the brink
of the heights overlooking the river, we would have been entirely cut off from water, and from behind these heights the
Indians would have swarmed in hundreds, picking off our
men in detail, and before mid-day of June 26th not one
officer or enlisted man of our regiment would have been
left to tell our dreadful fate, as we would have been completely surrounded.

With the prayerful hope that our petition be granted, we
have the honor to forward it through our commanding officer.

The above petition is endorsed by the surviving troopers
and thirty-six non-commissioned officers of the Seventh
Cavalry.

[The Reply to the Petition.

Headquarters of the Army of the U. S.
July 15, 1876.

The judicious and skillful conduct of Major Reno and
Captain Benteen is appreciated, but the promotions caused
by General Custer's death, have been made by the president
and confirmed by the senate; therefore the petition cannot be
granted.

When the Sioux campaign is over, I shall be most happy
to recognize the valuable services of the officers and men
by granting favors or recommending actual promotion.

Promotion on the field of battle was Napoleon's favorite
method of his officers and soldiers to deeds of heroism but
it is impossible in our service, because commissions can
only be granted by the president on the advice and consent of
the senate, and, except in original vacancies, promotion in the

regiment is generally, if not always, made on the rank of seniority.

W. T. SHERMAN, General.

E. D. TOWNSEND, Adjutant-General.

I will give here, in part, the version of the fight as rendered by the Indians who were with us when we visited the battle-field.* They had been carefully selected at the

---

*Considerable dispute has always been prevalent regarding the condition of the body of General Custer when found on the battle-field of the Little Big Horn. Some writers contend that his body was scalped and otherwise mutilated. Reliable and authentic information on this subject is given by Lieutenant James H. Bradley, Seventh Infantry, chief of scouts for General Gibbon's command, which was approaching the battle-field on the morning of June twenty-seventh. Lieutenant Bradley was riding in advance of the command some two or three miles to the left of Gibbon's column and personally made the discovery of the killing of the entire command of Custer.

In a letter to the *Helena Herald*, under date of July 25, 1876, four weeks only after the fight, he states that Custer's body was wholly unmutilated and that even the wounds which caused his death were scarcely discovered. Even the officers of the Seventh Cavalry (among them being Captain Benteen), who visited the field later in the day, before the bodies were buried, stated that they had not observed the wounds which caused the general's death. (He had been shot in the left temple and left side.) Lieutenant Bradley states that the expression on Custer's face was as peaceful as though he had just lain down for a rest and fallen asleep, the officers remarking: "You could almost imagine him standing before you."

Regarding the other bodies on the Custer field, of which there were a total of two hundred and eight, Lieutenant Bradley further asserts that beyond scalping of the bodies he saw but very little mutilation, and that in even the comparatively few cases of disfiguration it appeared to have been the result of blows with knife or tomahawk or war club to finish a wounded man, rather than deliberate mutilation. The bodies, he asserts, were all stripped, Custer's body also being entirely naked. Furthermore, several of the bodies were entirely clothed, as though the Indians had either overlooked them, or did not care to visit these bodies, some of which were at a distance from the main command.

However, many of Reno's men who fell in the fight in the river bottom were frightfully butchered. It must be remembered that Reno's engagement took place between three and four miles from where Custer fought; that there were probably five thousand warriors pitted against the two commands, armed with Winchester repeating rifles and other improved arms, while the troops were using the 45-70 Springfield single-shot carbine only; that the savages were between the two commands in full possession of that part of the valley, where their village extended up and down the Little Big Horn River for a distance of four miles, and contained approximately fifteen thousand

agency to accompany General Sheridan and his party. They were prominent chiefs in their tribes and all of them had taken active parts in the Custer fight. One of them had been badly wounded in the engagement.

These Indians stated that Reno's command was first seen about a mile and a half from the river. By the lay of the ground, he *could* have seen farther away. He was discovered by an Indian boy who was herding ponies. He had hastened on horseback to alarm the village, about a mile distant. The camp was at once in great commotion. The warriors hastened on foot and mounted to repel the attacking soldiers. The Indians had some little time to collect their senses before Reno could reach their village. This repelling force was small at first, but gradually increased until it outnumbered Reno greatly. Probably every available warrior in the camp at one time was fighting Reno's soldiers. Upon Reno's arrival at the ford he stopped to let his horses drink, which occupied from ten to fifteen minutes. He has been condemned for doing this, but, taking into consideration the circumstances, to my mind it was a case of necessity. His poor animals were nearly famished for want of water. They had been without it for twenty-four hours, and the water they had last drunk was so strong

---

men, women and children. With Reno were one hundred and twelve men; with Custer, two hundred and eight, the rest being with Captain McDougall and Captain Benteen, who were scouting the country to the left and never got into the fight until late in the afternoon, after Reno had reached his position on the bluffs. Neither Reno, Benteen nor McDougal knew what had become of Custer until Lieutenant Bradley made the discovery on the morning of June twenty-seventh, in person, and reported it to his commanding officer, General John Gibbon, who was marching up the valley with the expectation of arriving in time to take a part in the battle. Lieutenant Bradley's discovery of the bodies of the Custer command was the first inkling of their fate.

The battle of the Little Big Horn is a real study, and no person should read it hastily. Many things must be taken into account and every detail carefully followed before the student of western history can fully understand the "whys and wherefores" of Custer's defeat.

with alkali that they were unable to drink much of it. This made them more thirsty, and, to add to their misery, the day was extremely hot. In view of the condition the horses were in, it would have been almost impossible to force them across the stream without allowing them time to appease their thirst. In my judgment, the giving them some water could not have taken much time. Had Reno attempted to cross the stream without watering he probably would have experienced much difficulty.

Reno crossed the Little Big Horn some distance above the Indian encampment, and no doubt came in contact with some of the Indians sooner than he expected; at first only a few but gradually in increasing numbers, until they outnumbered him greatly. The first trooper to fall was about a half mile above the camp. His grave was pointed out to us. Apparently he was a non-commissioned officer, for lying near by was part of a trousers leg with a yellow stripe on it.* Reno found that he was greatly outnumbered and could not advance any farther so he dismounted in one of the many bends of the river, where there was considerable timber. Here he fought the savages for a while, then decided to cross the river and take the strong position which he later occupied. While fording the stream he lost several men, whose bodies fell from their horses and floated downstream. Many writers condemn Reno for not remaining in the timber. He might have done so and all might have been well if he had had sufficient ammunition. But he was on the ground, knew what he had to contend with, and doubtless some of his officers approved of the new position. Again, he might have been burned out. The Indians did start some fires, but the grass was too green to burn readily, although a good wind might have fanned the flames, and

*It is believed that this man was Sergeant Miles F. O'Hara of M Troop, who First Sergeant Ryan states in his narrative was the first man killed.

gradually the fire would have driven them out. Reno no doubt thought he might be burned out.*

It seems to me that the only thing Reno could do in the premises was to cross the river and occupy the position on the bluffs. He had lost many men before crossing the river, and a few more while fording the stream and taking his position on the bluffs—about thirty in all. Captain Ryan states: "In my opinion, if Reno had remained in the timber a short time longer, not a man would have made his escape, as the Indians outnumbered us ten to one."

Suddenly, and without warning, Custer and his gallant men debouched from a ravine about four miles below where Reno was fighting. This was the first intimation the Indians had that he was in the country. At this time, so they told us, the Indians thought they were fighting all the soldiers. Leaving a number of warriors to keep Reno's men busy, the rest swarmed down upon Custer. I do not believe he ever reached the river; at least, there were no men buried nearer than within fifty or seventy-five yards of it. Custer was swiftly driven back to the place where he made his last stand.

Reno was relieved on June twenty-seventh by General Gibbon of the Seventh Infantry. In the two days' fighting there were two hundred and sixty-five officers and men killed, and fifty-two wounded, as follows:

---

*In the retreat of Reno from the river bottom several men were left behind, their horses having become stampeded or lost. Among these men were Lieutenant Charles De Rudio, Scout William Jackson, Interpreter Fred Grouard and Private John O'Neil. They concealed themselves in the thick underbrush until dark, and then attempted to rejoin the command of Reno on the bluffs. De Rudio and O'Neil became separated from the others and underwent some thrilling experiences before they succeeded in joining their comrades, eventually getting into Reno's lines about two A. M., June twenty-seventh. Lieutenant De Rudio died in Los Angeles, California, some six or eight years ago. He has one daughter yet living in Seattle, Washington.

CUSTER'S LAST STAND
Painted especially for this work by Theodore B. Pitman, Boston, Mass.

CUSTER'S COMMAND: KILLED
Commissioned officers   13
Enlisted men   191
Citizens   3
Half-breed guide   1
                                         ————
    Total 208

RENO'S COMMAND: KILLED, WOUNDED
Commissioned officers 3
Enlisted men 48   52
White scout 1
Colored interpreter 1
Arickaree scouts 3
Crow scout 1
                                  ——   ——
    Total 57   52

RECAPITULATION:
Total killed 265
Total wounded 52
                                        ——
    Total killed and wounded............ 317

OFFICERS OF SEVENTH CAVALRY KILLED AT BATTLE OF THE LITTLE BIG HORN

Lieutenant-Colonel George A. Custer

CAPTAINS

T. W. Custer   G. W. Yates
M. W. Keogh

LIEUTENANTS

W. W. Cook   B. H. Hodgson
A. E. Smith   J. G. Sturgis
Donald McIntosh   W. Van W. Reilly
James Calhoun   J. J. Crittenden
J. E. Porter   H. M. Harrington

The bodies of Harrington, Porter and Sturgis never were found.

ASSISTANT SURGEONS

C. E. Lord   J. M. DeWolf

The body of Doctor Lord was never found.

The following civilians also were killed:
Boston Custer (brother of the General)
Armstrong Reed (Custer's nephew)
Mark Kellogg (newspaper correspondent)
Charlie Reynolds (chief scout and guide)
Frank C. Mann
Isaiah Dorman (negro interpreter)
"Mitch" Bouyer (half-breed scout)

INDIAN SCOUTS KILLED

Bloody Knife (Custer's favorite Indian scout)
Bob-Tail Bull   Stab

The Indians told us there were three thousand warriors pitted against the troops but doubtless there were fully a thousand or fifteen hundred more than that.

In this fight, Crazy Horse, Rain-in-the-Face and Gall were the head fighting chiefs, but Sitting Bull took no part in the battle. The position on the plateau back of the village where Sitting Bull "made medicine" was pointed out to us. He was back there while Crazy Horse was leading his warriors to victory. Crazy Horse was a great leader among his people. It was his voice that sang out, when his men were dropping back from Custer's fire, "Come on! It is a great day to die! Cowards to the rear!" It was the great bravery of Crazy Horse that first broke Custer's line.

The sole living thing found on the Custer field, two days after the fight, was "Comanche," the claybank horse ridden by Captain Miles W. Keogh of Troop I. Lieutenant G. I. Nowlan, of Captain Keogh's troop, who had been on detached service with General Terry's staff, was with the men gathering the dead, and discovered the horse standing in a ravine, severely wounded by bullets and half-dead from loss of blood.

The animal was at once recognized as Comanche, the

charger of Captain Keogh, who, with his whole troop had been killed in the fight. Lieutenant Nowlan caused the animal to be driven as humanely as possible to the steamer *Far West,* which carried the wounded of Reno's command down to Bismarck. Captain Marsh, in charge of the boat, provided a comfortable stall for him and a veterinary surgeon with the command extracted the bullets and dressed the wounds thoroughly. The horse commenced to improve rapidly, and reached Fort Lincoln, near Bismarck, safely.

After the Seventh Cavalry returned from the field special orders were issued regarding Comanche. These were to the effect that from that time to the end of his days no person should ever throw a leg over the animal's back. A man from Troop I was detailed as his keeper, to feed and care for him and to lead him, bridled and saddled and draped in black, on all dress parades and other functions of a regimental character.

Wherever the Seventh Cavalry went, Comanche accompanied the command. In 1888 the regiment was ordered to take station at Fort Riley, Kansas, where during the winter of 1891 or '92, Comanche died. His body was mounted by Professor Dyche, of the University of Kansas, at Lawrence, where Comanche may be seen to this day, as lifelike as ever. He was twenty-eight years of age at the time of his death.

The battle of the Little Big Horn has produced many alleged human "sole survivors." All are fakers, pure and simple. Not a white man of Custer's command escaped and even the story of Curley, one of the Crow scouts with the Custer command, can not be substantiated with any degree of accuracy. Just before Custer separated from the other commands "Mitch" Bouyer, in charge of the Crow scouts, told them they had done all that had been expected of them, that they had located the village, but were not expected to

take any part in the fighting unless they chose to; that he
advised them to go to the pack-train at once while there
was time.   Bouyer himself remained with Custer and was
killed.   Curley did not go with the other Crows but made
his escape down the Little Big Horn River to its junction
with the Big Horn, where the supply steamer, *Far West,*
was awaiting orders.   He could speak no English, but
through signs gave Grant Marsh, captain of the boat, to
understand that a big battle had taken place in which the
soldiers had been whipped.   Curley's own story is to the
effect that he escaped from the battle-field in the dust,
smoke and general confusion of battle by disguising himself
as a Sioux Indian.   The reader must form his own con-
clusions as to the truth of his story but it has no actual
foundation.   Curley died on the Crow reservation, Montana, May 21, 1923, aged sixty-six.   White-Man-Runs-
Him is now the only one left of the Crow scouts.

We located the spot where Custer made his final stand.
His brother, Tom Custer, Cook, his adjutant, Autie Reed,
Custer's nephew, Mark Kellogg, correspondent of the *Bismarck Tribune,* and two or three of Custer's officers, were
buried there.   The remains of their dead horses were lying
near by.   Captain Bourke and I cut off the hoofs of the
horse supposed to have been ridden by Custer (a sorrel
with three white fetlocks).   Bourke had his pair made into
ink-stands and gave one of them to a Philadelphia museum.
I placed mine in a grain sack, and, being ordered out against
the hostile Nez Percés in 1877, I left the sack, with some
other property, in our wagons, which were lost.

We went over the battle-field pretty thoroughly and
located the spot where Captain Keogh and several of his
men of Company I had followed Custer.   Here was a slight
depression in the ground.   Evidently at one time it had
been a buffalo wallow and the wind had blown out the dirt,

forming a semicircular depression covering several yards. The graves were around this depression. The men were buried where they fell, which clearly showed that their position had been taken for defense. This was the only position we found where it looked as if a defense had been made, for the men had fallen all over the battle-field, here and there.

Arriving at Fort Custer, we found Generals Sherman and Terry. General Buell, of Civil War fame, was building the post. There were three or four steamers unloading stores and material for the fort at the time, and the river was getting low, so much so that it alarmed the authorities, they being afraid the steamers would not be able to get back down the river. Our squadron, therefore, was detailed to assist in unloading the boats. They succeeded in getting away, but I have been told that they were about the last boats that ever reached Fort Custer.

CHAPTER XXIII

THE KILLING OF CRAZY HORSE*

O N St. Patrick's Day, March 17, 1876, Colonel J. J.
Reynolds, with troops of the Second and Third Regiments of Cavalry, attacked and destroyed, in zero weather, the village of the renowned Sioux chieftain, Crazy Horse, on Powder River. This chieftain had refused to come in and live on a reservation under the eye of the government, but lived far remote from either army posts or white settlements, hunting buffalo.

Crazy Horse's people suffered untold hardships after the destruction of their village. He managed, however, to recapture the larger part of his pony herd, which Reynolds, through gross carelessness, allowed to escape. It will be remembered that it was Crazy Horse who led in the attack against Crook's troops three months later to a day, June seventeenth, on the Rosebud. Crook was obliged to return to his permanent camp and this battle has been generally conceded a victory for the Indians. One week later, Custer fought his last battle against the forces of Crazy Horse and other allied tribes on the Little Big Horn River.

A few months after the Little Big Horn fight, Crazy Horse surrendered at Red Cloud agency, in northwestern

---

*I am indebted to Major-General Jesse M. Lee (retired) now living at the Presidio of San Francisco, California, for the facts regarding the killing of Crazy Horse.

Nebraska, yielding because he desired his people to have rest from the continual harassing by United States troops, and because the buffalo were getting scarce.   Furthermore, it had come down to a question of food for his wearied tribesmen.   His fighting spirit was by no means broken and he was yet looked upon as a great soldier-chief.

A few weeks prior to the surrender of Crazy Horse, General Crook promised the friendly and formerly hostile Indians that when matters were amicably settled they should have a great buffalo hunt together in the autumn.   After the arrival of Crazy Horse, he, too, was given this same promise, which, at the time, was considered a diplomatic move but which later developed into much trouble and danger.

At Red Cloud agency at the time Crazy Horse surrendered was a half-breed interpreter named Louis Richard (or Reshaw) who had a beautiful daughter with whom Crazy Horse fell in love.   The attentions of the renowned chief were reciprocated, and finally he sent the girl's father several ponies, as was the usual manner of obtaining a wife among the plains tribes.   The young woman immediately became an inmate of Crazy Horse's lodge.

The interpreter, however, did not look with favor upon the match, and demanded the return of his daughter.   Crazy Horse merely referred the matter to the maiden herself. She announced her determination to remain with the chief and the father was so notified.

Stationed at Camp Robinson, near the Red Cloud agency, was Lieutenant Philo Clark, an army officer of great popularity, who had general oversight of the late hostiles, particularly Crazy Horse.   Lieutenant Clark's specific duty was to keep a watchful eye upon his movements and report to General Crook anything that savored of trouble.

The hot days of summer were passing, and with the waning of the season came the desire of the Indians to start out on the promised buffalo hunt. There had been no trouble on the reservation, and peace seemed to have settled down. Crazy Horse was very eager for the hunt, which was now deemed an unwise procedure. It was thought that if both the hostiles and friendlies went out on a general buffalo hunt, some of the former might take the opportunity to slip away and join Sitting Bull's band of irreconcilables in Canada.

Chief Spotted Tail was loud in his denunciation of the proposed hunt, as was his right-hand sub-chief, Swift Bear. "The man who planned this hunt needs a heart and a brain," shrewdly observed the latter.

General Jesse M. Lee (now retired), agent at Spotted Tail Reservation, together with Major Burke, commanding officer at Camp Sheridan, near the agency, discussed the matter with the two chiefs. Spotted Tail held that if the Indians went out it might precipitate another Indian war, and that it was a dangerous experiment to make. The arguments which the shrewd old Spotted Tail presented were unanswerable, and it was thereupon decided to call the hunt off.

Crazy Horse was among the disappointed ones. However, no trouble arose at the time. It was then suggested sending the leading chiefs to Washington to hold a great pow-wow with the "Great Father." But when Crazy Horse was approached on the subject he declined to be among the number. "I am not hunting for any Great Father," he haughtily responded. "My father is with me, and there is no Great Father between me and the Great Spirit."

Toward the latter part of August an especial friend of Crazy Horse, named Touch-the-Clouds, whose honesty was beyond question, in the minds of both Agent Lee and Major Burke, informed the two latter that Lieutenant Clark had sent for him to go over to Red Cloud agency for some purpose which was not given out. This was about the time trouble was brewing among the Nez Percé Indians of Oregon. On the following day word was received at Spotted Tail agency that sixty Indian scouts were wanted to go out and fight the Nez Percés. This created much excitement at both reservations. The Indian scouts were made ready to leave, when an order came canceling it.

Major Burke on August thirty-first received a note from Lieutenant Clark stating that Touch-the-Clouds and High Bear had told him they were going to leave the agency and go north on the warpath. "Crazy Horse has worked Touch-the-Clouds exactly to his way of thinking," the note concluded.

Consternation reigned upon receipt of this information. The next day official word came from Red Cloud agency that the northern Indians were to be surrounded, and it was requested that the same thing be done at Spotted Tail agency.

Both Lee and Major Burke were greatly surprised to learn that Touch-the-Clouds was going north with Crazy Horse to fight the whites, and a conference was decided upon at Burke's house. There were present Louis Bordeaux and Charles Tackett (two of the most famous interpreters of the Sioux nation), Frank Grouard, Crook's famous guide, and Joe Merivale, an old-time scout and interpreter. The friendly, or loyal, Indians were represented by Chiefs Spotted Tail, Swift Bear, Two Strike and White Thunder; of the late hostiles, Touch-the-Clouds, Red Bear and High Bear. Major Burke and several army officers represented the government.

Touch-the-Clouds was asked to repeat what he had said and explain what he meant at Red Cloud on the previous day. Louis Bordeaux acted as interpreter, and the other interpreters were requested to note the conversation carefully and to follow every word. It thereupon developed that Frank Grouard had misinterpreted Touch-the-Clouds and given a wrong import to the chief's real meaning.

As soon as this became apparent to Touch-the-Clouds, he became furious and denounced Grouard as a liar, stating that he never had said he was going to fight the whites; that General Crook, the Great Father and others had deceived him, because they had been told when they came to the agency there would be absolute peace, and now he and his Indians were wanted to go out on the warpath, a thing which he violently condemned as a breach of faith. Touch-the-Clouds said that he had first been asked to surrender his gun and had done so; then he had been asked to enlist as a scout to keep peace and order at the agency, and he had done that; then he was asked to give up the buffalo hunt and he had acquiesced. Now, the Great Father (declared the chief), together with General Crook and Lieutenant Clark had "put blood on their faces and turned them toward war"; that both he and Crazy Horse had been deceived and lied to, but nevertheless, they would do as Clark said, and war it should be! They would all go north and fight—the troops would have to go, too, and when they met the Nez Percés "all would soon be peace."

Touch-the-Clouds repeated and explained all that both he and Crazy Horse had said, adding that Frank Grouard had given it a meaning they had not intended. It was an embarrassing moment for Grouard, who quite naturally disliked to acknowledge that he had misinterpreted Touch-the-Cloud's statement, but it was quite apparent that he had done so according to the interpretation of Bordeaux.

It was evident that the trouble originated in asking the northern Indians to go and fight the Nez Percés which they could not understand. However, Lieutenant Clark had acted on Grouard's interpretation, and additional troops were sent for to come to Red Cloud, until there was a total fighting force of about a thousand well-armed troops on the ground. The garrison at Spotted Tail was only about ninety men, a mere handful of fighters had an outbreak at that agency occurred, where there were six thousand Indians. But Chief Spotted Tail was standing by the government, and with his faithful allies was looked upon as a tower of strength.

Lieutenant Clark had suddenly lost all faith in Crazy Horse and Touch-the-Clouds. Agent Lee, at Spotted Tail agency, went over to Red Cloud on September second, and there was General Crook. It looked as if trouble were brewing. Crook was informed that there was some mistake, that all the Indians at Spotted Tail were quiet and that there was no intention on their part of taking to the warpath. Agent Lee was directed to see Lieutenant Clark and tell him all about the matter. This was done, but Clark was positive that Grouard had made no mistake. Lee repeated all that had occurred at the interview with Touch-the-Clouds, where Grouard had partly admitted that he had given a wrong interpretation, and wound up the interview with Clark by declaring that he could positively guarantee that no Indian from Spotted Tail agency would go north. Clark, however, smiled incredulously, plainly not believing Lee's statement.

General Crook finally remarked, "Mr. Lee, I am glad you have come. I don't want to make any mistake, for it would to the Indians be the basest treachery to make a mistake in this matter."

Lee felt easier when it was thought that he had accomplished enough to secure peace at Spotted Tail agency, although he could see that it was yet Clark's intention to have something done to Crazy Horse and his band—just at the time, it was not apparent what this was.

The following day four troops of cavalry came in from Fort Laramie, and on the afternoon of that day Lee was told confidentially that it was the intention to surround Crazy Horse's camp the next morning. He asked if word of this intended act had been sent to Major Burke at Spotted Tail agency and a negative reply was given. Lee urged the importance of getting word to Burke, that an Indian courier from the Indians at Red Cloud agency would probably get there first, with exaggerated news of the trouble; excitement would follow and trouble ensue.

Chief Spotted Tail was over at Red Cloud agency that afternoon, having been sent for by the authorities at Camp Robinson. Lee considered it important to have the chief back to his own camp as quickly as possible, and started in the morning at three o'clock to get him. When Spotted Tail and Lee were about to start for their own agency, the latter said to Lieutenant Clark: "Don't let Crazy Horse get away; he might come over to Spotted Tail agency." Clark replied, "Lee, don't you worry about that. Crazy Horse can't make a move without my knowing it and I can have him whenever I want him. I'll send the news of our success by a good courier."

Everything was quiet at Spotted Tail agency when Lee and the chief arrived there. Here Spotted Tail's sub-chiefs were called together, and told that probably some trouble might occur at Red Cloud that afternoon, but that it must not affect them. They were to keep the people quiet and have no fear.

News from Red Cloud was awaited with considerable anxiety. It was like waiting for a powder magazine to blow up; nobody could tell who would get hurt or what the result might be. About four o'clock the expected happened. An Indian courier mounted on a lathered panting pony arrived at Spotted Tail with the startling information that "their friends were fighting at Red Cloud and the troops were coming to Spotted Tail."

Joe Merivale, well known and respected by the northern Indians, was on hand to allay any excitement and prevent an uproar. With some of the chiefs he was accomplishing results, when word came that Crazy Horse had just arrived in camp! He had escaped from Red Cloud and fled to Spotted Tail agency!

Immediately pandemonium reigned. Here was their renowned leader—the undefeated Crazy Horse, the victor of every battle in which he had engaged during the 'seventy-six campaign; the idol of his followers and their one great hero. He was being hunted by the troops and was in the midst of his friends!

With magic swiftness the three hundred or more tepees came to the ground and had it not been for White Thunder and some of the more loyal Brules a stampede would immediately have resulted, followed by indiscriminate slaughter of the whites and the beginning of another merciless Indian war.

These chiefs, assisted by some of the reliable friendlies, harangued the aroused Indians, and finally order was restored. Word was sent to the Indians under Touch-the-Clouds to bring Crazy Horse to the post, about three miles distant from the Indian encampment. Agent Lee, Major Burke, Bordeaux, the interpreter, and Doctor Koerper started out to meet them. Half-way to the camp, Crazy Horse was overtaken. He was coming into the post, surrounded by about three hundred mounted and heavily armed Indians.

Just as the parade ground was reached, faithful old Spotted Tail, with three hundred trusted Brule warriors, armed with Winchesters, arrived on the scene. It was a moment of tremendous, tense excitement, and it looked as if serious trouble were about to occur. Old Spotted Tail was the coolest individual in the crowd. Garbed in a plain Indian blanket, and without any insignia of his rank as chief, he stepped in the circle and thus addressed himself to Crazy Horse:

"We never have trouble here! The sky is clear; the air is still and free from dust! You have come here, and you must listen to me and my people! *I am chief here!* We keep the peace! *We, the Brules, do this!* They obey me! Every Indian who comes here must listen to me! You say you want to come to this agency and live peaceably! If you stay here, you must listen to me! That is all!"

Can you picture the scene? Indian speech is hard to render, but could one have been there and listened to the telling points of old Spotted Tail's ringing words, and heard the pauses which were emphasized and punctuated by the click of loaded rifles, it would have struck the observer as the most dramatic moment of his life. At its conclusion Spotted Tail was greeted with four hundred vociferous *"Hows!"*

Obedient to the order that the crowds disperse, the Indians returned to their camp, and Crazy Horse was conducted to Major Burke's office to have a talk.

To digress a moment: It appears that soon after Crazy Horse had reached Spotted Tail agency a courier arrived from Red Cloud with a message from Lieutenant Clark to the effect that Crazy Horse's band had offered no opposition; they had surrendered their guns without any trouble at all, but that "Crazy Horse had skipped out for

Spotted Tail agency." Clark requested that Chief Spotted Tail have Crazy Horse arrested and he (Clark) would send over fifteen or twenty Indian scouts to escort the runaway chief back to Red Cloud. It was afterward known to be a fact that the scouts overtook Crazy Horse as he was riding leisurely along with his sick wife, and that when the scouts demanded that he accompany them back to Red Cloud the chief drew himself up proudly and haughtily retorted: *"I am Crazy Horse! Don't touch me! I'm not running away!"* The awed scouts did not dare enforce their orders.

In Major Burke's office Crazy Horse was assured that no harm should come to him; that there was no reason for any such apprehension, as the chief seemed to fear, whereupon he promised to return next day to Red Cloud. It was expected, and thought likely, that, if the chief could be conducted back to Red Cloud quietly, he would be granted an opportunity to talk with the authorities regarding his desire to come and live at Spotted Tail agency. Crazy Horse stated that he simply wanted to get away from trouble, that he had brought his sick wife to be treated and that he had come there for that specific purpose.

Agent Lee replied that he would remember what the chief had said and would repeat his words to the authorities at Camp Robinson the following day. Crazy Horse was thereupon turned over to several Indian chiefs for the night, they agreeing, under a binding Indian pledge, to be responsible for his safekeeping and reporting to Major Burke in the morning.

At the appointed time the following morning Crazy Horse reported at the office, but said he had changed his mind about going back to Red Cloud, giving as his reason that he was "afraid something might happen." He asked Lee and Major Burke to go down to Red Cloud without him and arrange matters satisfactorily. Crazy Horse was thereupon assured that he need have no fear about returning; that he owed it to his people to do so, and must return. The chief finally consented, with the understanding that neither he nor Agent Lee should take arms; that Lee should state to the authorities at Red Cloud all that had occurred at Spotted Tail agency, and that if Crazy Horse made a statement of facts Lee was to say to the soldier chief that Major Burke, Spotted Tail and himself were willing to receive him, by transfer, from Red Cloud, if the district commander so ordered, and furthermore, that Crazy Horse be permitted to state what had occurred—how he had been misunderstood and misinterpreted; that he wanted peace and quiet and did not want to have any trouble of any sort.

No promise was made to the chief that he would be transferred from Red Cloud to Spotted Tail agency, as both he and Agent Lee well knew this could only be done by a higher authority.

The start for Red Cloud was made on the morning of September fifth, Crazy Horse being allowed to ride on horseback. In the ambulance rode Louis Bordeaux, the interpreter, Black Crow and Swift Bear, two reliable agency chiefs, and High Bear and Touch-the-Clouds, Crazy Horse's friends. By consent, seven friends of Crazy Horse from among the northern Indians also went along. A few "reliables" rode with Crazy Horse to care for him and prevent any attempted escape.

During this ride Crazy Horse dashed ahead a few moments, and disappeared over the brow of a hill a hundred yards away. It is likely that here he obtained the knife which later figured in his last dramatic moments. When overtaken, he stated that he had merely ridden ahead to water his horse. He was then made to ride directly in the rear of Agent Lee's ambulance. As the distance to Red Cloud decreased the chief appeared extremely nervous and doubtful of the outcome, but was reassured that he need fear nothing.

When the party had arrived within fifteen miles of Red Cloud agency, Agent Lee sent a note to Lieutenant Clark by a swift Indian courier, asking if Crazy Horse should be taken to the post or the agency. It was stated in the message that great tact had been necessary in securing the chief without serious trouble, and that he had been promised he might state his own case. Clark was asked to arrange accordingly.

The courier returned with the information that Crazy Horse was to be taken direct to the office of General Bradley at Camp Robinson, but nothing was said about giving the chief a chance to state his case.

Agent Lee had built the post at Robinson, and knew the office of the commanding officer was next to the guard-house, and it at once came into his mind that Crazy Horse was to be imprisoned. When the party reached the post, Lee was informed by the adjutant that the general had directed that Crazy Horse was to be turned over to the officer of the day. Lee objected to this arrangement, stating that he desired Crazy Horse to see the commanding officer before anything else was done. This request was referred to the general himself. Lee entered his office, but was bruskly and in a few brief words informed that " 'Twas no use; orders were orders; he could not change them, nor could General Crook himself; nothing further need be said; Crazy Horse must be turned over to the officer of the day." To the inquiry: "Can Crazy Horse be heard in the morning?" the general made no reply, saying that, "Crazy Horse must be delivered to the officer of the day, *and not a hair of his head shall be harmed.*"

Seeing that further pleading was useless, Lee returned to the office, where Crazy Horse was informed that "night was coming on, and the soldier chief said it was too late for a talk; that he said for him to go with the officer of the day and he would be taken care of and 'not a hair of his head should be harmed.'"

Crazy Horse thereupon shook hands warmly with Captain Kennington, the officer of the day. Lee took Touch-the-Clouds and High Bear, friends of the chief, aside, and explained to them how he was powerless and subject to higher authorities at that post.

The chief made no objections whatever to following Captain Kennington. They stepped out of the office, followed by two soldiers of the guard. Kennington led the way to the guard-house and all passed through the main door. But here Crazy Horse caught a glimpse of the prison room beyond, the barred windows, the grated doors and the dungeon cells. Never before had his proud spirit been subjected to this sort of humiliation, and it is unquestionably true that into his mind immediately came the thought that he had been duped, tricked, lied to and trapped. Turning like a hunted animal at bay, Crazy Horse sprang with the agility of a panther into the main guard room, where he drew a long glittering knife from a hiding-place in his clothing and attempted to stab Captain Kennington. The latter diverted the blade with his sword, whereupon Crazy Horse sprang outside, fighting and striking right and left among the guard, struggling to make his way to where his Indian friends were standing.

The chief was seized by Little Big Man, a warrior comrade of Crazy Horse, who attempted to force him to the ground. The infuriated chieftain drew the blade across Little Big Man's wrist to free him from the treacherous grasp, then attacked a soldier of the guard. Three of the Brules caught and held him, and in the struggle Kennington shouted, "Kill him! Kill him!" An infantry soldier of the guard thereupon made a lunge with a bayonet, and Crazy Horse fell, mortally wounded, with a deep bayonet thrust in his right side.

The wildest confusion reigned. Crazy Horse's seven friends were barely prevented from firing upon the guard. Bugles blared and troops came rushing out, while the populous Indian camp poured hundreds of excited maddened warriors to the scene. Even the Indian enemies of Crazy Horse were highly wrought up over the dastardly murder. It was an inexcusable, deliberately planned attempt to "get Crazy Horse out of the way."

The dying chieftain was immediately carried into the office which he had just left a few moments before. Touch-the-Clouds, his firm friend, asked permission to remain with him. The request was granted on condition that he give up his gun, to which he replied with bitter sarcasm: "You are many; I am only one. You may not trust me, but I will trust you! You can take my gun!" The chief's old father and mother were also allowed to remain with him.

About ten o'clock at night, Crazy Horse sent word that he wished to see Agent Lee before he died. Lee went to his side. The chieftain was lying on his blanket on the floor. Grasping Lee's proffered hand, he gasped between his dying moans: "My friend, I do not blame you for this. Had I listened to you this trouble would not have happened to me." Before the end came, Crazy Horse said: "I was not hostile to the white man. Sometimes my young men would attack the Indians who were their enemies and took their ponies. They did it in return. We had buffalo for food, and their hides for clothing and our tepees. We preferred hunting to a life of idleness on the reservations, where we were driven against our will. [At this time steps had not been taken to teach them farming.] At times we did not get enough to eat, and we were not allowed to leave the reservation to hunt. We preferred our own way of living. We were no expense to the government then. All we wanted was peace and to be left alone. Soldiers were sent out in the winter, who destroyed our villages. [He referred to the winter before when his village was destroyed by Colonel Reynolds, Third Cavalry.] Then 'Long Hair' [Custer] came in the same way. They say we massacred him, but he would have done the same to us had we not defended ourselves and fought to the last. Our first impulse was to escape with our squaws and papooses, but we were so hemmed in that we had to fight. After that I went up on Tongue River with a few of my people and lived in peace. But the government would not let me alone. Finally, I came back to Red Cloud agency. Yet I was not allowed to remain quiet. I was tired of fighting. I went to Spotted Tail agency and asked that chief and his agent to let me live there in peace. I came here with the agent [Lee] to talk with big white chief, but was not given a chance. They tried to confine me, I tried to escape, and a soldier ran his bayonet into me. I have spoken." And then in a weak tremulous voice, Crazy Horse broke out into the weird and now famous death song of the Sioux.

Crazy Horse died about midnight, and with his passing went one of the bravest, gamest, most strategic Indian generals of all frontier history in America, a red man who could not and would not be reconstructed. Touch-the-Clouds folded the dead chief's hands on his breast and reverently said, "It is good. He has looked for death and it has come."

The old gray-haired father of Crazy Horse begged

that he might take the body away and give it an Indian burial. Consent was given and at daylight on the morning of September 6, 1877, the wailing, pathetic old father and mother followed on foot from the post an Indian travois, to which was lashed the body of their renowned son and protector. The offer of an ambulance was declined. They desired to convey the body to its burial-place in the manner they knew Crazy Horse would have desired, could he have been consulted in the premises. It was a pathetic scene not soon forgotten by those who witnessed it.

The real reason for attempting to confine Crazy Horse in the guard-house was not made public for many years. However, a captain of the Third Cavalry stated that his troop was detailed to take the chief from the guard-house at midnight, rush him rapidly to the railroad and convey him by train to the Dry Tortugas, Florida, far away from all his family and friends, doubtless for the rest of his days. General Bradley had received this mandatory order from the "higher ups" at Washington, and of course was compelled to abide by them. Had Frank Grouard not misinterpreted Touch-the-Clouds' and Crazy Horse's words, doubtless the whole tragic, lamentable affair would have been averted.

CHAPTER XXIV

AFTER THE NEZ PERCES AND A SCOUT FOR INDIANS

AFTER our trip to the Custer battle-field and Fort Custer we went back to the Clear Fork of Powder River, expecting to remain for some time. We were there only a few days, however, when we were ordered out to intercept the hostile Nez Percé ("pierced nose") Indians. We passed through Pryor Gap, one of the passes of the Big Horn Mountains. General O. O. Howard had been on the trail of these Indians several weeks. Other troops were ordered out to try to intercept them. Colonel Sturgis, with the Seventh Cavalry, was one of the commanders. Our expedition was composed of Troops B, H, I and L, Fifth Cavalry, commanded by Captain Montgomery Hamilton Kellogg and Lieutenant Rockwell, respectively, twenty-five scouts and Frank Grouard, a half-breed Kanaka, who had lived many years among the Indians.* Major V. K. Hart, formerly of the Seventh

---

*Frank Grouard was born in the South Sea Islands. His father was a white man and his mother a native of the islands. Frank was brought to this country when a small boy. At the age of nineteen, while acting as mail carrier between Forts Hall and Peck, Montana, he was captured by the forces of Sitting Bull. Because of his dark complexion, it was thought they had captured an Indian of some strange tribe. Frank said that when he was captured he was wearing a heavy buffalo skin overcoat. It was tied with strings around the wrists to keep out the cold. The Indians wanted to get the coat off uninjured before killing him, and some of them were trying to untie the strings. Suddenly Sitting Bull himself appeared, knocking the Indians right and left, and personally took possession of the captive. He took Grouard to the Sioux village and kept him a captive for several years, during which time Grouard familiarized himself with the

202

Cavalry, who was with Major Reno's command at the battle of the Little Big Horn, was in command.

On the Stinking Water, General Wesley Merritt joined us with the remainder of the regiment (save G Troop, which was stationed at Fort Washakie) and one hundred Shoshone scouts in charge of Lieutenant Hoel S. Bishop. Stinking Water was the name given the river owing to the strong odor of coal oil, which we scented long before reaching the stream.

When we arrived at the river the command was dismounted, while Colonel Hart and Lieutenant Andrus, his adjutant, were looking for a crossing. In the meantime I removed one of my boots and was about to put it on when there was a cry of "Indians!" Jumping up, I saw a dozen or more coming down the valley at a rapid gallop. I was somewhat excited (there were others). Not stopping to put on my boot, I gave the command to mount (nervy for a junior lieutenant). The order was promptly obeyed, when we discovered that Lieutenant Charles King*, our regimental adjutant, and Lieutenant Bishop were with the Indians. I must admit that I was somewhat frightened when the alarm was given and ashamed of it, as I was supposed to be an old Indian fighter. On looking around me I saw

---

Sioux tongue, and, to all intents and purposes, became one of the tribe, taking part in many of their battles against other Indian tribes. However, he did not intend to remain forever a captive, but was merely biding his time to make his escape. This he effected just before the Indian war of 1876, and immediately applied for work as a scout under General Crook. He did valuable work, his familiarity with Indian life being turned to good account. Crook is reported to have once said, "I would rather lose a third of my command than Frank Grouard." For several years after the Indian troubles, Grouard was stationed at Fort McKinney, Wyoming, in the employ of the government as interpreter. He died at St. Joseph, Missouri, several years ago, where he was undergoing treatment for failing eyesight.

*Retired as captain because of wounds, June 14, 1879. Brigadier-general in Spanish War. Author of more than fifty novels of western life.

several other officers looking about as pale as myself, so I felt a little better.

This was a hard trip, as we were having considerable rain and for several days we did not have a stitch of dry clothing on. We had only one mule on which to pack a month's rations for two officers and their bedding. Lieutenant Rockwell and I fared better than the other officers. As I had the only extra animal in the command (named Crazy Horse) I packed him with my portable mess chest. It contained dishes and cooking utensils sufficient for three officers. I also had a camp stove, a small tent and a 'paulin. I had provided myself with this outfit for just such occasions. On reaching camp my colored boy, Clay, would very quickly put up shelter for the kitchen and have a good fire burning. He would put dry stove wood into the oven before leaving camp, so we were sure of having a fire if our pack animal did not fail us. It would not be long before the officers would be coming around for hot coffee, having smelled the aroma. I finally had to ask them to bring coffee with them to replace ours.

We did not intercept the Indians. On our return, our scouts found the Nez Percés' trail and thought General Sturgis was following it, as they found a dead Seventh Cavalry horse and two or three Indian ponies. It was a fortunate thing that we did not meet the Indians. They would have outnumbered us greatly, were desperate fighters and well armed.

Shortly before this, they had repulsed Colonel John Gibbon, Seventh Infantry, in the fight at the Big Hole, Montana, killing and wounding quite a number of officers and men.* The colonel was shot through the thigh.

---

*Colonel Gibbon reported his loss in the Big Hole fight as two officers, six citizens and twenty-one enlisted men, killed; five officers, four citizens and thirty-one men wounded.

INDIAN WOMEN ERECTING TEPEE
SPOTTED TAIL, A BRULÉ CHIEF OF GREAT RENOWN
A SIOUX INDIAN VILLAGE

Colonel Mason, who was a member of General Howard's staff when he was pursuing Chief Joseph, told me that he (Joseph) showed remarkable generalship. He was quick to observe and prompt to take advantage of everything that favored or strengthened his position. When he went into camp at night he would throw up formidable defenses. The only way to drive the Indians out without great loss of life was to outflank them. We had several packers whose homes were in the Gallatin Valley, Montana. They told me that just before the Nez Percés commenced hostilities, Joseph sent word to the settlers not to leave their homes; that he would not harm them; that he was going to fight only the soldiers. I have been told that he kept his word faithfully, both as regards fighting the troops and not harming the Gallatin Valley settlers.

These Indians had been forced to leave their lands and go on an unproductive reservation, against their will. For years they had been friends of the government and the white men. They were self-sustaining and rich in cattle and horses. Who would not fight under such conditions? These Indians afterward surrendered to General Nelson A. Miles with the understanding that they would not be sent back to the Indian Territory (now Oklahoma) but this promise was not kept.

They were held as prisoners of war for a long time at Fort Leavenworth, Kansas, and from there were sent to Fort Sill, Indian Territory. That was a very unhealthy country at that time, noted for its chills and fever. The Nez Percés commenced to sicken and die off. It was thought at the time that the Indian Department sent them to that sickly climate, with the idea of taking that means of getting rid of them, and from all that I can gather they succeeded admirably. General McNeal, Indian Commissioner, told me at Fort Washakie that he was sent to

Fort Leavenworth to take charge of the Nez Percés and make arrangements to transport them to the territory. He found they had been promised they would not be sent there. They begged and pleaded not to be made to go and asked him to intercede for them. He communicated with the Interior Department, stating all the facts in the premises, but the authorities would not rescind the order. The Nez Percés must go. The general felt so badly for these poor people that he did not have the heart to move them and asked to be relieved and was sent elsewhere, and another man was sent to remove them. It was not until 1885 that the Nez Percés were sent back to their beloved mountain home, where Chief Joseph died September 22, 1904, practically of a broken heart.

After this expedition we returned to Fort D. A. Russell, Wyoming, via Fort Washakie, the Sweetwater, Laramie and the Chugwater.

While we were stationed at Fort McPherson, Nebraska, the winter of 1877-78, our commanding officer, Colonel Eugene A. Carr, Fifth Cavalry, was notified that a band of Indians was raiding the cattle ranches north of us. I was ordered to take a detachment of men and investigate the matter, and if I found the report true to make an effort to capture the Indians—without bloodshed, if possible. If not able to do so, I was to take such action in the premises as I thought best.

I left the post about six P. M. one day with a detachment of about forty men from Troop H, Fifth Cavalry, with pack animals and several days' rations, for North Platte, eighteen miles from McPherson, where I wanted to get information regarding the Indians who were supposed to be committing the depredations. I arrived at North Platte about nine o'clock. There were rumors afloat in the air but nobody seemed to know where the Indians were operating.

After some difficulty I found Dave Perry, a noted character, who informed me that the Indians had raided Barton and Keith's ranch, about forty miles distant, running off some of their horses, so I decided to go there. I had never been in that part of the country and Perry volunteered to accompany us as guide. I saddled up and left for the ranch at daylight, arriving there about eleven o'clock. I found about twenty cowmen at the ranch. None of these had seen the Indians, but they were quite sure they were in the country. Con Groner, county sheriff, was among the party, and doing most of the talking. He was spokesman for the cowmen. Afterward he was with a Wild West show as the cowboy sheriff, and a noted Indian fighter. It was on this occasion that he made his reputation.

I was informed that the cattlemen would work with me, and do whatever I thought best in the matter. I told Groner to take his men and try to locate the Indians' trail, and if they found it to wait until I came up and we would follow it. I wanted to feed my horses and give my men something to eat, so that in case they found the trail I would be in a position to follow it without delay—to the Indian reservation, if necessary. I carefully instructed the cattlemen if they located the trail not to follow it until I joined them.

As soon as my horses had eaten their grain and the troopers had had lunch, I saddled up and moved out to join the cowmen. In a few hours I overtook them, and to my great surprise they had found the Indians and fired upon them, the Indians escaping. I was greatly wrought up over their actions, and remarked that it was a "pretty howdy-do." I said, "If you had obeyed my instructions those Indians would not have got away."

They made some frivolous excuse and looked rather crestfallen. There were less than a dozen Indians, I learned, and only three or four were mounted. When the cowmen approached the Indians they were putting up some wickiups, and no doubt were preparing to remain all night.

I told the cowmen I was going to make an effort to capture the Indians, and that they had better go home. This was nearly at nightfall, and the Indians had scattered so that it was impossible to follow them very rapidly. Some of the cattlemen followed on after me. It was soon so dark that we could not distinguish the trail. We were satisfied by this time that the Indians were making for their reservation. In places there was some snow on the ground, so we could see that those who were afoot were making "some strides." I learned that the cattle ranch of "Buffalo Bill" Cody and Major Frank North was on the Dismal (the next stream). I told the cattlemen that I would make for the ranch, as it was on the direct route that the Indians were taking for their reservation. Here the cattlemen left me.

I arrived at the Cody ranch about one A. M. The ranchmen were up and halted me. They told me some Indians had come to the ranch about eleven o'clock. Hearing a noise out at the corral, the men got up to ascertain the trouble, and saw the Indians as they fled. No doubt they were trying to steal some horses. I knew there was little use following the Indians farther at that time of night, so unsaddled, feeding my horses some hay, and told my men to make themselves as comfortable as they could, and we would move out again at daybreak.

We started out bright and early. My men had had their coffee and my horses some rest, so I was prepared to follow the Indians speedily. I had no trouble in following their trail, for there was considerable snow on the ground. I went to Rankin's ranch, which was a ride of about thirty-five miles, arriving there about eleven o'clock. I learned that the Indians had been there about seven o'clock, pretty well fagged out, and the ranchmen had given them something to eat. They told the ranchmen that the soldiers were after them. The Indians were very tired. No doubt they had relieved one another with their ponies.

As the reservation was not many miles from the ranch, and as I was convinced the Indians had committed no depredations, I gave up the pursuit. On sober thought, I was glad that the Indians had got away from the cattlemen, for had I overtaken them at that time, when the excitement was on, I might have killed some of them.

I returned to McPherson by easy marches. I was in the saddle about twenty hours, and the distance marched was fully a hundred miles.

CHAPTER XXV

IN 1869 Camp Augur, a subpost of Fort Bridger, was established on the present site of Lander, Wyoming. It was named for Brigadier-General C. C. Augur, United States Army, then commanding the Department of the Platte. This post was established (at the earnest request of Chief Washakie) in compliance with the terms of a treaty with the Shoshone and Bannock Indians. Subsequently it was a separate post, named for Captain Frederick H. Brown, Eighteenth Infantry, who was killed at the Fort Phil Kearny massacre, December 21, 1866.

It was deemed advisable to relocate the post, and the commanding officer, Captain Robert A. Torrey, Thirteenth Infantry, was enjoined to select a site for the new post. This was done June 26, 1871, the location being on the south bank of the south fork of Little Wind River, near the junction with the north fork. Adobes were the material selected for the construction of the post. Later a valuable rock quarry was discovered near the post and all the new construction material was from this quarry.

In December, 1878, the designation of the post was changed to Fort Washakie, for the illustrious chief of the Shoshones. A few years ago the military post was turned over to the Interior Department and it is now the agency for the Shoshone and Arapahoe Indians.

In December, 1878, my troop was ordered to Fort

Washakie. I remained at Washakie until June, 1880. Green River was the nearest railroad station.

While stationed there, I was the quartermaster, commissary, ordinance officer and post treasury officer and was also in command of my troop part of the time. I partly rebuilt the post, erecting a large storehouse, guardhouse, stables and an administration building, which included an officers' club room; also a recreation room for the enlisted men—bowling alley and a chapel, which was provided with a stage for amusements. Most of the work was done by soldier labor. The men went into the mountains, felled the trees and hauled the logs to the sawmill, which was provided with a planing and shingle mill. I employed a citizen sawyer and a carpenter. These were all the civilians employed, except the blacksmith and a few teamsters.

While in charge of the bakery, I purchased flour from a little mill near Lander City, made the flour up into bread and sold it to the Indians. Taking some of this money, I sent to Salt Lake City for a hundred trees and set them out around the parade ground. To-day they are immense trees. I had to send the adjutant-general a quarterly report of the finances of the bakery. My tree transaction was disapproved. I was informed that the government did not approve of that kind of business, and directed not to do it again. I didn't care. I got the trees. Had I been permitted to continue that kind of work I should have made other improvements to add to the appearance of the post.

I took great interest in these Indians. They called me "the little chief with the scar on his face." I put in the first irrigation ditch for the Arapahoes. General Jesse M. Lee told me while in the Philippines that the Indians had informed him when he was at Fort Washakie investigating some of the Indian grievances, that I was the one who surveyed and showed them how to make the ditch. This was their first farming, and if the government had taken the interest in them that I did they would now be self-sustaining.

I inspected all the fresh beef and cattle issued. The issue day was every Saturday morning. I went over to the agency, superintended the weighing of the meat issued, and had to certify to the weight and see that it was up to the contract. This certificate was sent to the Indian Department at Washington. I inspected and received for these Indians about three thousand head of stock cattle. They were divided among the families.

One day I was riding around the reservation, and upon passing a thicket I happened to see an Indian therein, branding two or three calves. I asked him what he was doing. Pointing to the brand, he replied laughingly: "Oh, me branding, all same white man." It looked to me very much as if he were branding mavericks. There were several large herds grazing on the reservation.

While at Fort Washakie, I took baths in an Indian sweat-house. The use of the sweat-bath by means of heated air and steam seems common to all tribes, and with all it is used not only to cure physical disease, but as a form of worship and supplication. The sweat-house at Washakie was a small bower, constructed by sticking the ends of sharpened willow branches in the ground, then bending them over and fastening them together at the top, over which buffalo robes were thrown. The bower was about eight or ten feet long and six feet wide, and the height was such that when a person sat down his head would nearly touch the top. A hole was dug in the center of the bower in which to place stones that had been previously heated. These stones were carefully selected, were as nearly round as possible and were never used more than once for this purpose.

Lieutenant Cummings and I decided that we would try one of these baths. It was in January, with snow on the ground. Dry grass was first placed inside the sweat-lodge for us to sit on. We stripped and went inside with four or five of the Indians, the medicine man coming last. The hot stones were passed in on a forked stick and put into a hole in the center; then a bucket of water was handed in. The medicine man now placed on the hot stones some sweet grass, which emitted a fragrant odor. He then commenced to sing incantations. Finally, taking a cup of water from the bucket, he filled his mouth and sprayed it over the hot stones, which filled the place with a dense steam and made it very warm. The thermometer we had with us showed a temperature in the bower of one hundred and twenty degrees. It became so hot that we had to put our faces down in the grass, in order to breathe. After a thorough sweating we came out of the bower dripping with perspiration, threw buffalo robes over ourselves, ran down to the stream (Little Wind River) about fifty or seventy-five yards away, and jumped in. We did not remain very long in the water, but the sensation was pleasant. Then we went back to a tepee and thoroughly rubbed ourselves down. I never felt better in my life.

The post surgeon wanted to try one of the baths and went down to the Arapahoe camp with us. Before entering the sweat-lodge we told him he must keep his head up, let come what might. We had been in the bath but a short time when the surgeon commenced to perspire. He told us he could not stand the excessive heat much longer. Cummings and I had our faces down in the grass, where we could stand the heat very well. First one would bob up, and then the other, asking the doctor "how he was making out." He stood it as long as he could, then made a break, remarking that it "was the damnedest hottest place he ever was in," as he bolted through the side of the sweat-lodge.

During my stay at the post, Sharp Nose, the head chief of the Arapahoes, fractured his thigh. The commanding officer sent me down to tell him that if he chose to come up to the post he would be put in the hospital, but that his family must not accompany him. When I arrived at the Indian camp I found the Indian doctors attending him. They had made a splint by taking many willow twigs, about as large around as a lead pencil, and stringing them in the same way as the Chinese and Japanese make their screens. They had set the leg and wrapped these willow twigs around it, and had made a strong tea out of sage, and occasionally sprayed the concoction on the limb. This relieved a great deal of the inflammation and soreness. All this time there were about a half dozen Indian doctors in attendance, beating tom-toms and blowing their whistles. The music was about as confusing and noisy as Chinese music. Nevertheless, Sharp Nose duly recovered, although his leg was about an inch shorter than the other. Indian doctors also "cup" for headaches and other complaints, by using the base end of a buffalo horn.

During the spring of 1879 I captured the roving remnants of the Bannock Indians, at the end of hostilities with that tribe. There were about forty men, women and children. I had to use some diplomacy in capturing them without loss of life. I had been informed that these Indians were about forty miles away from the post, and started out after them with Troop L, Fifth Cavalry, leaving the post about two or three in the afternoon. I also had about a dozen Shoshones and Arapahoes. We reached the Bannocks' camp about daylight and surrounded it. I then sent word by a scout to inform them that we were all around them, and that they must surrender. After some little talking, they decided to accompany me. I told them no harm should be done to them, and that we had other prisoners at the post. I ordered them to make preparations to break camp and go with me. Some of my own Indians were much excited and I could hardly keep them from firing into these people, but I started back to camp, and that night I put my men on guard over both the Bannocks and the turbulent scouts, keeping this guard over them until I arrived back at the post.

One of the greatest Indian chiefs of modern times was Washakie, chief of the Shoshones, after whom Fort Washakie received its name. He was born about 1804 and died at Fort Washakie February 20, 1900. His father was a Flathead and his mother a Shoshone. Washakie became a chief at nineteen or twenty years of age, but was not distinguished or well known until 1863, after General Connor's defeat of the Shoshones and Bannocks on Bear River, Utah, January 29, 1863.

In this fight there were about three hundred Indians engaged. Colonel P. C. Connor's command numbered about the same, all California volunteers of cavalry and infantry, with two howitzers. The Indians were strongly entrenched in a deep ravine, and Connor had much difficulty in getting to them. The obstacles were finally overcome, however, and the soldiers killed all but a few Indians, who jumped into the river and escaped. Many were killed in the stream while attempting to swim across.* Only the women and children were spared. One officer and twenty soldiers were killed and three officers and forty-four men were wounded.

---

*Narcott, the Shoshone interpreter, who was very cross-eyed, was in this fight. He related to me that while swimming the river he kept looking back over his shoulder, and became so frightened that his eyes were never again normal.

For this victory over the Indians, Colonel Connor was promoted to a brigadier-generalship. The Mormons sided with the Indians and gave them aid and encouragement, supplying them with food and ammunition and information of the soldiers' movements. The campaign was the outcome of depredations on the overland trail and the killing of immigrants and miners.

After this fight a much larger number of Indians congregated on Bear River, but Washakie, after much persuasion and entreaty, finally induced many of the young warriors to withdraw, and he then led them into Fort Bridger, Utah. From this time on, he was absolutely chief.

A treaty, called the "great treaty," was made with the Shoshones and Bannocks in 1868. By the terms of this treaty these tribes were given the Wind River country for a reservation. It was understood that the treaty should provide military protection for the Shoshones in the country they were to occupy, but for some reason this was not inserted in the treaty. To my knowledge, the Indian Department wanted the soldiers removed from the reservation on several occasions, but Chief Washakie insisted upon their remaining, asserting that they were his friends and that he could rely on their friendship and protection. Although not actually inserted in the treaty, it was intended to be a part thereof. In after years, however, this stipulation was canceled by the War Department.*

Throughout his life Washakie was the steadfast friend of the white man, but was almost constantly at war against other Indian tribes, the Sioux, Cheyennes and Arapahoes in particular. He was generally on the defensive, as the tribes mentioned were much stronger than his own. It is not known that he was ever defeated, although at times closely pressed and besieged.

---

*I am indebted to my old friend, J. K. Moore, for many years post trader at Fort Washakie, for the above information.

Red Cloud and Crazy Horse admitted that Washakie was the greatest general of them all. He took part in the campaign of 1876 with General Crook, tendering the latter scores of his young men for use as scouts with the expedition, and they rendered valuable service. They were under the charge of Tom Cosgrove, as Chief Washakie was too old himself to take an active part in the campaign.

Washakie was a great leader and always had complete control of his people. The latter part of his life was spent in the quiet enjoyment of his people and surroundings. He was a man of excellent character and endeavored to exercise a good influence over his people. He was extremely fond of his family and enjoyed the peaceful life. A story often told, as well as written, that he killed one of his wives, is an error. His disposition was most kindly. He was dignified and commanded the respect of all.

Washakie was known to all the early pioneers and pathfinders, and they sought his friendship. Kit Carson appears to have been his favorite. No Indian of mountain or plain was more extensively and favorably known. His remains rest in the post cemetery at Fort Washakie, where a monument, erected by the United States Government, stands to his memory.

CHAPTER XXVI

IN THE issuing of annuity goods, the Indians were arranged in two parties. On one side were the women, with small children who were unable to leave their mothers. In the next row were girls from eight to fifteen years of age. In the third row were the old women. The men were placed on the opposite side, the young men in the inner and the older men in the outer circle. Head men were selected who issued the articles by placing each allotment in front of the person for whom it was intended, and all were obliged to remain in their places until the distributions were completed. The women had to be watched closely, for occasionally they would attempt to secrete things and then claim they had not received them.

The Indians were always much pleased at receiving their annuities, and the fact that I was in charge of the issues caused one of them to present me with a horse; or rather, with a stick that represented the value of a horse, for all I had to do was to hold on to the stick, go to the herd, select the best horse there, and then surrender the stick. I did not know this at the time.

After this presentation two of the chiefs led me out into the center of the ring, and from the opposite side a man led out a beautiful Indian maiden, magnificently dressed in Indian costume, wearing a handsome buckskin garment covered with beads and elk teeth. Thirty or forty of the teeth ornamented the tunic, and in those days they were valued at from two to three dollars each. The moccasins of the maiden also were covered with beads and her arms were thickly encircled with silver bracelets. Her costume must have been worth one hundred and fifty to two hundred dollars. Her face was painted in such a manner that it greatly enhanced her natural beauty.

As she was being led out, several queries ran through my mind. As it was the custom among the Indians, when they were pleased, to give their friends their daughters, I thought this might be what they intended to do, and of course I could not accept her. Really, I did not know what to do. They led her up and she stretched her arms toward me. I thought she was about to throw them about me and kiss me. I thereupon dodged back, throwing up my hands, one of which held the stick I was supposed to present for the horse, when she quickly grabbed the stick from my hand and ran gleefully away with it. The whole multitude of some two or three thousand Indians commenced laughing uproariously.

At the time I did not understand the cause of their mirth, but I was told by Friday, the interpreter, that it was the custom in cases of this kind to give the officer in charge of the distribution the blessing of the tribe. The young woman had come out to confer this blessing upon me, and had merely extended her arms with the intention of placing them on my head and pronouncing a benediction; but when she grabbed the stick, as I dodged, the horse became hers. So I got neither horse nor blessing!

As in other nationalities, the Indians have their love affairs, and it is an old custom among them to sell their daughters in marriage when they reach the proper age. There was a girl who had been sold when she was a child to another Indian, but she had fallen in love with a young warrior and they ran away, returning as man and wife. One issue day they were going up for rations, when the Indian who had purchased the girl struck the young "warrior-Lochinvar" with a whip. The youthful groom killed his assailant on the spot and then fled to the mountains with his wife, telling his enemies if they wanted him to come and get him. This caused a great commotion among the different bands of Indians, and it looked as though there was going to be serious trouble. The Indians went to the commanding officer, Major John Upham, Fifth Cavalry, who had great influence over them, and asked for advice. He suggested that they send two or three old men, who were friends of the warrior, out to him, and try to prevail on him to accompany them in to the post with his wife, not as prisoners; that the commanding officer would put them into a room in the guard-house and keep them there where they would be safe from their enemies. The head men would then try to get the two factions together to see whether they could not settle the matter with the dead man's relatives without further bloodshed.

One morning, about daybreak, I was awakened by a noise and looking out saw the young warrior and his wife surrounded by about a dozen Indians who were singing a war song, a custom of theirs when they effect a capture. I was officer of the day, and confined the couple to the guard-house. They had a very fine buffalo robe with colored porcupine quills. Around the edges were loops about three inches in length, on which were strung the cleft hoofs of more than one hundred deer.

Our Indians got together and held a council with the relatives of the prisoners, and the matter was finally settled by the friends of the young warrior presenting ten ponies to the relatives of the murdered man. When the young couple were released from the guard-house I again happened to be officer of the day and released them, whereupon the squaw made me a present of the decorated buffalo robe. I was offered one hundred dollars for it on several occasions.

At one time I had probably one of the largest individual collections of Indian curios in the world. They were deposited for several years in the museum on Governor's Island, New York harbor. They were also on exhibition in Glasgow, Scotland, and in London. At Governor's Island the collection was not properly cared for, and the valuable furs and clothing were so ruined by moths that there was scarcely any hair left on my prized buffalo robe. Another robe captured by Colonel Cody in the fight at Summit Springs, Nebraska, July 11, 1869, which he gave me later, was also ruined. This robe was covered with paintings, evidently the life history of some Indian. I also had a memorandum book captured by my first sergeant, James Turpin, Troop L, Fifth Cavalry, in the fight with Dull Knife's Cheyennes in the Big Horn Mountains, in the winter of 1876.

I sold this collection of Indian curios to a French artist who had a studio in New York. He broke up his studio and sent the curios to France, together with his wife and child. All were lost en route by the sinking of the French steamer, *La Bourgogne,* off the coast of Newfoundland, in 1898.

CHAPTER XXVII

IN 1881, I was detailed to the school of application, Fort Leavenworth, Kansas, when it first opened, rejoining my troop at Fort McKinney, Wyoming, in 1883.

I was stationed at Fort McKinney for several months. The post was named for Lieutenant McKinney of the Fourth Cavalry, who was killed in MacKenzie's fight with Dull Knife's band, November 25, 1876, on Powder River. This post has been abandoned several years. The town of Buffalo was established adjoining the military reservation while I was there, and is now one of the important towns in the state of Wyoming.

While at McKinney I had several important details, one of which was to proceed with a detachment of men to Rawlins, Wyoming, a station on the Union Pacific Railroad, a distance of one hundred and seventy-five miles or more, to receive a hundred horses for my regiment and to conduct them safely to the post.

At that time the country was infested with horse and cattle thieves and stage robbers. Horses had even been stolen off picket lines during the night time while a sentry was walking the line. This was accomplished during dark and stormy nights. Great precaution had to be taken, therefore, to prevent animals being driven off during the night as well as day.

I was not expected to lead the horses (as is usually

222

done) with a small detachment such as mine. I was to conduct the horses attached to a line, thereby saving the use of a large number of men. My detail was small, on account of the work on post and the number of men on detached service. I suggested to the commanding officer the scheme of using a line such as I had seen used when quite a lad during the Civil War. As I remembered, a rope was run from the tongue of one wagon to the axle of another; but my scheme was to do away with the wagons and attach two teams to a line, the driver riding one of the horses. Of course, it required more skill to manage a pair of horses in this way than it would to drive them to a wagon.

Before leaving the garrison I provided myself with a coil of rope, some harness and the necessary equipment which I expected to use. On my way to Rawlins the only incident that occurred was when one of my mules was taken with wind colic. Having no drench, I bled the animal in the mouth, as I knew that in that ailment they were sometimes relieved by swallowing the blood; but in this case it did not help matters. The animal, in great agony, lay down and refused to move. Not having a trocar, I punctured the mule with my knife, on the right side where the intestines were attached, which gave the animal immediate relief.

I found the horses awaiting my arrival, and at once made preparations to leave the next morning on the return trip, selecting suitable horses for my teams that were to be attached to the lines. The horses conducting the column had to be fastened to the rope by means of doubletrees, so I let out the tugs to the last hole, as a precaution against the doubletrees striking the horses' heels when the rope slackened. I prepared the harness for the teams that were to be attached to the other end of the line, by attaching straps to the collars, and to these straps the line was tied. These horses were supposed to hold back and keep the line taut, which was going to be very hard on their necks, and in order to protect them as much as possible I ran straps from the breechings across the horses' backs, fastening them to the rings in the harness.

The next morning we were up bright and early. We harnessed and hitched the horses to the line. I had two lines, each of which was about one hundred and seventy-five feet in length, and of course had to fasten one line at a time. During this operation everything ran smoothly, but when we commenced to tie the horses to the rope our trouble commenced. The line was so long that the attached horses could not keep it off the ground, and no sooner would we get some of them secured than others would step over it, and scarcely would we get the latter back in place when others would repeat the error. Several times four or five horses became tangled up and we had to unravel the bunch. At times it looked as if I would have to abandon the scheme and ask for more men, but I kept that to myself, not wanting to discourage my men, and worked all the harder. I finally succeeded in getting all the horses on the first line, but had to leave three men with it to keep the animals quiet.

I then commenced on the other line and then did not have quite so much trouble, although I had fewer men to work with. But we had gained some experience. For instance, I commenced to tie the horses to the center of the line and also had the halter shanks tied shorter and more securely. This kept part of the line off the ground so the horses could not so rapidly step over it, and kept the straps from slipping, which no doubt also saved a mix-up.

After working several hours we were ready shortly before noon to start out. We had some trouble in moving out, for the horses did not know what was required of them, but the lead teams were good pullers and were well handled, so we at last got on the road. Some of the horses were headstrong and wanted to pull ahead, while others were inclined to hold back; but this turned out to be an advantage to the rear teams, as they had very little work to do. We had one or two pretty bad tangles, and in straightening out one of them my hand was caught in some manner between a halter strap and the line, breaking one of the bones, but, nevertheless, I kept at work as best I could.

We got into camp rather late, having made a march of fifteen miles. In camp I had to use the same ropes for the ground lines that had been used on the road, fastening them to the ground by means of iron pins driven well into the soil to hold them firmly. In doing this, all the horses had to be taken off the lines; so we tied them here and there to the scattered sage-brush until we got the lines down. The horses were "recruits," never having been on a ground line before, but they behaved fairly well. I had plenty of hay on the line, which kept them occupied, but occasionally one would want to step over the line, so I had to keep two or three men walking it most of the night to prevent any of the animals injuring themselves.

My hand was rather painful. I put on a splint and bandaged it, and on my arrival at the post I showed it to the surgeon. He said it was doing nicely and that he could not have treated it better.

We got an early start in the morning, the horses giving very little trouble. We traveled pretty well, trotting quite a little, and got into camp about twelve o'clock, having made about twenty miles. At this camp quite a number of cowboys called on us commenting on what fine horses we had. If one saw a particularly fine horse he would call it "his" horse. One of them told a member of the guard that he would be around that night to get "his" horse, that he needed a good one in his business.

On the next day the horses worked splendidly and we made about six or seven miles an hour, arriving at Fetterman before noon. Crossing the Platte River, I went into camp. After getting something to eat and seeing that everything was in shape, I left the camp in charge of a non-commissioned officer and went to town to see some friends and learn the news. While I was there, an ex-sergeant named Wolf, who had served in my troop (L Fifth Cavalry) and who was then in the employ of the stage company, came to me quietly and informed me that I had better keep a good lookout on my horses, as the town was full of cowboys, many of whom were out of employment, and that some of them would not mind running off with my stock if given an opportunity. The sergeant said he didn't want to alarm me, but he had overheard some of them saying that now was a good time to get a mount and get out of the country. It might be only talk, but, at the same time, it would do no harm to be on my guard. I, of course, appreciated this warning and thanked him sincerely.

After remaining in town several hours, I went to my camp. There had been several cowboys in camp, and about half a dozen were there yet, but they soon got on their horses and rode away. I found that the horses had been watered and fed and everything was in good shape. I did not feel particularly alarmed, as I had been "through the mill" before, but I had made up my mind if any horse thieves came around my camp that night, they were going to be disappointed, for I did not intend to be there. However, I kept this to myself.

Before going to bed I went around to give some special orders, after which I returned to my tent but did not undress. I lay down on my bunk for an hour or so, then got up, called the sergeant and told him I was going to break camp at once, informing him what was up. We broke camp quietly and soon were on the move. I left the sergeant and one man to follow me, not too closely, explaining to the sergeant that if the rustlers should come to our camp and find the bird had flown they might follow us up, and if they did so, he was to run them off.

I never stopped going until daylight. The night was nice and bracing, the horses never acted better, and we must have made at least forty miles. I then went into camp and remained until afternoon, when I started out again for Wild Horse Creek, the headquarters of Mr. Franklin's horse ranch. Here I got permission to feed my animals in his corral. The next day we went to the old Fort Reno cantonment just across Powder River, and the following day I drove into the post, thirty-five miles.

Some little time after, I learned that the warning given me by Sergeant Wolf was "straight." A party visited my camp and was much surprised at not finding me there. However, if I had remained in camp I do not believe I would have lost any of my horses, as I would have taken every precaution to prevent their being stolen.

CHAPTER XXVIII

ESCORTING GENERAL GIBBON

U PON my return from Rawlins, I went on another
trip, escorting General John G. Gibbon, our department commander, and his party, from Fort McKinney to
Fort Washakie. This was in November, 1883. Among
the number was General Robert Williams, my old esteemed
friend, who was very much interested in me when I entered
the service.

(To digress a moment: I was in Rio Janeiro, Brazil, in
May, 1916, and called on the American minister, Mr. Mor-
gan. The minister himself was at Sao Paulo, but I there
met Lieutenant Robert Williams, the naval attaché at the
embassy. In the course of our conversation, he inquired
whether I knew General Robert Williams. I told him the
general was a very dear friend of mine, whereupon he
said General Williams was his father.)

Others of the party with General Williams were Thad-
deus Stanton, paymaster general; Colonel Mason of the
Fourth Infantry and Major Lord of the quartermaster
department. I had taken the first wagons over the mountains to Washakie some time before this with Major E. C.
Mason, the inspector-general of the department. This was
for the purpose of seeing whether it were feasible to do
so. The major had been General O. O. Howard's chief
of staff during the Nez Percés' uprising, and was known
to be very devout.

I told the men of my detachment before starting that

I wished them to be very choice of the language they used on this trip, telling them that the major was a very religious man. On the trip, in ascending one of the mountains, our elevation being several thousand feet, my mules did not pull as they should and there was some question as to whether we would be able to get all the wagons up. No doubt the rarefied air had a great deal to do with their trouble in pulling. This had not occurred to me. I lost my temper and commenced to cuss the mules in good old western style. This did not better matters very much, but old "mule-skinners" used to say that a few cuss words encouraged the mules to pull harder. While I was applying the blacksnake freely and every man was doing all he could to help the wagons up the mountainside, I came to my senses and thought of my request to the men to be careful of the language they used. I felt ashamed of my conduct and looked around to see whether the major had heard me. He was coming down the mountainside rapidly. I felt sure he was going to reprimand me for my language, but he grabbed a stick and helped pound them along. With the major's assistance, the mules were "got down into their collars," and we reached the summit.

Arriving at Washakie, I was complimented by the party for getting them safely there. Colonel Mason told Major Lord to tell me if I would transfer his regiment he would make me his regimental quartermaster. General Gibbon and his party thoroughly enjoyed their outing. The trout fishing was excellent and considerable large game was killed, including elk and mountain buffalo. These were the last buffalo I ever saw, to my regret. The mountain buffalo was not so large as the plains animal. We saw several bands of elk; one band must have numbered at least a hundred head. General Williams killed one, which pleased him very much.

On my return I had some trouble getting my wagons over the mountain because of the snow. I was very anxious to overcome this, as it was getting late in the season and if I did not succeed I would have to make a long detour to get back to Fort McKinney. I finally overcame all obstacles, reached the top of the mountain and went into camp among the pines. The snow had to be shoveled away where my tent was pitched. The men built a large fire; I sat in my tent facing it; it was not cold. The snow was falling, and the beautiful pines, the snow and the cheerful fire made one of the prettiest camp scenes in my memory.

The snow ceased during the night. It was at least a foot in depth. We could not look down into the valley, several thousand feet below us, because of the bank of clouds. It was a beautiful morning. I had never seen anything like it before, nor have I since.

Before starting down the mountains, I had to take every precaution against an accident, as the snow had made the traveling very slippery. In going down the very steep places I had to lock the four wheels and take the lead mules off the wagon. In the sliding places I had to throw a rope clear over the wagon, attaching it to the reach, and keep three or four men at the other end above the wagon, pulling at times with all their strength, to keep the wagon from tipping over and sliding down the mountainside. In other places I had to attach a rope to the axle and have men hold it to keep the wagon from running against the mules. It was wonderful how easily two or three men could let a wagon down steep places by the aid of a long rope. Before I had taken this precaution one of the wagons slipped off the trail and landed against a tree about eighteen inches in diameter. We were not able to move it from the position it was in without unloading it, so

I thought it would be better to fell the tree, leaving a stump about six inches in height. The stump was blocking the wheels, so we decided to pull the wagon over it. The hill was steep, and I concluded to attach a rope to the axle to keep the wagon from running against the mules when the wheels went over the stump. I passed the rope around a near-by tree, telling the men when the wheel went over the stump, having a fall of a foot or more, to let the wagon down gradually. The mules were started, but when the wheels went over the obstacle the men at the rope were not quick enough in allowing the rope to slip. It broke, and both wagon and mules went sliding down the mountainside a few yards and lodged with a crash in some small trees. The driver jumped in time, which doubtless saved him from a severe fall. The mules were bruised considerably but no bones were broken.

The wagon did not fare so well. The tongue was broken and also a few of the bows. The question then arose, "How are we going to upright the wagon without unloading it?" We overcame this difficulty by passing two lariats over the wagon, attaching them to each wheel and hitching a pair of mules to these ropes. We then started them up the hillside and they uprighted the wagon safely. While the accident delayed us an hour or two, we reached the bottom of the mountain without further accident.

CHAPTER XXIX

FIRST LIEUTENANT—BACK EAST

I WAS promoted to a first lieutenancy, October 13, 1884, joining my new troop, H, Fifth Cavalry, at Fort Robinson, Nebraska, my old station in 1876. While there I superintended the construction of the new telegraph line to Fort Laramie, Wyoming. The poles were all cut by soldier labor. The distance was sixty-seven miles.

We remained at Robinson until the latter part of May, 1885, when the Fifth Cavalry was ordered to change station to the Department of the Missouri. The troops at Fort McKinney, Fort Washakie and Fort Robinson mobilized at Fort Laramie, preparatory to marching to Fort Riley, Kansas, which was to be our station. Lieutenant-Colonel C. C. Compton was in command of the regiment. Our colonel, Wesley Merritt, was the superintendent at West Point at that time.

I was detailed on special duty as assistant to our regimental quartermaster, now General William P. Hall, adjutant-general, retired. I had charge of the transportation on the march, and was commended by the inspector-general, Major Joseph P. Sanger, for the efficiency with which the wagon train was handled. We had forty six-mule teams and three or four ambulances drawn by four mules each. I had nearly all soldier teamsters, many of whom had never pulled a "jerk line" (single line) over a six-mule team. I had to go into the mule corral, where there were several hundred mules, to select a number for my transportation. Many of them had just been purchased by the government and had never been worked in a six-mule team

In making the selection I had to match them according to their formation and color. A six-mule team consists of the "wheelers" (large mules), "swings" (not quite so large), and "leaders" (still smaller)'. They are trained to be driven by a single line, the driver riding the near wheel mule. There is what is called the "jockey stick," about four feet long, between the lead mules, fastened to the bits by a small chain in such a manner that it indicates to the mules which way the driver wants them to go. If to the right, he jerks the line a few times; if to the left, he pulls on the line. The driver also has command of the wheel mules by short reins, which usually rest over the pommel of the saddle. All mules become so well trained that they are managed with great ease.

Many people think a mule is obstinate, vicious, unreliable and ready to kick on all occasions. This is not the case. Mules are naturally of a gentle disposition, as much so as a horse, although they may not be quite so intelligent. They can stand more hardships than a horse and require less feed. The government's allowance of grain for a horse is twelve pounds daily and for a mule, nine. The driver becomes much attached to his mules and has pet names for each.

On one expedition we had to negotiate a very steep hill, so steep that many of the teams had hard work to overcome it. There had been a great deal of unnecessary whipping and yelling at the mules. Presently a driver came along requesting the men to keep quiet and not touch his mules. He started up the hill, speaking gently to the animals, calling them by their names, to which they readily responded. Some of the men commenced yelling, and it

looked as if one or two were going to strike the mules.
The driver pulled his six-shooter and threatened to shoot
the first man who struck his mules. There was no more
yelling at those mules, and I am quite sure that the
majority of the men approved of the teamster's action. If
we had more such men handling live stock it would be a
blessing.

We were about a month on the road marching to Fort
Riley, and had no sooner reached our quarters than
Colonel Compton, with seven troops of the regiment, was
ordered to proceed at once by rail to Christfield, Kansas,
then the terminus of the Atchison, Topeka & Santa Fé
Railroad. I was the quartermaster and commissary of
the command.

Over one-half of our little army of twenty-five
thousand men were mobilizing at Christfield. The Indians
on the reservation were supposed to have broken out (or
were going to) and had been raiding the settlements. We
were ordered to scout westward and along the southern
boundary of Kansas. As we were marching through the
settlements we heard all kinds of wild rumors regarding
depredations the Indians were alleged to have been committing, but no one had seen any redskins. It was always
somewhere else they had been committing their deviltry.
We met several small parties of men armed with squirrel
rifles, shotguns and pistols, who thought we might be Indians, seeing our advance guard and flankers from a distance. Not one of them had seen an Indian, but they
"knew they were in the country." Seeing two or three
wagons coming from the south, I waited for them to come
up and asked the parties whether they had heard the news,
that the Indians were raiding the settlements. They replied that it was strange; that they had not seen or heard
an Indian since leaving the agency three or four days

previously. We scouted to Dodge City and beyond there, but did not see an Indian.

We crossed the Canadian River into the Indian Territory and went into camp at Deep Hole, an old stage station, where there were several springs. After remaining a few weeks, scouting the country thoroughly, we went to Camp Supply, Indian Territory, Colonel Potter, Twenty-Fourth Infantry, in command. We left Troops F and H there, together with some of our transportation, and proceeded to Fort Reno.

I had some trouble in crossing the Canadian River, because of quicksand. I unhitched my mules and drove them back and forth two or three times across the river to loosen the sand so that it would wash down-stream with the current. I did this until all the quicksand was washed out, thereby giving a hard bottom. I had to raise the wagon beds as high as possible to keep the water from running into them. Then I hitched twelve mules to each wagon, with instructions to the teamsters to keep them going, even if one went down. It is dangerous to stop a minute with an animal or wagon in quicksand. If a wagon gets stalled it is hard work to get it out. We crossed without accident, although I thought at one time that I was going to lose a twelve-pound Parrott gun and carriage, which I was taking to Fort Reno. It sank out of sight but "bobbed up serenely." Had the driver allowed his mules to stop, I might have lost it for the time being.

After the Indian flurry we returned to Fort Riley, Kansas. We marched about fifteen hundred miles that summer.

I remained on duty at Fort Riley several months, and then received the regimental recruiting detail, with assignment to duty in New York City. I was on duty there more than two years, and then joined my troop at Fort Elliott, Texas, in August, 1887.

CHAPTER XXX

THE CHARGE OF THE WAGON TRAIN*

I AM inserting in this place a chapter on the famous Charge of the Wagon Train, made by my friend, Lieutenant Frank D. Baldwin, later General Baldwin. It is not very well known by the public generally, but should be remembered as one of the most thrilling of the incidents in the warfare with the plains Indians.

We have all heard of the charge of the Light Brigade and of Pickett's charge, and many of us have heard of other charges, but hardly any of us have heard of the charge of the Wagon Train, resulting in the awarding of that much coveted decoration, the Congressional Medal of Honor, to the infantry lieutenant who led his gallant wagons in the fray.

This six-mule team charge, unique and thrilling, took place in Kansas. But let us turn back for a moment to the state of Georgia.

The Germaine family, consisting of father, mother, two grown daughters, Sophie and Catherine, two boys and two younger girls, Julia and Adelaide, had left Georgia in 1874 to find a home in Colorado. Their route lay via the Smoky Hill River, Kansas, and they reached Fort Hays without encountering any one, save friendly soldiers and cowboys.

---

*By Colonel W. C. Brown, United States Army, retired, in *The Quartermaster Review.*

236

Early on the morning of September eleventh, just as the family had gathered around the camp-fire for breakfast, they were suddenly attacked by a bunch of hostile Indians known as "dog soldiers," composed of renegades from various tribes, all under the leadership of Kicking Bird.

Four members of the party were killed and scalped in the presence of the four terrified young girls, who were then hurried off into captivity, the two elder ones in one direction and the little ones, Julia and Adelaide, in another.

On November 4, 1874, the headquarters and a portion of the troops composing the Indian Territory Expedition, commanded by General Nelson A. Miles, then colonel of the Fifth United States Infantry, were camped on the north bank of the Red River, bordering the "Staked Plains" of Texas. The term Staked Plains came from a series of poles or stakes that had been driven to outline a route for cowboys and their herds, making a practicable route which led by water holes, springs and small lakes.

A detachment of this command was organized composed of Troop D, Sixth Cavalry, Lieutenant Gilbert E. Overton commanding, and Company D, Fifth Infantry, Lieutenant H. K. Bailey commanding. Lieutenant Frank D. Baldwin, Fifth Infantry, who was chief of scouts, was assigned to command the detachment. General Miles' oral instructions to Lieutenant Baldwin were:

"I want you to take this detachment of cavalry, infantry and scouts, one mountain howitzer and a train of twenty-three six-mule teams, with empty wagons, and proceed northward and eastward. Should you run across no Indians or trails which you deem advisable to attack or follow, you will convoy the train to the supply camp on the Washita River. Should you find any considerable body of Indians, you will communicate with me, and attack or pursue, *as you deem expedient.*"

Under these instructions the detachment left the main camp at ten P. M., November 4, 1874. The personnel of this command could not be considered an offensive fighting force. It was intended only to act on the defensive as a convoy to the large wagon train. This was the real mission of the detachment. A train is always a great impediment to an active command when in the field and moving through a country infested by an active cunning enemy, never encumbered with any surplus equipment that impedes instant and rapid movement, either in attack or escape.

Before going further, let it be vividly impressed upon your mind that this detachment was only of the proper strength to insure the safe convoying of the train through a section of country overrun by large bands of hostile Indians. To divert any portion of the troops constituting the convoy for any purpose that would prevent their defending the train would be hazardous, if not almost unwarranted, except under unusual conditions. It would only be risking the destruction of the detachment, and above all the train and property, with very doubtful chance of success.

From information gathered from spies and captured hostile Indians, it was certain that the four Germaine girls were alive. They were held by their captors, and were with Grey Beard, head chief of the strongest hostile band in the field in that section. His exact whereabouts were not known, but it was more than probable that he would be found in the most out-of-the-way and inaccessible place in the country. Under the conditions, no command or detachment moved that did not have in mind the meeting of Indians, but foremost in the minds of all was the rescue

Lieutenant Frank D. Baldwin's Charge on Grey Beard's Camp, McLellan's Creek, Texas, November 8, 1874

of the white captives, whatever the risk or hazard might be.

After leaving the main command, Lieutenant Baldwin moved as rapidly as possible, infantry in wagons, through the hills and valleys, following no trails, thus taking advantage of a natural screen. After three days and nights of marching, camp was established in a dense forest of cottonwood on the banks of McLellan's Creek. Only fires necessary for cooking coffee were lighted, although it was a bitter cold night.

The following morning, November eighth, scouts were sent out before daylight, so as to examine carefully, before resuming the march, the country to the north and east, which was very rough and hardly passable for wagons. The command had just started from camp when Scout Schmalsle came back at breakneck speed, reporting that the advance guard had discovered a large camp of hostiles.

"We are sure it is Grey Beard's band; his tepee is there," he reported.

Schmalsle was at once despatched to find General Miles to inform him that Grey Beard's camp had been located and would be attacked at once, although it was evident that the convoy was greatly outnumbered by the hostiles.

Whatever the result might be, it was reasonably certain that General Miles with his entire command would soon be within supporting distance. The large number of wickiups and tepees and herds of ponies grazing in the vicinity caused the first realization of the desperate situation and task in hand, and the degree of responsibility involved in determining to attack so large a force, which outnumbered the convoy at least two to one.

It seemed almost rashness to attack, but Lieutenant

Baldwin knew his men, and knew they would fight. He also knew that he had the important element of surprise in his favor.

The train guard was brought to the front, the train forming in double column with lead teams on a line with the most advanced troops. The wagon-master was informed that he would have no train guard and that the safety of the train depended on its keeping abreast of the front-line troops. Thus the wagon train for the time being enjoyed the distinction of being in the "front line."

Without halting a moment, this formation was completed. The fighting force was in single line, trains and howitzer in the center. Under the circumstances, this was the best formation for an offensive attack, but to succeed it must be expeditiously carried out.

Without hesitation, Lieutenant Baldwin rode ahead a few yards, and the hostile camp was discovered less than a mile away. It was a reckless undertaking but there was no time to think of that. The troops having reached the crest of the divide, the trumpeters sounded the charge, and as the clear shrill notes of that thrilling call echoed through the valley, reaching the ears of the Indians, which was evidently their first warning of any danger, yelling troopers, wagon train and all rushed madly down the slope, into and through the Indian camp like a hurricane.

The charge was spectacular, grand and most effective in results. Old soldiers believe it is the first instance in an engagement where every man, hoof and wheel was used in the first onslaught on an enemy's camp. There was a stampede on the part of the Indians, and not one of them was found in the camp, except those who had been disabled.

They retreated to the westward, reaching the Staked Plains only a short distance away.

The command closely followed, not stopping an instant at the camp, but keeping on to where the warriors made a stand. The Indians held their position for some time, thus enabling their squaws and children to get out of reach of the troops. Taking then only the time necessary to re-form the command as at the start, the advance was resumed. It was not difficult now to force the enemy back, although there was a constant fusillade of shots poured into the advancing lines at long range, which fortunately was not effective.

This was returned with deliberation and effect by the troops, and the hostiles were driven back in much confusion. After reaching this position, the command was on the plain, and the view presented, as far as the eye could reach was a vast expanse of comparatively level country covered with squaws and children in full flight, from one to three miles away. The obstinate braves, however, were gathering again to contend the advance, keeping between the troops and the fleeing squaws and children.

Here the infantry was put back into the wagons, and all hands had a short rest. Then the aggressive forward movement was resumed. All efforts to impede the advance of the troops were now feeble; the howitzer was brought to bear upon the Indians, and finally the mounted troops were ordered to charge, which was done with most satisfactory results. The Indians were breaking up and no subsequent demonstration was made by them that was at all formidable or that retarded the command in the least.

After being followed for about twelve miles, the Indians scattered, and shortly not a brave was in sight. The pursuit was then discontinued, owing principally to the utter exhaustion of both men and animals. The troops had been four hours under fire, all this time advancing as rapidly as possible.

Subsequently, General Miles with four troops of cavalry joined the convoy.

The results of the engagement were the utter defeat and scattering of Grey Beard's band of more than three hundred warriors; the capture of his camp with its entire paraphernalia and many ponies, and last, but most important of all, the rescue of the white children, Adelaide and Julia Germaine. There is no doubt that the Indians would have murdered these girls had it not been for the sudden attack of the troops.

The spectacle presented of twenty-three six-mule teams and wagons in double column, flanked by the cavalry, charging as foragers, coming down the slope at a run (the wagons, it should be remembered, were empty, save for a few infantrymen in each) was extremely terrifying. Instead of being a source of weakness, as is usually the case, the train was actually an asset in this instance.

According to the rules laid down in the military manuals, the train should have been left under cover at the rear, under a small guard. This measure, however, would have depleted Lieutenant Baldwin's already too small attacking force, and any guard which he could have left would have been too small adequately to protect the train from any serious attack. He had to make his decision on the spur of the moment and he did so.

The children were found in Grey Beard's abandoned tepee by a soldier of Company D, Fifth Infantry. Their story was heart-rending, and they were in a most pitiable condition, scared, bruised and sunburned so as to be beyond recognition; their clothes in rags and they were in a starving condition. They were taken in charge and carefully looked after by Doctor James L. Powell of the medical department, now colonel United States Army, retired, and were soon restored to normal health.

For this service Lieutenant Baldwin was, for a second time in his military career, awarded the Congressional Medal of Honor. The citation accompanying it reads:

"The Congress of the United States, to Captain Frank D. Baldwin, Fifth United States Infantry, for rescuing with two companies two white girls, by volunteer attack upon Indians whose superior numbers and strong position would have warranted delay for reinforcements, but which delay would have permitted the Indians to escape and kill their captives."

In this campaign Lieutenant Baldwin was also awarded the brevet of captain, the citation, as shown by the "Army Register," reading for "gallant services in action against Indians on the Salt Fork of the Red River, Texas, August 30, 1874, and on McLellan's Creek, Texas, November 8, 1874."

Lieutenants Overton and Bailey were brevetted, the former for "gallant services in leading a cavalry charge in action against Indians on McLellan's Creek, Texas, November 8, 1874"; the latter for "gallant services in action against Indians on McLellan's Creek, Texas, November 8, 1874."

PART THREE: SOME FAMOUS WESTERN CHARACTERS

CHAPTER XXXI

WILLIAM COMSTOCK AND JOHN WHITEFORD

WILLIAM COMSTOCK was employed in 1868 in the government service at Fort Wallace as chief scout and interpreter. He was born in Wisconsin, of good parentage, and left home at an early age.

Comstock was one of the original pony express riders at the time Cody and Wild Bill Hickok were similarly employed. He was the first owner of the Rose Creek Ranch, situated on that stream, about eight miles from the post. At that time the land in the western part of Kansas had not been sectionized, and the ranch was held by a squatter title "possession." It was a valuable holding, for two or three hundred tons of hay were annually cut there. This was a small gold mine, as it was the only available spot for hay of any consequence in the immediate vicinity of the post. The contractors were receiving from twenty to twenty-five dollars a ton, delivered at the post. Wood was worth fully as much a cord and had to be hauled thirty or forty miles. This high cost of fodder and fuel was due, in a large measure, to Indian hostilities, as help was very scarce. Everything had to be hauled into the country from long distances.

In 1867, prior to my arrival at Wallace, Comstock had shot and killed the wood contractor. They had some difficulty over a business transaction. The contractor had agreed to pay Comstock a certain amount if he could show where sufficient wood could be cut to fill his contract. Comstock showed the man where wood could be cut in various places, one of which was Big Timbers, about forty miles from the post. Several hundred cords were cut and delivered. The contractor failed to pay Comstock as promised, and it appeared that the latter feared he was to be swindled.

The day prior to the shooting, the post trader received a note from Comstock, stating that on the following morning he would have a "black tail" for his dinner. The trader thought nothing about the matter, as Comstock frequently brought in game. It appeared that Comstock intended to warn him that trouble was brewing, and took this method of so doing, as they had been very friendly. The shooting followed, the contractor falling dead on the porch of the trader's store. This man had often boasted that he was a member of the Quantrill guerrillas, which sacked Lawrence, Kansas, August 21, 1863, and posed as a "bad man."

The commanding officer of the post had Comstock arrested and turned over to the civil authorities at Fort Hays, Kansas, for trial. When arraigned before the court and asked how he would plead, Comstock answered, "Guilty, sir." The judge immediately asked him if he did not wish to alter his plea. The scout replied, "No, sir." The judge immediately exclaimed, "I discharge you for want of evidence." Comstock smiled, thanked the court and walked out. A horse was waiting for him, which he immediately mounted and rode off into the desert. It was thought that his friends intended to help him to escape, and doubtless the court thought that to dismiss the case was the easiest and best way out of the tangle. V. L. Todd, the main witness for the prosecution, related this incident to me. The judge in the case was afterward city editor of the *Leavenworth Times* and I later knew him well.

Comstock returned to his ranch but did not dare go in to the post, fearing arrest. Shortly after this episode Indian troubles began. One of the government teamsters named Curry was killed while hauling rock from the quarry, and some of the settlements were raided.

General Phil Sheridan, the department commander, came to the post on a trip. He wanted to see Comstock, and asked the trader if he knew where he could be located. The trader told the general that he thought he could find the scout, so he went out to Comstock's ranch, but the latter would not come in to the post, sending word by Todd that he would meet the general in a certain place, but that he must come out with Mr. Todd and unaccompanied by an orderly. The general laughed and said, "He ought not to be afraid of me, but I will go out and see him." This Sheridan did. Comstock was promised by the general that he would not be molested, which induced him to return to the post, where he was given his old position.

A few months after my arrival at Wallace, Comstock and another scout named Abner T. Grover, known as "Sharp" Grover, were sent out to see if there were any signs of Indians, and I came very near going with them. About fifty miles from the post they found a friendly band on the Solomon River whom they knew, as they belonged to the tribe into which Sharp Grover had married. While there, a runner came in and notified the chief of the village that Roman Nose and his dog soldiers were raiding the settlements. The chief, whose guests Comstock and Grover were, told them they had better leave the camp, as his young men were greatly excited, and he was afraid he could not control them, expressing a fear that they might harm the two scouts. An Indian's code of honor is to protect his guests, and the chief told him he would do all in his power for their safety, but thought it best for them to leave the camp. Comstock and Grover were anxious to start, in order to report what they had seen and heard.

Thereupon the chief sent his son and three or four other Indians to escort the scouts from the village. A short distance out they were joined by several other redskins. The escort left them but the new arrivals continued on with the white men. As they were riding along, conversing in a friendly manner, two or three of the Indians dropped back and fired on them. Comstock was instantly killed, and Grover was shot through the back and left lung. On looking back and seeing that Comstock had fallen off his horse, Grover dismounted, thinking that possibly his partner was "playing possum." The Indians fled after the shooting, which seemed singular. Some people had an idea that Grover killed Comstock to obtain his position. Another story was that Comstock was perhaps killed that the Indians might obtain possession of a beautiful ivory-handled six-shooter which he had exhibited while in the village, which caught the fancy of the red men. Grover made his way to the nearest railroad station, whence he was brought in to the post.

General Bankhead sent out a detachment to bring the body of Comstock in to the post, where the remains were properly interred.

Sharp Grover was later killed by a man named Moody, who had charge of the quartermaster's corral and with whom Grover had quarreled over a halter. The shooting occurred in Pond Creek, Kansas. Grover was in one of the stores, drunk, when Moody came in. Grover made for him, calling him several vile names, whereupon Moody fired and killed him. It was considered a cowardly act, as

Grover was not armed, having placed his pistols under the counter when he came into the store. Moody claimed he thought Grover was armed. The latter was buried in the Fort Wallace cemetery.

Frank Dixon, a half-breed Mexican partner of Comstock, was the next victim to die with his boots on. He and his wife lived on the Rose Creek Ranch. At the death of Comstock and Dixon, Mrs. Dixon fell heir to the ranch.

Pond Creek was a little town of three or four hundred inhabitants located near Wallace. The Kansas Pacific Railroad was supposed to make this its station, as it was the most desirable place because of the water. However, when the railroad was completed to this point the station was located about a mile and a half nearer the post, for the convenience of the fort people, although the water had to be pumped up to the station at considerable expense. When the station was established, the town of Pond Creek disappeared from the map, if indeed it had ever been on it.

Pond Creek started, as most western towns did at that time, with a bad element. The inhabitants, fortunately, had in their midst a man named John Whiteford, who acted the rôle of peacemaker. He had been appointed a justice of the peace by the governor of the state, and was the only law the townspeople had. He was naturally sustained by the better element of the community in his efforts to keep the peace. He owned a jewelry store and was a manufacturer of moss agate jewelry. The agates were found in that vicinity and Whiteford was one of the first jewelers to make articles of that description.

Whiteford killed Frank Dixon one day when the latter attempted to ride a broncho into his store. He also killed a colored soldier who had broken into one of the stores and resisted arrest. He was said to have killed one other person and wounded two or three more. He certainly administered the law himself. He was a Christian gentleman, and belonged to the Episcopal church. He was a terror to the tough element but had the respect of all law-abiding people.

Pond Creek was probably one of the best conducted towns in the West, due almost entirely to John Whiteford's efforts. He performed all his executions with an old Civil War Enfield rifle, which never missed fire.

It was said that Whiteford came from Arkansas, where he had been a United States marshal during the Civil War. When Pond Creek was abandoned, I believe he went to Manhattan, Kansas, and later represented his county in the legislature. His daughter, a very bright woman, was at one time state librarian.

CHAPTER XXXII

CAPTAIN GEORGE W. GRAHAM'S troop (Tenth Cavalry), with others of his regiment, was stationed at Fort Wallace, Kansas, where I first met him. He had a wonderful career. When a boy he was employed in driving mules on the towpath of the Whitehall Canal, connecting Lake Champlain and the Hudson River.

When the Civil War broke out Graham was serving a sentence in a penitentiary. Soon thereafter he was pardoned, with others, and enlisted in a New York regiment. He served his enlistment and was employed in the secret service of the United States, doing good work in Virginia and the Carolinas. During his service he came under the eye of General Grant and through him was appointed a lieutenant in the army. My cousin, V. L. Todd, former post trader at Wallace, was employed as clerk at Grant's headquarters, City Point, Virginia, at the time of Graham's appointment, and assisted him when he was preparing his examination to enter the service.

Lieutenant Hammond, Third Cavalry, who was serving in the same squadron with me in the celebrated winter campaign of 1876, asked me one day if I ever knew a Captain Graham of the Tenth Cavalry, to which I replied that I knew him very well. He said that Graham was a native of his town, and thereupon related what he knew of Graham's early life. He informed me that his (Hammond's) father was one of the commissioners of the penitentiary in which Graham was serving at the outbreak of the war, and recommended to the governor of New York State that certain prisoners, Graham among the number, be paroled for good behavior. All of the men enlisted. At the close of the war, to the great surprise of all who knew him, Graham returned home as a captain in the army.

At various times while I was on scouting parties with Graham, he told me some of his history, and I am going to relate some of his experiences and doings while serving in the Tenth Cavalry, and tell of his dismissal from the army, as nearly as I can remember these matters.

He told me that he was from the South, and when the war broke out was living at Charleston, South Carolina, he then being a lieutenant in the Charleston Cadet Corps; that being a Union man, he resigned and went into the United States service; that he raised a company of mountaineers who equipped and armed themselves, although I think they were regularly enlisted soldiers. Their duties consisted in acting as guides and scouts, making raids into the enemy's country, tearing up the railroads, destroying bridges and running off contraband (slaves). He stated that at the close of the war he had thirty thousand dollars, which he had made by enlisting negroes for soldiers to supply the demands of the authorities of the New England States; those authorities being required to furnish a certain quota of troops, based on population, used this method of obtaining them. I had heard of this before. Graham said that when he was mustered out of service he went to Saratoga Springs, New York, where he lost his money playing the races.

While stationed at Wallace he received the brevet of major for gallantry in an affair with Indians while escorting General Eugene A. Carr, then lieutenant-colonel of the

Fifth Cavalry, en route to join his regiment on Beaver Creek, Kansas.

Graham had a good troop and did much good service. He had a way of his own in disciplining his men. Upon one occasion when I was with him on one of his scouts, two of his men engaged in a lively quarrel. They were brought up before Graham by a non-commissioned officer, and Graham, after hearing their versions of the quarrel, sent the sergeant to the wagon-master for a couple of blacksnake whips. Placing one in the hands of each man, he told them to go to work on each other, and put the men in positions where they could use the whips to the best advantage. When Graham thought they were not laying on the lash strenuously enough he would inform them that if they did not work more rapidly and strike harder he would have them whipped in a way they would remember, and which would remind them of the old slave days, many of the colored soldiers in those days having been slaves. At this they put more energy into the work, and as the whiplashes began to hurt the men became "good and mad" at each other and used the whips most vigorously. When the captain thought they had been sufficiently punished he stopped them, and asked if they thought they could now behave and be good soldiers. Upon receiving an affirmative reply he made them shake hands and sent them back to the troop. I was told that at one time a soldier of his command tried to shoot Graham—who afterward made the man a non-commissioned officer!

On one of his scouts the captain had gone into camp on Sand Creek, Colorado, on the site of the Chivington battle. The Indians tried to run off his horses, but he, with Lieutenant Amick and Sergeant Burke, pursued them, recovering all the horses and in addition an Indian pony. Three Indians were killed, one of them being "made good"

CHEYENNE CHILDREN
Note dresses trimmed with elk teeth worth several hundred dollars.

by Burke, who clubbed him with the butt of his carbine. Burke, in the excitement of getting started from the camp, had forgotten his cartridge belt, and had no ammunition. He was the troop quartermaster-sergeant, and could neither read nor write, but he took good care of the troop property. He had the boxes containing the property marked with hieroglyphics of his own devising, so that he could easily ascertain what each contained. Burke had wonderful strength. I once saw him place his back against the rear wheels of a wagon loaded with forage, take hold of the spokes and raise the wheel off the ground with apparently very little effort. Nobody else was able to do it.

Accompanying Graham when the Indians tried to run off his horses was Doctor Turner, the post surgeon. The doctor was greatly interested in craniometry, and was procuring Indian skulls for the Smithsonian Institution, Washington. He had informed some of the soldiers that if they came across any Indian burying-ground he would like to get some skulls. Quite frequently, in scouting, we would find places where the Indians had placed the bodies of their dead in the trees on scaffolds. After a few months this support would rot and fall down or the wind would blow it down, and the bones would be scattered on the ground.

On the evening after the Indians had tried to run off the horses, Doctor Turner was lying down in his tent, when he heard a scratching on the canvas and upon inquiring who was there, the reply was, "Sergeant Burke, sir." He was told to enter, the doctor thinking perhaps he wanted some medicine. When the sergeant entered the tent he carried a gunnysack on his shoulder. Remarking that he had a present for the doctor he emptied the sack, and to the astonishment of the surgeon out dropped the heads of the three Indians killed in the chase after the horses! They were taken to the post hospital, prepared and sent to the Smithsonian museum.

After Captain Graham left Wallace he was tried by courtmartial for selling government horses, was convicted and dismissed from the service. He must have had considerable money, for at one time he had in our safe about four thousand dollars. Afterward he went to Denver, Colorado, and while there must have gone broke, as he tried to rob the government paymaster, Major Brooke, at Lake Station, Colorado. The major was en route to pay off the soldiers who were camped near there and was making the trip in an ambulance with Captain Irwin of the Sixth Cavalry, commanding officer of the camp, two or three officers, Nicholas Roberty, manager of the sutler store at Lake Station, Mrs. Roberty and her baby. It appears to have been a part of Graham's plan to frighten the mules so that the ambulance would be overturned into a gulch as they were passing around the head of it. The scheme failed, however, and Graham fired into the ambulance with a shot-gun loaded with buckshot. Captain Irwin received most of the charge in the shoulder but Major Brooke caught one or two of the bullets. Mrs. Roberty was carrying her infant in her lap, with one hand grasping the bows of the ambulance. One of the buckshots passed through her hand. A soldier who was riding with the driver shot at Graham but was not aware at the time that he had hit him. The mules ran away but by good handling the driver managed to guide them into camp, where they arrived just about dark. A party was immediately sent back to the scene of the attack and found Graham badly wounded. A bandit companion who was with him escaped. The following morning Graham was put on a train, taken to Denver and placed in the hospital, not being expected to recover. While there he managed to escape, and he was at large for some time, but was finally captured in a saloon wearing his favorite disguise, that of a negro. He was recognized by a United States marshal, according to the statements of the newspapers at that time. Graham was tried and sentenced to the penitentiary at Canyon City, Colorado, for a term of years.

With one or two other prisoners he finally escaped from the prison, but some time after was recaptured in St. Louis Park. He had stopped at a roadhouse which was erected for the convenience of freighters. On the morning of his capture he arose early, going out, no doubt, to ascertain whether the road was clear. He carried a Winchester rifle which he had taken from one of the prison guards when he escaped. He was ordered to surrender, and upon his refusal was shot through the neck by the posse which had trailed him down and had surrounded the cabin. He was returned to the penitentiary and served out his term, after which he returned to Denver.

Some time after this, I was in Denver with some army officers attending the fair and races, and found that Graham was there, taking an important part as one of the judges of the horses and the races.

While I was adjutant and quartermaster for General Eugene A. Carr at Fort McPherson, Nebraska, the general told me the following incident about Graham which occurred in the Beaver Creek fight with Indians in October, 1868, indicating the great bravery and daring of the man.

The general was en route from Fort Wallace, Kansas, to join his regiment, the Fifth Cavalry, supposed to be on Beaver Creek. He was escorted by Captain Louis H. Carpenter, Tenth Cavalry, and two troops of the regiment. I remember very well the occurrence I am about to relate, as I was at Fort Wallace at the time. Moreover, I had heard Captain Graham's version of the affair prior to the time it was related to me by General Carr.

The expedition was camped on the Beaver for the night

and broke camp early in the morning. Graham started out with two troopers to reconnoiter before the command had moved out. His object was to ascertain whether he could find any signs of Colonel Royall's command, the latter being in command of the Fifth Cavalry. Graham was moving down the Beaver and had reached a point which was not beyond the view of the camp, when several Indians suddenly dashed over the hill in his rear, with the apparent intention of cutting him off, and began firing on the party.

Three bullets passed through Graham's clothes, one through his hat, one through his shirt and one through his leggings. The horse of one of the soldiers was shot. Graham was riding a very fine mount known as "Red Eye," which had a very deep chest and a thin barrel, rendering it very difficult to keep a saddle from slipping backward. Red Eye jumped over the bank, which was several feet high, into the creek. The saddle slipped, and kicking clear of it, Graham grasped the horse's mane, hanging on for dear life, finally alighting in the bed of the creek. The horse ran toward the camp, and Graham began firing on the Indians. Just as he fell from his horse, Lieutenant Amick came up, charged the Indians and drove them off. This quick action of the lieutenant, no doubt, saved Graham's life and the lives of his men.

General Carr told me that Graham was one of the bravest men he ever saw; that he often would amuse himself by concealing men in hollows of the ground, taking away their horses, until the Indians came up for them to shoot at, and then charging up with the horses and bringing them off.

Graham lost his life while in the employ of some bankers for whom he was guarding a mine near Rosetta, Colorado, to prevent it from being "jumped." He was shot and killed from ambush on his way to Rosetta. It was said he had been warned not to go to the town.

CHAPTER XXXIII

I FIRST met "Wild Bill" (James Butler Hickok) at Fort Wallace, Kansas, in the fall of 1869. He came to Wallace as one of the scouts with the Fifth Cavalry. William F. Cody ("Buffalo Bill") was the chief scout at that time. The regiment was at Wallace a few days and then went to Fort Lyon, Colorado, where it remained during the winter, and while there went on several scouts, the most important of which was the rescue of General Penrose's command.

When the Fifth Cavalry was relieved from the Department of the Missouri, all the scouts were discharged with the exception of Cody, who went to old Fort McPherson, Nebraska, with the regiment. Hickok, on his discharge from the service, returned to Fort Hays, Kansas (via Fort Wallace), where he had been employed as scout, and shortly after was appointed marshal of that city. In 1872 I met him again in Abilene, Kansas, the great cattle mart of the West. He was city marshal there. I was in Abilene buying cattle. One of my cowboys tried to run the town in good old western style, shooting off his gun and declaring that "he was a wolf and it was his night to howl." Hickok arrested him and placed him in the lock-up. The cowboy had my revolver, which was returned to me. When I left Abilene this cowboy was serving his sentence.

Hickok was born in La Salle County, Illinois, and grew

257

to young manhood there. During the time that I knew
him he did not indulge in liquor. He was not a profane
man and was affable. He had the respect of the citizens
and especially the cow men. While he may have had a
habit of shooting up the saloons in his younger days, he
certainly put a stop to that sort of sport in Hays City and
Abilene. Upon my leaving Abilene with my cattle,—which
by the way, was the first herd that went into western Kansas,—I lost touch with Hickok. I heard that he had gone
to Deadwood, South Dakota, at the first outbreak of the
Black Hills gold excitement. There he was assassinated in
a cowardly manner by a cheap gambler named Jack McCall,
while sitting in at a game of cards. It appeared that
Hickok and McCall had, on the previous day, been playing
cards, and that Bill had won all his money. McCall
acknowledged that he had been beaten fairly, but nevertheless, Bill, because of his well-known generosity, insisted
upon returning to McCall ten dollars of the money.

The following day, August 2, 1876, Wild Bill was engaged in another game of cards with three men in the
saloon of Nuttall & Mann. Upon this occasion he was
sitting with his back to the door, something he was never
known to do before. Unseen by Bill, McCall entered by
the back door, and came around behind Hickok, where he
jerked out his gun, placed it close to Wild Bill's head and
fired, killing him instantly. It was a treacherous, cowardly
act. Great excitement prevailed in Deadwood and a lynch-
ing was freely discussed, but not carried out.

McCall ran out of the front door of the saloon, to
where a horse was tied near by, and tried to mount it, but
the cinch was loose. The saddle turned, and he fell to
the ground. He jumped up and ran along the street into
a meat market, where he hid. He was finally found by
a man named Isaac Brown; after a scuffle, the latter

dragged McCall out, and called for help to take care of him. Several armed men responded. They confined McCall in an old cabin, which they kept heavily guarded. A mass meeting of citizens was called at the Deadwood theater building, to consider what action might be taken to punish the murderer, there being no legally constituted courts. The presiding officer stated the object of the meeting. He was then elected judge to preside at the trial of McCall. A prosecuting attorney and one to defend the prisoner, and a jury of twelve men, were chosen to sit in the case the following day. After listening to the evidence and the arguments of counsel, the jury retired. After being out a short time they brought in a verdict of not guilty.

It is said that immediately the prosecuting attorney accused the jury of selling out, and said he could prove that two thousand ounces of gold dust had been secretly weighed out that day for their "private" benefit. He declared he would follow the assassin until justice was done, and he "kept the faith," for it was largely through his determined personal efforts that McCall was indicted by a Federal Grand Jury on October 7, brought to trial on November 27, sentenced January 3, and executed March 1, 1877, at Yankton.

Hickok was buried on the side of a hill now known as "Ingleside," Deadwood, South Dakota. His old "pal," Charley Nutter ("Colorado Charley"), wrote on the slab that was placed at the head of the grave:

Wild Bill

J. B. Hickok

Killed by the Assassin

Jack McCall

Deadwood City

Black Hills

Aug. 2, 1876

> Pard, we will meet again in the Happy Hunting
>   Grounds to part no more
>   Good Bye.   Colorado Charley.   C. H. Nutter

It has always been contended that self-aggrandizement
was McCall's reason for murdering Wild Bill.

At McCall's first trial by the Deadwood jury, he was
acquitted, alleging that he had killed Wild Bill for the
reason that the latter had shot his (McCall's) brother.
Following his acquittal, McCall went to Laramie City,
where he began boasting of his murderous deed. He was
immediately rearrested and sent to Yankton for trial where
a verdict of guilty was rendered almost without deliberation by the jury. McCall was hanged on March first,
1877, the execution being the first legal hanging in Dakota
Territory.

It subsequently developed that McCall was the scape-
grace son of respectable parents in Louisville, Kentucky.
Correspondence with the McCall family by the Yankton
authorities developed the information that Wild Bill had
not shot McCall's brother, nor ever had any trouble with
him. Some historians have brought out the information
that McCall did not even have a brother.

Mrs. Hickok was very instrumental in prosecuting Mc-
Call for the murder of her husband. She was a most
estimable woman and had been the wife of a circus man
named Lake, having herself been a noted bareback rider
at one time. The last I heard of her she was the owner of
a very fine stock ranch near Salina, Kansas. This account
of the killing was told me shortly after the tragedy by a
reliable business man who lived in Deadwood at the time.
I was in Wyoming and read the account of the murder in
the Cheyenne and Deadwood papers, which declared it was
a dastardly murder, and even the bad element condemned

it. Buffalo Bill and Wild Bill were great friends, although the latter was nearly ten years Cody's senior, and they rode the Pony Express together. Cody speaks of Hickok in the highest terms of praise, in his memoirs.

Had Hickok been the coward that some of his critics try to make out, he would not have been a friend of Cody, nor would he have been able to fill the honorable position of city marshal of Hays City and Abilene. He did kill several men, but those who malign him can not prove that it was not done in self-defense or in the execution of his duties as marshal. If, in his younger days, he was inclined to be rather wild, he atoned for it in later years. At his death, Hickok was about thirty-nine years of age.

Many untrue stories have been circulated in eastern magazines regarding Wild Bill, such as declaring that at one time at St. Joe, Missouri, a man had pulled his nose and dared him to shoot, and had called him a coward, and that Wild Bill had slunk away. It was further said that he had never been a scout. All such stories are false, as old timers who knew Hickok personally have reason to know.

Wild Bill had done splendid work as a scout in the western sections during the Civil War. I think he did his first killing in Montana while an express rider. His greatest feat, however, was his terrible fight with the McCanles gang at Rock Creek Station, Nebraska, while riding the pony express, which will always form an interesting chapter in the thrilling history of the West. It was written by Buffalo Bill, in *Hearst's Magazine*, January, 1917:

"Coming into his swing station at Rock Creek one day in December, 1870, Bill failed to arouse any one with his shouts for a fresh mount, which was an indication of trouble. It was the stock tender's business to be on hand with the relief pony the instant the rider came in. The Pony Express did not tolerate delays. Galloping into the yard,

Bill dismounted and hurried to the stable, where he found in the doorway, the stock tender lying dead. At the same instant a woman's voice rang out from the cabin near by. Turning about, Bill found himself face to face with a ruffian who was rushing from the house, brandishing a six-shooter. Bill asked no questions, but pulled one of the two guns he carried, and fired. No sooner had the man fallen, however, than a second man, also armed, came out of the cabin. Hickok disposed of this fellow also, and then entered the place, where he was met with a regular fusillade from four others. Although the room was thick with smoke and Bill had to use extreme care to avoid hitting the woman, who was screaming in the corner, he managed to kill two of his assailants, who were armed with revolvers, and to ward off the blow which a third had leveled at him with a rifle. The blow knocked his own weapon from his hand, but his knife was still left him, and with it he put the man with the rifle out of the way. His troubles were not at an end, however, as another man appeared at the window and started to climb in and avenge his fellow gangsters. Bill reached for a rifle which lay on the floor and shot first. When he had taken count a few minutes later he discovered that he had killed five men and wounded the sixth, who escaped, in the fight.

"The woman, who had been rendered unconscious by one of the desperadoes, soon revived. She was the stock tender's wife, and had been attacked by the gang as soon as they had slain her husband. The passengers of the overland stage, which rolled in as Bill was reviving the terrified woman, were given a view of western life which none of them ever forgot. Bill was the hero of the occasion, and a real hero he was, for probably never has a man won such a victory against such overwhelming odds in all the history of the war against the ruffians of the West. The man in that day who was not quick on the trigger had little chance with the outlaws among whom he lived."

Hickok never was known as a "bad man" by those who were acquainted with him, although he had several notches on his gun, reminders of men he had killed, all in the line of his duty. He was a man over six feet in stature, of magnificent physique, and had the keenest steel-blue eyes I ever saw. He never indulged in liquor, was quiet in manner, a man of nerve and steel, and had the instincts of a gentleman.

I will add here that there were frontiersmen and daredevil fighting men on the plains who were a race of men bred by the prairies and hard conditions of western life. They became man killers from stern necessity.

One of the overland stage superintendents was Alf Slade, a man of nerve and courage, who, having earned the reputation of being a gun fighter, became too eager to live up to it, eventually becoming an outlaw. He was easily the best superintendent of the line, but his habit of man killing got him into trouble, which resulted in his own execution on the gallows.

I was riding one day with Ed Lane, of whom I have heretofore spoken. I asked him how quickly he could shoot. He answered, "As quick as this," pulling his gun from its holster and firing six shots almost instantly, to my great surprise. He commenced to shoot while answering my question.

CHAPTER XXXIV

"BUFFALO BILL"

T HIS incident about my old friend, Buffalo Bill, I think, has not been published in this form. It was told me by my former general, E. A. Carr.

On October 16, 1868, the Fifth Cavalry left Wallace for Fort Lyon, Colorado. Previous to their arrival, Colonel Penrose, captain Third Infantry, left with a command of about two hundred and fifty men to scout the Cimarron country as far as the Canadian River. The command had not been heard from for several weeks and the military authorities were getting anxious about the safety of the command, so General Carr was ordered out with his command to try to locate them.

On one of the tributaries of the Cimarron they found one of Penrose's old camps. They followed this stream to the Cimarron River and found other camps. They also found the trail leaving the stream and going south toward the Canadian River. After two or three days' marching they found Penrose's command encamped on a branch of the Canadian, half famished. They had been living on short rations, and many of their mules had died from fatigue and starvation. They were lost.

Penrose had sent couriers and a Seventh Cavalry company to Fort Lyon for rations, but had not heard from them. As soon as the general had taken care of Penrose's command, he wanted to send despatches to General Sheridan, who was at Camp Supply, notifying him that he had found the missing command. He therefore sent for his scouts to come to his tent. At this time, Cody was ill with chills and fever, and was lying in a tent near the general's. The scouts demurred against taking the despatches out, saying it was extremely dangerous; that they knew nothing about the country, and so forth. Cody overheard the conversation, arose from his sick bed, went to the general's tent and said, "General, if no one is willing to take those despatches, I will carry them myself."

The general told him he had not thought of sending him, as he was a sick man; that the extremely cold weather would be hard on him and therefore he did not want to send him. However, Cody insisted upon going, and as the general was very anxious to send the despatches he decided to let Cody go. The ride was through an unknown country.

When asked how many men he wanted to take with him, Cody replied that he would prefer to go alone, and that all he wanted was a lead horse; that if necessary he would lay over during the day and travel by night, and if there were several in the party they would be more likely to be seen. Cody carried the despatches to Camp Supply, more than three hundred miles distant, and while he did not encounter any Indians he saw many evidences of their recent occupancy of the country.

I will relate another little episode which pleased me very much. While I was stationed at Fort Oglethorpe, Georgia, in 1909, Cody, with his Wild West Show, was exhibiting at Chattanooga, Tennessee. He had been there three or four days, and on the last day of his stay several of the officers and I decided to go and witness the performance. Upon arrival, I took several of the young officers to call on Cody. He asked me why I had not been down before, and I told him that I had just finished the officers' test ride of thirty miles a day for three days, making each ride in about five hours. Cody laughed and said: "Wheeler, when I first knew you, you used to ride that far in a day." I had never told any of these young officers of my earlier experiences on the plains.

In 1872 I spent the holidays in St. Louis. At that time Cody and "Texas Jack" Omohondro were playing in Ned Buntline's (Colonel Judson) drama entitled, *The Scouts of the Plains*. Linggard's company of New York was also there; also *The English Blondes*. All were stopping at the Southern Hotel.

One evening after the play we went out for some refreshments. An actor named Hudson of Linggard's company accompanied the party. Of course, we went into one of the fashionable resorts. Cody had a way of knotting his hair under his hat so that people would not recognize him. Hudson was wearing Texas Jack's sombrero, and passing himself off as Texas Jack.

An elderly gentleman who had been imbibing rather freely joined our party. He addressed most of his conversation to Hudson, under the impression that he was talking to Texas Jack. He told him that he admired him very much, but that he did not have much use for Buffalo Bill. This, of course, caused us much amusement. Presently, he took from his finger a very nice old-fashioned seal ring and gave it to Hudson as a token of friendship.

A day or so later one of the hotel employees asked me if I was connected with *The Scouts of the Plains* company. I told him no, that Cody and I were old friends on the plains, and while in the city I was passing quite a little time with him. The clerk then stated that there was a prominent man and his family living at the hotel, a man who, at times, drank too much; that he had been out a few nights before, and while in his cups had given away a valuable ring; that he had had it for a number of years and was very anxious to get it back. The gentleman had an indistinct idea that he had given the ring to one of the members of the *Scouts of the Plains* company.

I told the clerk that I knew all about the transaction and would be pleased to assist in recovering the ring. I went to Cody about it, and he said that of course the ring must be returned and that he would see Hudson and get it. He went to Hudson and told him the ring must be given up. Hudson replied that he had given it to his sister in the presence of the ladies of the other troupes, and that under the circumstances he disliked to ask her for it. This young lady was called "Laughing Eyes" by Cody and Texas Jack. She was indeed a very attractive person. In the meantime, I had been introduced to the gentleman who had given the ring to Hudson. He told me he was willing to get the young lady another ring. I replied that I did not think Cody would permit that, although neither he nor Texas Jack had anything to do with the transaction.

To shorten the story: We got the ring back and the man gave me an order on Jackard's jewelry store for a ring to cost not more than one hundred dollars. I bought a very pretty ring for less than one-half the amount.

One evening, after the play and refreshments, Laughing Eyes was presented with the ring before quite a number of the show people. In the next morning's *Globe-Democrat* was published an article to the effect that Buffalo Bill and Texas Jack had presented the young lady with a very valuable diamond ring. The gentleman appreciated my services and before I left the city he gave me and some of my friends a very nice dinner.

Colonel William F. Cody was buried on Mount Lookout, near Denver, on June 3, 1917, when thousands paid homage to the famous scout. The burial services were conducted by the Masons. "Taps" was blown over the grave, and a salute of eleven guns sounded the knell in the life of a hero and maker of history. The salute, which was that of a brigadier-general, was given in recognition of that title which had been conferred upon Colonel Cody by the governor of Nebraska. A monument has been placed over the grave by the people who knew him so well.

He rests atop Mount Lookout, where below can be seen the stretches of the plains of Kansas and Nebraska, the hills of Colorado and the hummocks of Wyoming, his old roving places of other days.

CHAPTER XXXV

JIM BRIDGER'S STORY

JIM BRIDGER, for whom Fort Bridger and Bridger's Pass were named, was a well-known frontiersman who was among the Indians from his fourteenth year. He was reticent and hard to know, but a genius in many ways.

One day the overland stage from Omaha arrived at Fort Bridger, Utah, and an Englishman stepped out and inquired in the sutler's store for both the post trader (Judge Carter, well known of the older officers) and General Anson Mills. He had a letter from General Sheridan, stating that he was a captain in the British army, on a journey around the world, for the purpose of writing a book, and that he wished to see Jim Bridger.

We called on Bridger, who lived alone in the quarters of one of the officers. We found the old man looking grave and solemn. Our English friend plied him with questions, stating he had been told by General Sheridan that he, of all others on the western plains, could relate the most thrilling reminiscences regarding the exciting scenes of the settlement of the frontier.

Bridger made no advances, appearing like a child reluctant to "show off." The captain requested the old scout to tell them something interesting. Finally Bridger told the following story:

"Well, I think the most exciting adventure I have had on the frontier was in the winter of 1855, when Jack Robinson and I went trapping about two hundred miles down

the Green River, in the Ute country. We knew the Utes
were unfriendly, but we did not think they were warlike,
so we got two horses and a pack outfit, and in December
went into camp on Green River. We spent two months
in trapping and were about ready to return, when early one
morning we saw a large war party coming up the stream.
We only had time to saddle our horses, gather our rifles
and ammunition and mount. We estimated their party at
about a hundred, and started out the horses at full speed,
abandoning everything we had in camp

"As we became hard pressed one of us would dismount
and fire, and so continuing, checking our pursuers until we
gained some ground. Their horses were not only fresh but
they had lead horses with them, which gave them great
advantage over us, who had but one animal each.

"We continued this method of defense all day, and by
night had killed thirty of the Indians. But our horses were
so tired we feared the enemy would take us. At the foot
of the mountain there was a dense timber. Here we took
shelter about dusk, knowing the Indians would not follow
in the dark. We spent the night in great fear as to what
would become of us next day. Knowing that at dawn they
would be after us, we started to lead our horses out of the
valley, but had no sooner started than we heard the Indians
behind us.

"We continued our defense until about two o'clock,
when we had killed thirty more Indians. This only left
about forty to continue the pursuit, but they did not seem
at all discouraged. If anything, they were more active
than ever.

"By this time our broken-down horses began to give
way at the knees. Observing a narrow canyon, we concluded to follow it, as it gave us a better defense than in
the open. This canyon was narrow, with a swift stream

running down it, and we made our way as far as we could, for two or three miles, when looking around, we saw immediately in our rear, the whole force of Indians. Matters were desperate. The canyon walls were high and nearly perpendicular for three hundred feet, and growing narrower every mile. Suddenly, around a bend in the canyon, we saw a waterfall two hundred feet high, completely blocking our exit."

Here Bridger paused. The captain, all aglow with excitement, cried anxiously, "Go on, Mr. Bridger, go on. How did you get out?"

"Oh, bless your soul, Captain," answered Bridger, "we never did get out. The Indians killed us right there!"

This closed the interview. I have never known whether the captain included this story in his book. This incident is taken from the book of General Anson Mills, published in 1918.

CHAPTER XXXVI

SHERIDAN was the terminus of the Kansas-Pacific Railroad, and remained so for nearly two years. In less than a year it numbered two thousand population.

It was a genuine frontier town. All freight for Colorado and New Mexico, and some for Arizona, was transported from Sheridan to points in those territories by mule and bull train. On the return trip the trains would bring wool, hides and valuable ores. At times as many as a thousand wagons were camped in the vicinity of Sheridan.

A very bad element congregated there, gamblers, horse thieves, murderers and loose women. Saloons, gambling and dance houses flourished, and scarcely a day passed that there was not a shooting scrape. It was a common saying each morning, "Well, we'll have another man for breakfast!" In time, conditions became so bad that a committee of safety was organized, and all the tough characters were notified, in a letter signed by the committee of safety, to leave the town within forty-eight hours. Ed. Dizart, secretary of this committee, was afterward employed as a bookkeeper in the trader's store with me.

On the night following the issuance of this letter of warning, three of the worst characters were hanged. There were four desperadoes who were to have been strung up together, but while the noose was being adjusted around the neck of one man he slipped it over his head in some manner,

272

and disappeared in the darkness. After the others had been executed, it became unnecessary to have any more hanging bees for some time. The regulators were composed of the business men, who had to take the law into their own hands to protect themselves.

An incident that happened about this time forcibly illustrates the conditions which prevailed in Sheridan. An ex-scout named "Hank" Whitney, whom I knew very well, was running a dance-hall. One night he was shot in a drunken carousal. The man who did the shooting was immediately arrested by members of the committee of safety and taken into a near-by saloon for trial. While the court was in session, "Hank," having had his wound dressed, entered the "court room" and placing a pistol against the back of the prisoner's head fired. The man jumped up, his head nearly striking the ceiling, and fell dead. "Hank" was at once escorted to the nearest railroad trestle and hanged. Next morning a brief funeral service was held over the bodies and both men were buried in the same grave.

An incident I saw illustrates how little life was valued in that wild country in those days.

I went down to Sheridan once with some of the scouts. Sharp Grover, the post guide and interpreter, went into a barber shop with me. While there, we heard shooting outside. Grover and I went to the door and saw a discharged soldier of the Fifth Cavalry running amuck and shooting in the street. Grover shouted, "Stop that shooting!" The man tauntingly yelled back, "Hunt your hole or I'll kill you!" At the same time he fired upon us. Grover drew his revolver and shot the soldier dead. He then returned to the barber shop and sat down in the chair, remarking, "I don't believe that man will do any more harm."

The commanding officer of the post sent Lieutenant

Bache of the Fifth Cavalry down to arrest Grover. He was taken to Wallace and placed in the guard-house. I accompanied Lieutenant Bache to Wallace, and at the investigation by the commanding officer related my version of the affair. Several other witnesses who saw the shooting were called and Grover was exonerated.

When the town was removed to Kit Carson, Colorado, all that remained of the once prosperous Sheridan was the section house, pumping plant and cemetery. There were nearly a hundred graves in the cemetery, and with but one or two exceptions, the occupants had died violent deaths. A very few had been killed by Indians.

"Buffalo Joe" North was a hunter and came from a very good family living at St. Joe, Missouri. I had known him for some time, had had business transactions with him and had many reasons to know he was a "square" man.

One Sunday evening in 1873 he came into the post trader's store with a "piece of calico" on his arm and told me that he wanted to get married. He asked me to take him to the post chaplain, which I did, and he was married. After the ceremony Joe said to me, "Homer, have you a 'fiver' in your vest pocket?" I happened to have one, and turned it over to him, whereupon he gave it to the chaplain.

Some few months after this he killed a man named Jones, who formerly had worked on my ranch. Jones was a good worker, but addicted to drink, and when under the influence of liquor was likely to do almost anything that entered his mind. It seems that he had been showing Mrs. North some attention, whereupon Buffalo Joe killed him.

Shortly afterward, a party of buffalo hunters and others were in one of the stores at Wallace drinking, and it was suggested by some of the party who claimed to be friends of Jones, that they string Buffalo Joe up for the killing of

Jones. This they did, hanging him to a telegraph pole near the station. The body remained swinging from the pole until after the passenger train came in the next morning.

As soon as I heard of the hanging I went to the station. The body had been taken down and was lying in the freight depot, with the rope still encircling the neck. I made arrangements for burial in the post cemetery.

There had been considerable horse-stealing going on, and the proprietor of the store was supposed to be implicated. Horse thieves, professing to be hunters, were accustomed to steal animals on the Platte River in Nebraska, drive them down to Dodge City, Kansas, on the Arkansas River, and dispose of them. Then, when they had spent their money, they stole more horses and drove them north. Wallace was the half-way station. This merchant, it was alleged, harbored these thieves en route—in fact, was their agent—and helped them to dispose of the stolen stock. Inasmuch as Joe North knew of some of their transactions, they were afraid of him and took this means of getting him out of the way.

In those wild days there was no law. Wallace County was not organized. There were cases where hanging was justifiable, but there was no doubt in the minds of the good people of Wallace that the hanging of Joe North was cold-blooded murder. I am glad to state that shortly afterward the county was organized and the outlaw band broken up. Wallace then became a law-abiding town.

CHAPTER XXXVII

THE typical "bad man" of the West is not a tough, although he has killed his man. It is hard for eastern people to understand the environment that produced the western bad man in perfection. In the settlement of the West many small towns sprang up, their nucleus being a trading store, usually, where ammunition, flour, clothing, bacon, candles and bad whisky could be obtained at ruinous rates to the consumer.

After the store had become established a gambling hell soon became its neighbor; if, in fact, it was not a more or less thinly disguised adjunct of the store. Here the stage-coach discharged its passengers or stopped for meals, and the occupants who had survived the ride could take fresh chances for their lives with tough meat fried in grease and saleratus biscuits a month old, at a dollar a meal. The proprietor of the store, his clerks, the faro dealers and professional gamblers formed the bulk of the permanent population.

The honest miners, ranchmen and cowboys were in the hills or on the prairie, attending to their respective callings, and came to the "city" only for supplies, a desire for a change of scene, to "spree" or for a general "hurrah."

Where all men go armed politeness is very general and every one is courteous and respectful of the rights of others, and although every one always carried a six-shooter one might have lived in the toughest of western towns for many years without having any use for a gun—but when one was wanted, it was wanted mighty bad!

The man who acquired a reputation for being a bad man in such a locality generally got the notoriety by having it thrust upon him. No man ever lived very long with that reputation without having many sterling qualities. He had to be a good deal of a success or some one would "wipe him out," as they expressively said in the West in those days. He was a man slow to quarrel and one who avoided all trouble until it was actually forced upon him. Then he was quick to "draw" and quicker to shoot, and in the early days a man never drew his gun until he intended to kill, and kill quickly. It was the unwritten law of the West that a man who made a motion to draw his gun was at the mercy of his opponent if the latter could "get the drop" on him. You will therefore see that it very soon grew unfashionable to carry one's handkerchief in the hip pocket. It was likely to give a wrong impression.

Men will not allow wanton murder in any country, and in killing his man the "bad man" had to be sustained by public opinion. A reckless murderer would soon be assassinated or lynched, no matter how much he was feared. If you killed your man, even in what was considered fair fighting, you still had to consider the enmity of his friends.

It was this carelessness which led to the death of Wild Bill Hickok. Bad men were usually the killers of bullies and criminals and they generally performed good service to the country at large in ridding it of dangerous people. The wild cowboy, who got drunk on the vilest of whisky, was of another type entirely. It was his delight to ride into bar-rooms, shoot out the lights and dash madly through the street, shooting in the air and yelling that "he was a wolf and it was his night to howl." But he was often regarded only as an object of amusement. Of course, he created a wild sort of excitement, but, as a matter of fact, he was perfectly harmless. But if a bully wantonly insulted and threatened inoffensive men and tried to be "bad" and run the town his shrift was a short one. He soon met his match and "died with his boots on." Moreover, his taking off was approved by the community.

I recall an episode that occurred at Wallace, Kansas, many years ago. One day a large amount of bad whisky had been consumed by the transient population, and a keg of nails had been emptied on the floor of the trading store. Two men seated themselves facing the pile and were pulling nails, one at a time, with both hands. The man who picked up the last nail was "it," and had to buy the drinks for the crowd. There were many who were very much interested in this game of chance. Some of the bystanders amused themselves by dropping counterweights and other objects into the pile. Finally, a boy about nineteen years of age playfully dropped a package of crackers and cheese among the nails. The owner of the parcel immediately fell into a rage and rushed at the boy with upraised bowie knife. As he was about to strike, the boy shot him dead. It all took place so quickly that no one could interfere. The authorities investigated the shooting and found that it was done in self-defense. Several bad men grew jealous of the boy's reputation and he sent costly floral tributes to their funerals. This young man grew up with the country and later became one of the prominent citizens.

The right of a man to take the law into his own hands also was thoroughly recognized. At Fort Washakie we had at one time a post guide named McCabe. He was sent down to Rawlins, a station on the Union Pacific Railroad, on government business. One night he fell in with a tough named Allison. The latter was drunk and abusive. McCabe was much the older man of the two and Allison thought he could whip him with impunity, and proceeded to do it so thoroughly that there was no mistake about it. McCabe was brought home and was in the hospital for several weeks.

Some time after this, business again took him to Rawlins. He remarked to a friend of mine that if he met Allison in town he would kill him. Allison had been staying at Rawlins off and on, and, as luck would have it, was there at the time. McCabe ran across him in a saloon, and, walking up to Allison, asked if he knew him. "Certainly," rejoined Allison, "and if you want anything out of me, just turn yourself loose." As he said this, he drew his gun. McCabe did not make a motion, apparently, but, as Allison drew, McCabe shot him dead. The latter wore his gun thrust through his belt, where it was in plain sight, but he also had a short pistol in his overcoat pocket and it was pointed straight at Allison when the latter drew his weapon.

A little incident about McCabe is interesting, at this point. Three notorious train robbers made their escape from the Laramie City penitentiary. One of them was called "The Kid" because of his extreme youth, and he was noted throughout Wyoming for his daring exploits. The three were serving life sentences for holding up and robbing a Union Pacific train, killing and wounding two or three train employees. The desperadoes overpowered the prison guard and killing one of them and securing their arms, made their escape. A heavy reward was offered for their capture, dead or alive. It seems that the bandits were making their way to the Jackson's Hole country, which was then well known as a rendezvous for outlaws. If the bandits once got into that country they would be comparatively safe from capture.

Early one morning a man went to a milk ranch near

the post (Fort Washakie) and wanted to buy some salt, stating that he was a prospector. He was a total stranger in that part of the country and his actions aroused the suspicions of the ranch people, for they had just read the poster offering a large reward for the capture of some convicts who had recently escaped from the penitentiary. It also seemed rather strange for a man to call at a ranch for salt when the post trader's store was so near by. Had the men been content to have lived on fresh meat for a time until they had reached the Jackson's Hole country this story probably never would have been written.

A day or two later McCabe, who was a deputy United States marshal, learned that the men had been at the milk ranch. He inquired of the Indians at the agency if they had seen any strange white men around and learned that they had seen three men. McCabe got some Indians and began to look for the trail of the convicts, to see in which direction they were going. He found the trail shortly. The men were headed toward Grey Bull Lake, which was the only trail that would take them to Jackson's Hole.

McCabe came to me and asked for three horses, stating the purpose for which he wanted them and saying he hoped to get the reward by capturing the bandits, as he needed the money in his business. He had made arrangements for two Shoshone Indians to accompany him. He got the horses although I had no right to loan government animals.

He started out to follow the trail and found two or three places where they had stopped to rest and get some sleep. He was quite sure they were the convicts, for they had no camp equipment or horses. When McCabe got as near as possible to his quarry as he dared to go without fear of detection (being able to judge their distance fairly well by the freshness of their footprints), he left the trail and made a long detour to get ahead of the bandits and cut them off. He succeeded in his undertaking and concealed his party in a thicket in a ravine through which the trail passed. Here he waited for the bandits to come up. They made their appearance quite early in the morning, coming along the trail carelessly and thinking, no doubt, that they were so far away there was no danger.

McCabe and his faithful Shoshones raised up, covering the bandits and demanding that they throw up their hands and be in a hurry about it. The desperadoes were so taken by surprise that they did not have time to make any defense. Their arms were taken from them and the prisoners were taken in to the post and confined in the guard-house. It was hard work to guard their prisoners while en route to the post. McCabe told me he did not get a wink of sleep for three days, as the capture was made at a distance of a hundred miles from the post. After a day or so of rest McCabe and his two Indians took the prisoners to Laramie City by way of Green River Station, one hundred and sixty miles from Fort Washakie by stage, and turned them over to the prison authorities.

While they were confined in the guard-house at the post one of the three prisoners, a large man, was saying what he "was going to do" when they were first captured. The Kid suddenly said, "Well, why in hell didn't you do it, then? I have been listening to all of this talk and am tired of it, and if you don't shut up, I will beat your brains out with these shackles!" There was no further loud talk from that man.

McCabe not only secured the reward for the capture, but he and his men were highly commended for their good work. McCabe shortly after was given an important position in the territorial penitentiary.

Horse and cattle stealing by the "rustlers" (thieves)

was frequent. I lost a dozen horses which were stolen within two years and never recovered any of them. They were worth at least one hundred and twenty-five dollars each, and could not have been replaced for that sum. Six were stolen in one night during the autumn of 1873. The foreman told me of the loss the following morning. He had found their trail leading north and thought two or three men had run them off, as there were tracks of two or three extra horses, making nine animals. My men were feeling about as badly as I was over the loss of the horses, as they were all good mounts and a cowboy's main delight is to ride good horses. Each herder had three good animals which he could call his own, and no one else was supposed to throw a leg over them without his permission. I held each man responsible for the care of his horses and great care had to be taken of their backs. I never would keep a herder long in my employ who did not look out for his horses. A cattle outfit that had good horses usually had good men.

With two of my men, Asa Lathrop and Joe Edwards, heavily armed, I started out at once, prepared to follow the rustlers several days if necessary. At times we had trouble following the trail, as they tried to throw pursuers off the track by dividing the band of horses and then meeting again at prearranged places. On the second day we saw a horse grazing near the ravine we were in. It was about a mile from us and it now looked as if we were getting close to the thieves. If so, they must be in the gulch below. We therefore rode as far as we could up the ravine, taking great care not to be seen. Here we dismounted, lariated our horses and proceeded up the gulch on foot. Presently we came to an abrupt bend and my foreman went ahead to explore the premises, for we suspected that the thieves must be around the bend of the ravine, and if so we were going to fire on them without warning, as we did not propose to take any chances. We knew they were desperate men, who would not give up without fighting.

The precautions observed in approaching the supposed rustlers were without avail, however, for there was nobody in the ravine. We were at once very much disappointed and very much relieved. The animal which we had seen evidently belonged to the rustlers and they had no doubt abandoned him. He was not a very good horse. We were now sure there were only two men with the horses, so this gave us the advantage over them. The horse was picked up shortly afterward but the owner never was located. It had been my intention to secure the animal upon my return.

We followed the trail for four days, when a snow-storm came up and the pursuit had to be abandoned. It may have been a good thing for us, as we were getting near the rendezvous of the "Doc" Middleton's band of rustlers, who were then the most notorious horse and cattle thieves in all the West, with agencies in several states, where they disposed of their stolen stock. The state of Nebraska, in which they were located, finally, at great expense, broke up the gang. Middleton served a term in the Nebraska penitentiary and later was arrested in Wyoming for selling whisky without a license. He was sent to jail in Douglas, Wyoming, and died there.

PART FOUR: IN COMMAND OF
INDIAN SCOUTS

CHAPTER XXXVIII

MAKING SOLDIERS OF INDIANS

I JOINED my troop, H, Fifth Cavalry, at Fort Elliott, Texas, in August, 1888, after a detail of nearly two years and a half in New York City. While at Fort Elliott I was detailed as post adjutant, treasurer and ordnance officer, and was in command of Troop C, Indian scouts, numbering about fifty, composed of mixed tribes, principally Cheyennes and Arapahoes. Very few of them could speak English, so I had to communicate with them through interpreters. The scouts were enlisted for six months and received the same pay as the white soldiers, $15 a month, including clothing and rations. They furnished their own mounts, receiving forty cents a day for their use (one horse) and the government furnished the forage for the animals.

When I took charge of the scouts there were some drinkers among them, including the first sergeant, Meat. When drunk he was in a fighting mood, and the other scouts were afraid of him. I told one of the non-commissioned officers, who spoke English, to let me know next time the first sergeant was drinking and I would put a stop to it. In the meantime, I told the other scouts, I would not permit any drunkenness in camp.

One evening about nine, shortly afterward, it was reported to me that the first sergeant was drunk and creating a disturbance in camp. I went to the camp and found him in his tent, drunk. As I entered he picked up his knife and commenced to flourish it. I told him to put up the weapon or he would get into trouble; that I was not afraid of him. I told him that if he killed me it would be a very bad thing for him as well as for the other Indians, as he would be killing one of his best friends. He then replaced his knife, and I gave orders for the other scouts to fall in for inspection, to ascertain whether any of them had been drinking. While they were formed, and as I was making the inspection, the first sergeant came reeling out of his tent, seized an iron rake and made for the scouts. They all ran, leaving me alone with the sergeant, "an officer without a command."

Sergeant Goodman, the senior sergeant, came up, and, catching me by the arm, exclaimed: "Post, post! First sergeant heap—" I took the sergeant's advice and went back to the post. Next morning I went down to the camp, and found the first sergeant hard at work in his garden. I called him up and gave him and the other scouts a good temperance lecture, and had very little further trouble with them while at Fort Elliott.

During the autumn and winter of 1888-1889, one of my duties while in charge of the scouts at Fort Elliott was to drive drifting cattle out of the Indian Territory. We were only a few miles from the border. In the "panhandle" of Texas were many cattle and they were continually drifting into the territory, which their owners had no right to allow them to do.. The cattlemen had not been very active in driving them out; in fact, it was a big job and an expensive one to do it. About the only way they could have been kept out would have been to fence the boundary line for several hundred miles, and this the cattlemen could not afford.

The scouts had driven the cattle over the line a great many times, but they would no more drive them out than they would be back. This work was, of course, very hard on their ponies.

On the first trip out I met some of the cattlemen, and found them good people. They requested me not to let my scouts set prairie fires, and I told them I would try to prevent it. Having been in the cattle business myself, and being then interested in a herd in Kansas, I knew by sad experience what it meant to have the winter grazing ground burned off. However, upon my arrival in camp, I failed to caution my scouts.

In the morning I sent my men out in different directions to drive the "drifters" out of the territory, but we had hardly started when, to my dismay, fires started up in several places. I immediately put a stop to this but it was too late; the damage had been done. I discovered that my first sergeant, Meat, had given the firing orders and I called him to account for it. He told me that it was the only way the cattle could be kept out of the territory, and that it had been resorted to only after the men had tired out their ponies in a vain attempt to keep the cattle out. The fires lasted several days, when luckily a storm came up and extinguished them. I never did know the amount of damage that was occasioned but it must have been quite heavy. After that there were no more fires.

There was a creek running parallel to the border line, where the cattle had been accustomed to go for water, using the intervening strip of land, a mile or so wide, for grazing. I told the cattlemen that if they would not let the cattle cross the creek they might continue to let them graze there. I had no right to do this, but I knew it would save me lots of hard work as well as considerable horse-flesh. The cattlemen carried out their agreement and I had no further trouble.

LIEUTENANT WHEELER AND COMPANY A, CHEYENNE INDIAN SCOUTS, AT FORT ELLIOTT, TEXAS, 1889

In May, 1890, I was ordered to change station with my scouts from Fort Elliott to Fort Reno, Indian Territory, and there form an experimental company of a hundred men, with a view to ascertaining whether the American Indian could adapt himself to military discipline; the object being, in case the experiment proved successful, to make soldiers of the Indians. Lieutenant F. W. Casey, Twenty-second Infantry, was to form a similar company composed of Cheyennes, Sioux and other tribes in the North. I was to select my men from the southern Cheyennes, Arapahoes and the different tribes in the Indian Territory.

On January 27, 1891, following the "ghost dance" excitement at Pine Ridge reservation, South Dakota, Lieutenant Casey was shot from behind by a young Sioux Indian named Plenty Horses,* after Casey had talked pleasantly with him and had turned his horse to ride away. His body was recovered by his scouts, who were devoted to him.

I left Fort Elliott, Texas, May 17, 1890, for Fort Reno, with forty scouts and their families. We were escorted out of the post by the Thirteenth Infantry drum corps, which pleased the Indians very much, as they were exceedingly fond of ceremonies.

A few days after leaving Fort Elliott I had to cross the headwaters of the Washita River and camp on the river bank. Upon my arrival there I found that the near side afforded the best camping ground, and I had concluded to stop for the night on that side. However, I thought of the old rule, and decided it would be better to cross and camp on the other side, for had it rained during the night

---

*Plenty Horses was arraigned before a United States court but was acquitted on the ground that the Sioux were then at war, and the officer being practically a spy upon the Indian camp, the act was not murder in the legal sense of the word. Lieutenant Casey's death was greatly deplored by his Cheyenne scouts as the insane act of a boy overcome by the excitement of the times.

(and it was threatening for several days) the chances were that the stream would rise and I should have difficulty in crossing the next morning, and possibly might be delayed a day or more.

As a matter of fact, it did rain that night and by morning the banks of the stream were running full. Needless to say, I was greatly pleased that I had crossed over the night before. Even if there is no danger of high water it is considered the wise thing, when on the march, to cross a stream before going into camp, especially if the crossing is difficult and there are heavily loaded wagons with the command. Animals will not pull so well early in the morning and if one has trouble in crossing, a wagon or two stuck in the mud or quicksand, it changes one's disposition remarkably and puts a damper on the whole day's march. If the wagons are late getting into camp and every one is tired and hungry "the devil is to pay."

I moved out of camp early in the morning and had been on the road but a short time when Corporal John D. Miles, named for a noted Quaker Indian agent appointed by President Grant,* and who had wonderful control of his Indians, came running back to inform me that we would have to cross the river again, and that if we hastened we might be able to cross before the flood water reached the ford, which it had not yet done. I was astonished at this, but it developed that at this particular point, the Washita in its course formed a large peninsula several miles around and we were crossing the neck of it, and the flood water had not yet appeared.

The corporal informed me that the crossing was not very good, the banks being quite steep, and he suggested

---

*At that time there had been a great deal of dishonesty in the Indian service, and President Grant conceived the idea of appointing Quakers as agents, with a view of doing away with the dishonest practises.

taking some of the scouts, with picks and shovels, and leveling the banks down somewhat. About a dozen wagons belonging to the scouts were being driven by their women, and, besides, there was a six-mule team hauling my belongings. I hurried up the wagons and went ahead with the corporal to see about the crossing.

Scarcely had I arrived there when one of the scouts came running up and told me there had been an accident. From his gestures and signs I concluded that a wagon had run over somebody's head, so I hastened back and discovered that one of the wheel mules had fallen down and the wagon had partly run over his neck!

The wagons came up just barely in time to cross the river before the flood water came rushing down in an immense volume, fully seven or eight feet deep. Each team with its particular wagon had to be helped up the bank. One of the wagons became stuck midway of the stream, and I was afraid it would have to be abandoned, but the scouts managed to get it out. I did not attempt to superintend the crossing, as it was in good hands, one of the sergeants, William Elk,* being actually in charge.

---

*On March 12, 1924, I received a letter, at Los Angeles, California, from him; he wrote that he was sixty-five, and that of the hundred scouts only forty-nine were alive.

CHAPTER XXXIX

MY MEN AND THEIR FAMILIES

UPON my arrival at Fort Reno my company was disorganized and was consolidated with the new company of Indian scouts being known as Company A, Indian Scouts, which gave me a force of a hundred men. Most of the scouts in A Company had been enlisted shortly before my arrival but had received no military training. They also had more than their share of non-commissioned officers, so I reduced some of them to the ranks to make places for my own Indians. This caused some discontent, although I told them I would remake them at the first opportunity.

I found that the scouts had not only brought their own families into camp but most of their uncles and aunts as well, making a camp of over five hundred people. The celebrated Cheyenne chief, Whirlwind, and his family were among the number. I ordered all these "extras" out of camp, save those belonging to the scouts' immediate families. This caused some bitter feeling, especially among those who had to go. I told them it was unpleasant for me to send them away, but that it was a military duty, that they well knew that soldiers were not allowed to have their families in camp, save a special few. I am quite sure several of the scouts approved of my action, as they did not care to feed all their relatives. My Fort Elliott scouts stood by me and told the disgruntled ones I was doing it for their own good; that I had taken more interest in their welfare than any other officer who had ever had charge of them.

One of the first things I did was to take into consideration the sanitary condition of the camp. This was something new to them. Indians never thought of cleaning up their camps. When they became uninhabitable they moved to new camps. I think this had something to do with their nomadic life.

The camp was situated on a very pretty stream near some beautiful springs, the outflow of which formed the creek. I had the springs cleaned out and the stream policed for some little distance below the camp. I also put up latrines, special ones for the women and children. This also was something new to them and it was some time before I succeeded in making all of them use them. I divided the camp into two sections. The sergeant in charge of the platoon took charge of the policing. I had a general inspection on Saturdays, mounted and dismounted. After this was over I inspected their tepees, which the women were required to keep neat and tidy. This was up-hill work at first, as they were inclined to put their dishes away unwashed and leave the bedding unrolled. After a while, however, they took great interest in it.

One day I was making my usual rounds inspecting the tepees, when I saw the wife of Little Hawk putting something into her stove oven. From the manner in which she was acting I was aware that she was hiding something she did not wish me to see. I made her open up the oven door, and there in the baking pan were five or six young puppies, which she was preparing to bake! I must say they looked quite edible, too.

Indians are very fond of barbecued dog, which is prepared in the following manner: A fat-looking dog is selected and tied fast in some selected place for several days,

given nothing to eat and only water to drink. He is
then fed with a mixture of meat and dried fruit, made into
a soft moist paste, and allowed to eat all he wants. This
is to serve as a stuffing or forcemeat. The dog is killed
by knocking him in the head with a hatchet before digestion
commences. His hind legs are tied together and he is hung
up by a cord, head down, from a pole supported on two
forked sticks over a low fire. With a firebrand the hair is
burned off his body close to the skin, and the body is then
rubbed with buffalo or other fat. It takes many hours'
turning and basting the carcass with melted fat. The
dog is then roasted whole, for he has not been disem-
boweled. When the dog is thoroughly barbecued the guests
are assembled for the feast. The dog is cut up and the
guests all gorge themselves to their full capacity. The
most desirable morsels seem to be the bowels and other
soft parts. When the eating is all over the feast is celebrated by the beating of drums, chanting of songs and
dancing. This is kept up for many hours. Those who
have tasted roasted dog claim it is quite edible. The Indians prefer it to any other meat.

The Igorrotes of the Philippines barbecue dogs in a
similar manner.

One day White Wolf came to me and begged for the
loan of a dollar. I asked the interpreter what he would do
with it and the reply was that he (White Wolf) was sick
and had no appetite and he wanted to buy an unborn calf—
that he thought he could relish some of that! It is considered a great delicacy among many different tribes of
Indians. He got the dollar. I found that the post butcher
was doing quite an extensive business in selling unborn
calves at one dollar each.

Occasionally I had to discipline some of my scouts but
I rarely confined any of them in the guard-house. When

they had committed some breach of military discipline I would give them a good lecture, tell them what was right and what was wrong and what I expected of them. This was usually all that was necessary. There were, however, two or three cases where talking did no good. These men I would not reenlist, and this served as a good object lesson, for nearly all of them wanted to be reenlisted.

Meat was my first sergeant all the time I was in charge of these scouts, about two or three years. He was a natural born soldier, over six feet in height, with a magnificent figure. When he entered my office with the morning report his hair was always nicely combed, his clothes were neat, his shoes well blacked and he wore white gloves. It was said that he and Sergeant Major Seymour of the Fifth Cavalry were the finest specimens of soldiers on post.

I had a scout in the troop named Swallow who had given us a great deal of trouble. One day the first sergeant came up with an interpreter, and told me he had been having some trouble with Swallow; that he was no good, and that if I said so, he would take him down the creek and shoot him. I told the sergeant that I thought Swallow ought to be killed; that he was worthless, but that I didn't care to shoot him, because if we did both of us would get into trouble. I intimated to the first sergeant that when I came down to camp I would put Swallow in the guardhouse, and that if we could not make a good soldier of him I would not reenlist him when his time expired.

Upon my arrival in camp Swallow was in his tent, where Sergeant Otterby and two or three scouts were guarding him. They had been sent out to arrest Swallow, who had been absent two or three days and had missed muster for pay. The first sergeant came up with his gun ready for business. I was just about to go into the tent, when Sergeant Otterby, who could speak English, advised me not to; that Swallow had his gun and might shoot me; that he had been singing his death song, and had threatened to shoot any one who went into his tent.

I therefore thought it best to parley with him. Sally, his wife (who spoke English), and his old father were in the tent with him. I called them out, and told them they had better advise Swallow to come out of his tent and decide to go to the guard-house; that he had done wrong and knew it; that he was a soldier and would have to be punished the same as a white soldier. He finally decided to go to the guard-house with the first sergeant. Had I used forcible means instead of trying diplomacy there might have been some bloodshed.

Sally was a devoted wife. While Swallow was in the guard-house he had to work with the other prisoners unloading grain. The sacks were quite heavy. Sally came to me and pleaded to be allowed to take Swallow's place, saying that he was not very strong nor accustomed to hard work, but that she was "heap strong" (showing me the muscles of her arms). When I refused to grant her request she went away, greatly disappointed. Swallow was one of the first scouts to cut his hair. He enlisted as a soldier in Troop L, Fifth Cavalry.

While at Fort Reno I had for a "striker" (or servant) an Indian named One Horse. He blacked boots for myself and Lieutenant Wilhelm, and also cared for our horses. He was very neat about his person, as I had told the Indians it was necessary to be. One day my cook heard the water running in the bathroom. Knowing that the tub had been removed she opened the door, and there was One Horse taking a bath in her bread pan! I called his attention to the fact that it was not the proper thing to do, and he replied, "You know, Lieutenant, you are always telling us we ought to be clean and neat about our persons. I looked all around, but could not find anything else to bathe in but the bread pan, but I washed it out afterward."

Lieutenant Wilhelm, my assistant, occupied the same quarters with me. He had several pairs of boots and shoes. One Horse polished them up in good shape and placed them on the mantel of his room, after removing the photos of Wilhelm's best girls.   He then called the lieutenant's attention to "how nice they looked!"

The non-commissioned officers and privates of Company A, Indian Scouts, composed of Cheyennes, Arapahoes and a few Utes and Sioux, commanded by me at Fort Reno, Oklahoma, were as follows:

FIRST SERGEANT

Meat

SERGEANTS	CORPORALS
Goodman	John D. Miles
Flacco	Long Neck
John Otterby	Tall Son
John Washer	Benny Keith
Woolworth	Bald Eagle
William Little Elk	Nathan Seegar

TRUMPETERS	FARRIER
White Buffalo	Thunder
George Little Bear	

PRIVATES

One Horse	Little Cup
Big Nose	Man Hat
Bird Chief	Old Bull
Brave Bear	Star
Bull Thigh	Tony
Creeping Bear	Ute

PRIVATES

Alfred Brown
Red Man
War Path
White Antelope
Frank Murphy
Ernie Black
Red Eagle
Antelope Skin
Big Knee
Thomas Otterby
Swallow
Miller Red Wolf
Short Nose
Little Man
Little Hawk
Tall Bear
Crooked Nose
Kias Redwolf
John Stanton
Spotted Calf
White Crane
Little Bear
Long Hair
Red Wolf
Bow
Circle
Pawnee
Sam Johnson

Theodore North
Clarence Powderface
Francis Lee
Jan Hutchison
White Bear
Red Man, Jr.
Two Spear
Rabbit
Red
David Tabor
James Monroe
Bottle Nose
Bad Man
Joe Weesner
Bird Seward
Edward Campbell
Richard Bearsheart
Young Man
Sleeper
White Log
Traveler
Big Horse
Osage
Small Rib
Little Bear, Jr.
Kiowa
Bobtail Coyote
Black Bull
Short Nose, Jr.

Camp of Cheyenne Scouts and Families at Fort Elliott, Texas, in 1889

NAMES OF SOME OF THE INDIAN CHILDREN
BELONGING TO THE SCOUTS

Martin Chance Alone

Noah Horse

Victoria Holy Rock

Julia Afraid-of-Hawk

Mary Brown Ears

Julia Crazy Ghost

John Left Hand

Lizzie Shot-to-Pieces

Mercy Yellow Shirt

Emma No Fat

Julia Stand-Up

CHAPTER XL

OKLAHOMA was opened for settlement April 22, 1889. Some time previous to this President Harrison issued a proclamation prohibiting cattlemen from grazing their herds on Indian lands, and other parties from going into the territory for the purpose of locating homesteads. These latter were called "sooners." Quite frequently, parties would sneak in and build dugouts in some secluded place where they intended later to locate their homes. These "sooners" hoped, of course, that they would not be discovered by the military, whose duty it was to drive them out.

A portion of my duties, while at Fort Reno in command of Indian scouts, consisted of patroling a part of the territory with my scouts. Whenever I found cattle I would drive them out over the state line into Kansas or Texas, and when I came across "sooners" I would escort them to the line and turn them loose, on their promise not to return. If they did not promise, I would turn them over to a United States commissioner for proper punishment. Furthermore, I always destroyed whatever improvements they had made. Usually they would go with me quietly, but always protesting, claiming that the government had no right to move them off the lands they had squatted on. Occasionally, however, I would find a party who would be quite abusive and dare me to put them off. However, by using a little diplomacy, I generally could cool their wrath and induce them to move out, without much trouble.

Upon one occasion I found a man with quite a family who had made extensive improvements. Naturally, he was loath to leave; in fact, he declared that he would not go; that he would die right there first and that I did not have sufficient scouts to put him off. Although I had about a dozen Indians with me, the more I argued with him the more stubborn he became. He was well armed and handled his gun as if he meant business. I did not think he would dare shoot but at the same time I thought it quite possible that his gun might go off accidentally, so I did not propose to take any chances.

I had a sergeant, John Woolworth, with me. He was an Arapahoe who had attended school at Carlisle, Pennsylvania, and was the only English-speaking scout in my party. My Indians had previously been instructed just what to do when a situation of this kind arose. They were to appear as if they had no interest in the controversy. (Indians do, naturally.) In case of impending trouble they were gradually to place themselves in such positions that they could "jump" a man and disarm him when I gave the signal.

Finally, I came to the conclusion that "forbearance had ceased to be a virtue" in dealing with this man, so, watching my opportunity, I gave the signal, whereupon three of my scouts, including the sergeant, jumped him like so many cats after a mouse and took away his gun. I never saw a man so completely surprised. Inasmuch as he had given me so much trouble, I told the sergeant to tie him; that he was a bad man and I was not going to take any chances.

The scouts took a lariat, tied it around his ankles and wound it around him several times, binding his arms by his side, and fastening the end of the rope around his neck, until they had the man so trussed up that he could scarcely move a muscle. He had a boy about fifteen years of age but I did not consider it necessary to tie him. I then packed up everything of value and movable about the place, loaded it in his wagon and destroyed his improvements.

When we were ready to start the sergeant asked whether I intended to let the old man ride on his wagon. I said no, that he was a dangerous character and we had better take no chances, so we would strap him on a mule. The scouts thereupon brought one up and this brought the old man to time. He then commenced to beg that I would not put him on a mule, promising, by all that was above and below, if I would untie him and let him ride on his wagon, he would not give me any further trouble. I therefore relented and told the sergeant to unbind him, although I was strongly tempted to make him ride the mule for putting me to so much trouble. In the meantime, I had assured his wife that I would not hurt him if he would behave himself. She laconically remarked, "Stranger, ef you kin make the ol' man give in, it's more'n I was ever able to do!"

We were about fifty miles from El Reno and twenty-five from the state line. It was my intention to take my prisoner before the United States commissioner at El Reno, but he begged so hard and promised so faithfully that he would never go into the territory again until it was opened for settlement, that I, feeling sorry for his family, decided to turn him loose. I am quite sure he was a grateful man and well he should have been, for had I turned him over to the commissioner it would have gone hard with him. If he could not have given a bond he would have been sent to Fort Smith, Arkansas, and held for trial before the United States court, which would not have been in session for some weeks.

While the scouts were stationed at Fort Elliott, Texas, I had among their number an Indian named Yellow Bull, who complained one day that one of his horses had either been stolen or had strayed away. It was reported to me at the time and I gave Yellow Bull permission to be absent two or three days in an endeavor to locate the animal. He returned unsuccessful and shortly afterward I was ordered with the scouts to proceed to Fort Reno to take station.

We had not been at Reno very long when Yellow Bull reported to me that he had seen his pony at the trader's store in the possession of a white woman. I went at once to investigate the matter and found that Yellow Bull was right. I recognized the pony as the one his little daughter had formerly ridden.

I questioned the woman, who stated that she was living on a ranch near El Reno. She said that her husband had purchased the pony from an Indian for twenty-five dollars, and that it had been in their possession for a long time. I told her it belonged to Yellow Bull and had been stolen from him at Fort Elliott. However, the woman refused to give up the animal.

As we were on the Indian reservation, I thought of taking it forcibly from her possession but reconsidered the matter. The next day Yellow Bull and I went before a justice of the peace at El Reno and swore out a writ of replevin.

When the case came up the defendant was not willing to let the justice decide it, but insisted upon having a petit jury (six men). I had decided to represent Yellow Bull before the court, but the justice advised me not to do so, as I was not familiar with the procedure involved. I therefore procured a lawyer, whose fee was ten dollars.

Yellow Bull and his wife both swore that the horse in question was theirs and that they had never disposed of

it. Several scouts swore that the pony at one time belonged
to Yellow Bull and even the Indian from whom Yellow
Bull had purchased the horse testified that he had sold it
to him and also identified a brand that was on the animal.

I swore that I knew the pony as one Yellow Bull's little
daughter formerly rode at Fort Elliott. For the defense
the woman herself was the only witness, her husband not
being in the territory at that time. She swore that they
purchased the horse from an Indian when it was a three-
year-old colt, for twenty-five dollars, and at the time of
the purchase branded it with a brand-iron that came
through the mail to them in a pasteboard box from her
father, who was a ranchman living in Utah. She declared
that the horse had been in their possession nearly a year
and a half.

We cited to the jury that a brand-iron of the size used
on the pony was too large to come in a pasteboard box.
We proved by an expert horseman who examined the pony
in the presence of the jury that the animal was at least
eight years old, and was worth at least seventy-five dollars.

In spite of all our testimony, the jury decided in favor
of the woman! The expense of the trial was about forty
dollars, which I had to advance.

Yellow Bull was puzzled. He told me he could not
understand the white man's law, that the Indians had been
told they should give up their unlawful ways of living and
walk the white man's road; but that if this was a sample of
the white man's justice he preferred to remain an Indian,
as he thought they were more honest than the whites.

When the Cheyennes and Arapahoes received the money
for their land several of them bought horses, mules and
wagons with which to start farming, as they had received
their lands in severalty. Yellow Bull, who had some harness and a wagon, bought a pair of mules and I asked the

government hay contractor to let him haul hay into the post, which he did. As he was entirely without experience in this line of work I went into the field and loaded his wagon. I remained on the load and the haymakers pitched it up to me, while I spread it about and explained to Yellow Bull just how to load the hay on so it would ride securely.

In this way Yellow Bull earned more than enough to repay me the money I had advanced him in the lawsuit.

It has been my experience that an Indian has very little show of getting justice in the courts. While at Fort Elliott I had a case where a negro had been selling liquor to my Indians. I interviewed him and he acknowledged the fact and promised me if I would not prosecute him he would not do it again. He was the man who sold Sergeant Meat the liquor. Shortly after he gave me this promise there was more drinking among the scouts. Upon investigation I found they were getting their liquor from the same man. I had the negro indicted and took him to Graham, Texas, to be tried before the federal court. While I had two or more witnesses who swore that the darky had sold them the liquor, the bootlegger was found "not guilty!" I might add that in those days a Texan had very little use for an Indian.

CHAPTER XLI

THE following description of my company of Indian scouts is taken from the official report of Major J. P. Sanger of the inspector general's corps, made after visiting Fort Reno on a tour of inspection.

"The company is commanded by Lieutenant H. W. Wheeler, Fifth Cavalry, who, apart from the special qualifications for this duty, which he possesses in a marked degree, is an officer of much experience in the western country, and thoroughly interested in his work. It is generally admitted that Lieutenant Wheeler has been indefatigable in his efforts to make a good company, and it affords me pleasure to report that he has succeeded as few officers in the army could have done. He understands the character of the Cheyennes and Arapahoes, is fearless and just in his intercourse with them, and apart from instructing his company in military exercises, which they perform most creditably, has interested himself in their family and tribal affairs, and endeavored to give them better ideas of conduct.

"Lieutenant Wilhelm, Tenth Infantry, has been on duty with the company since August sixteenth, and Sergeant Lynch, Troop G, Fifth Cavalry, since the organization. Lieutenant Wheeler reports that they have given him valuable assistance. I visited the camp on Sunday morning, and inspected the company on foot and in their tepees. I had previously seen the company mounted, both at drill and review, and on all occasions their appearance and performance were most creditable, and I found the camp and tepees in as good order as any military camp I have ever been in.

"By authority of the department commander, the scouts were ordered to march from Fort Reno to Fort Sill, and I accompanied them. Ninety men were in the ranks, a majority of whom had two ponies. This is important to their efficiency, as they cannot do much field service with but one pony, and Lieutenant Wheeler, by making it a partial condition of reenlistment, has not only furnished an inducement for a profitable investment but has provided against a serious weakness of organization in case of sudden arduous campaign.

"The company left Fort Reno at nine-thirty A. M., September twenty-ninth, and reached Fort Sill at twelve-thirty P. M., Wednesday, October first, a distance of seventy-two miles. Three camps were made en route, in each of which the scouts spread their shelter tents, pitched the officers' tents, cut wood and brought water with as much willingness as the best soldiers would have done. When the character and past history of these Indians are remembered, this is surprising. Among the last to yield to the government, they have been the most reluctant to adopt the ways of white men, and are still very independent, and, I am told, dangerous Indians. Be this as it may, Lieutenant Wheeler has them under such good control that they do with alacrity all that he requires. The march was very well conducted, and brought out in some degree the peculiar aptitude of the scouts for military service."

Fort Reno, O. T., Nov. 15, 1890.

Official extract copy respectfully furnished First Lieut. H. W. Wheeler, 5th Cavalry commanding Company A, Indian Scouts, for his information.

By order of Major Russell.

C. H. WATTS,

1st lieut. and adjutant 5th
Cavalry, post adjt.

4930 D. Mo. '90.

Extract from report of an inspection of the post of Fort Reno, O. T. made by Major J. P. Sanger, inspector general, on September 23 to 29, 1890.

THE COMMAND OF THE POST

Military bearing and appearance at reviews: Co. A., Indian Scouts—Excellent.

Arms and Accoutrements: Co. A, Indian Scouts—Very good.

Undress Uniforms—Co. A, Indian Scouts—Very good.

Appearance of Horses—Co. A, Indian Scouts—Excellent.

Horse Equipments—Co. A, Indian Scouts—Very good.

Company Property—Co. A, Indian Scouts—Very good.

Books and Records—Co. A, Indian Scouts—Very good.

POLICE OF BARRACKS, COMPANY GROUNDS AND STABLES

Company Grounds—Company A, Indian Scouts—Excellent.

Individual and Company Drill—Co. A, Indian Scouts—Very good.

Discipline—Co. A, Indian Scouts—Good.

HEADQUARTERS OF THE ARMY

Washington, D. C., December 2, 1890.

Brigadier-General Wesley Merritt,

Commanding Dept. of the Missouri,

St. Louis, Mo.

General:

Major J. P. Sanger, inspector general, has reported to me personally a full account of his inspection of Company A of the Indian Scouts, composed of Cheyennes and Arapahoes, serving in your Department.

He informs me that their conduct has been "Excellent" and that they are considered very reliable men when on duty, executing their orders to the very best of their ability: And the major has explained to me very fully the character and conduct of the Scouts and their ambitious desires to be in all respects good and valuable soldiers.

The account he has given me is very gratifying, and assures me of what I had before believed—that these Indians can be trusted for any service which I may hereafter require of them, either in our own country, or in the event of war with any foreign nation.

I would be glad to have you communicate to the Cheyenne and Arapahoe Scouts this gratification which I feel at their good conduct, and my confidence in their character and qualifications as United States soldiers.

Also please convey to their commanding officer, Lieut. H. W. Wheeler, Fifth Cavalry, my cordial commendation of his efforts and appreciation of his success in the organization and training of these valuable troops.

Yours very respectfully,
(Signed) J. M. SCHOFIELD,
Major-General, Commanding.

HEADQUARTERS DEPT. OF THE MISSOURI

St. Louis, Mo., Dec. 5, 1890.

Official copy respectfully furnished the commanding officer Reno, O. T., who will communicate to the company of scouts and to the officer concerned, the foregoing commendations from the major general commanding the Army.

BY COMMAND OF BRIG.-GEN. MERRITT.
(Signed) WM. J. VOLKMAR,
A. A. Genl.

Fort Reno, O. T., Dec. 9, 1890.

Official copy respectfully furnished to the commanding officer Company A, Indian Scouts, for his information.

BY ORDER OF COLONEL WADE.
(Signed) C. H. WATTS,
1st lieut. and adjt. Fifth Cavalry,
Post Adjutant.

PART FIVE: INDIANS AND THEIR WAYS

CHAPTER XLII

FAMILY LIFE OF THE INDIANS

INDIANS, as well as their white brethren, have their love-affairs. It was quite comical to watch the young men and women flirt, as I have often seen them. They dressed up in their very best, colored blankets, beaded leggings and moccasins; their hair carefully combed and ornamented; their faces painted with yellow ochre, on each cheek a heart, a star or a round spot in red, according to their individual tastes. Their blankets were worn over the head in such a manner that only the eyes could be seen.

The young men of the plains do most of their courting in a standing position. An Indian lover will stand and wait near the lodge where abides the object of his admiration until she appears, when he walks up alongside her and throws his blanket over her. If she reciprocates the tender sentiment they will thus stand for hours, his blanket covering both and closely wrapped around both bodies. While so waiting or standing outside a lodge, they usually have the head entirely covered with their blanket, except only a little hole for one eye. If the girl likes to be held she gives some reply to the first greeting. The embrace under the blanket excites no comment or annoyance.

"In 1877 it became necessary for the military authorities to know something of the movements and plans of the great war-chief of the Sioux, Crazy Horse, and to discover this one of the enlisted scouts suddenly became smitten with the charms of a dusky maiden who lived in the tepee adjoining that of the chief. As she reciprocated the tender feeling, the scout would stand just outside of Crazy Horse's lodge, holding the girl in a fond embrace, while his quick ears took in every word that was uttered in the lodge. He discovered a conspiracy, which, if it had not been for his cunning shrewdness and prompt and loyal action to the whites, would in all probability have terminated in the murder of a white officer, but which eventually led to the necessary killing of the chief himself."*

The women drew the rations; so on ration days the "dudes" came out to flirt with them, making eyes at them or peeking around the corners of the store buildings. Before young men could get married they must have some means, in the way of ponies, to offer for a wife. The number of ponies a young man gave depended upon the rank of the girl's family and her beauty. They could be had for from three or four ponies up, together with a few presents.

All arrangements, including the amount to be paid, were made through their friends. Their likes and dislikes were taken into consideration by their parents. If everything was agreeable, the day was set and preparations made for the marriage and feast. The town crier went through the village announcing the event and inviting all to the feast. There was usually very little ceremony, if any. If the groom was well to do, he gave the poor people a few presents. If, as was sometimes the case, a young man did not have a sufficient number of ponies

---

*From *The Indian Sign Language,* by Lieutenant Philo P. Clark.

to buy a wife, he went to some of his friends to help him out by advancing a pony or two, but the lender retained an interest in the bride by way of security until he had been repaid for the ponies.

Quite frequently the bride and groom did not get along very well together, and the wife returned to her parents, who in some cases were to blame for the separation, not being satisfied with the amount given them by the groom. If the young wife went home to her parents she could not get married again unless the prospective husband was willing to recompense her own husband in some way. If they could not agree on the amount it was left to arbitration. If any one who advanced a pony at the time of the prior wedding had not been paid he must be appeased in some way. If any man was known to be committing adultery with this woman he had to compensate the husband by giving him a pony or a money equivalent.

Upon one occasion one of my scouts complained to me that one of the Indians had taken his horse and would not give it up. He asked me to go to the agent about it. I inquired about the matter and discovered that the scout had been too intimate with the Indian's wife. Upon my asking if he did not know the "rules of the game" and the consequences of violation thereof, he acknowledged that he did, and I thereupon told him it served him right; that he ought to have a wife of his own and that under the circumstances I would not do anything about the matter. I never heard any more from it.

I knew a case one time wherein a white man was caught committing adultery with an Indian woman. A few days afterward his horse was found dead, shot through the head, and it was supposed that the husband had shot the animal for revenge. That settled the affair, there was no suing for damages.

Among the Apaches the mode of punishing a squaw for committing adultery was by cutting off her nose (the Blackfeet Indians included the lower part of the ear), whereupon she became a public woman. I have seen three or four squaws with their noses cut off. A man was sometimes whipped and usually had to pay roundly for his misdeed. If the wife of a chief dishonored him, she as well as her paramour would sometimes be killed by the enraged husband. I do not know of any people on the globe who are more chaste than the Cheyennes, Sioux and Shoshones, but I am sorry that I can not say as much for the Arapahoes, Snakes and Crows.

Indians have some peculiar customs. At one time the wife of one of my scouts did my laundry work and I wanted to give her some instructions about it. I asked one of my interpreters, a sergeant named Otterby, whose father was a Mexican and a noted scout, to tell her what I wanted. I observed that he acted rather diffident about it and inquired what the difficulty was. He answered, "I can't tell her that; she is my mother-in-law." I asked what difference that made and he replied, "Lieutenant, you know that mothers-in-law make lots of trouble between man and wife; that is the only reason I can give. It is an old custom of the Cheyennes."

No Apache will speak to his mother-in-law, a custom which the woman reciprocates. There are times at the agencies when Indians have to be counted for rations. Even then the rule is not relaxed. The mother-in-law will take a seat with her son-in-law and the rest of the family, but a few paces removed and with her back turned to them all. References to her are by signs only. She is never mentioned otherwise.

I do not believe that any race of people exists on earth who are more fond of their families than the American

Indians. They rarely punish their children, who are brought up to obey and respect the older people, especially the head men of the tribe. If one wants to gain the confidence of Indians, he should be kind to them, especially to their women and children, and they will remember it and show their gratitude in many ways.

I think the secret of my success in controlling them was my treatment of their women and children. I interested myself in their welfare and tribal relations. If any of them were ill I would get the post surgeon to see them, especially their children, although at times it was up-hill work, for they had great confidence in their medicine men, who accomplished some really wonderful cures.

My first sergeant, Meat, had a very pretty little girl five or six years of age who, at one time, was very ill. I asked the post doctor to see her. He said she had stomach trouble and he was afraid he could not do much for her as she was a delicate child and needed proper food and good nursing, which she could not get in an Indian camp.

He said if I would have her brought into the post he would do all he could for her. I did this, pitching the first sergeant's lodge in my back yard. I instructed my colored cook to see that the child had nourishing food and to prepare it herself.

This change of living and care soon had its effects and the child commenced to improve wonderfully. Very soon she was able to return to camp. The doctor said that for a while they would have to be very careful about her food and this was explained to the father and mother. Several days after I inquired how the child was doing and what food they were giving her. His answer was that she was pretty well and that they were giving her all the beef and eggs she could eat! That was their idea of "proper food." The child, however, fully recovered. The mother went to the doctor's quarters and insisted upon working for him. The father was a good hunter and quite frequently sent the doctor game. Their actions in every way showed their gratitude.

When I had charge of the Indian scouts, I used to marry and divorce them. One of my Indians, Red Eagle, fell in love with one of the two wives of Thunder and their love was mutual. Thunder was my blacksmith. Red Eagle wanted to marry the woman and offered Thunder three ponies and about twenty-five dollars in money, but he refused to sell her. Thunder had had some trouble with his wife and had tried to whip her, but he told me that he did not hurt her very much, because some of the other women pulled them apart.

After investigating the case thoroughly I decided to let this woman go and live with Red Eagle. I brought the parties all up before me and told them that they knew the white man's ways, which allowed only one wife, and I didn't see why Thunder should have two wives and Red Eagle none, and that I believed one wife was enough for any man to care for. Therefore I would divorce this woman from Thunder and give her to Red Eagle. I told Thunder that if he would not accept the ponies and money at that time he would never get anything. However, he would accept nothing and I married the squaw to Red Eagle.

Some few weeks later I was making an inspection of the Indian camp, and Thunder's remaining wife, Julia, hailed me. This was the first I knew that she could speak English but it seemed that she had been a Carlisle girl. She told me that Thunder had changed his mind and now wanted those ponies and the money for the other wife. I reminded her that I had already told Thunder if he did not take the ponies and money at the time I divorced the second wife from him he never would get anything; and then I said to her, "Julia, you know very well that you don't want that woman to come back." She replied, "I don't care whether she comes back or not; she didn't treat Thunder right, anyway." I presume Julia had been promised some of the money and ponies if she could have prevailed upon me to make Red Eagle pay Thunder.

Another case of a somewhat similar nature in which a couple of my scouts figured was as follows:

Sergeant Chester A. Arthur wanted to marry a certain Indian girl, but he lacked the necessary number of ponies to pay for the squaw. He went to Corporal Long Neck and asked for the loan of a pony to consummate his matrimonial venture. Long Neck gave Arthur the pony, but according to the Indian custom he retained an interest in the bride until Arthur should have paid him back the pony. Arthur and his bride did not "hitch" very well and he shortly abandoned her.

Then Scout Big Knee fell in love with the woman and married her. Arthur thereupon went to Big Knee and demanded five ponies from him as payment for his late wife. Big Knee gave the former husband two ponies and ten dollars in cash, but Arthur was not satisfied and demanded the full five ponies.

The parties came to me to have the matter settled. It appeared that the squaw was the favorite sister of another of my scouts named Waldo Reed. Reed was not at all pleased that Arthur had abandoned his sister and did not want Big Knee to give the five ponies to Arthur. Both Big Knee and Reed wrote me letters about the affair, or rather, one wrote both letters, as the other could not write. These letters are interesting. Although somewhat incoherent to the average reader, they are good specimens of the manner in which the red man expressed himself in writing.

The custom of making the woman the head of the house and investing her with the care of the property is unusual among the aboriginal races. As far as I know the Hopis and Zunis are the only tribes that do so. Their women are vested with the power of divorce. If the husband is uncongenial out he goes and his personal belongings follow him. His only recourse is to return to his mother for sympathy, telling her how cruelly he has been treated.

The docile Hopi is compelled by their tribal laws to aid his father as long as the old man can find work for him, and it is said that he rarely fails to do so. The Hopis and Zunis are few and growing less numerous, while the more democratic Navajos are flourishing. They let the women do most of the work, and the young men are by no means amenable, like the Hopis, to paternal advice.

One time Professor Welch, of Philadelphia, one of the Indian commissioners, came to Darlington agency on a tour of inspection. He was trying to get the Indians to consent to have their children go to school at Carlisle. Most of these Indians objected to it, preferring to have them remain at the agency and go to school there. We got the Indians together and had a feast. Cattle were killed and roasted. The professor talked to them regarding their children and after he had finished an old Indian got up and said he believed it was a mighty nice thing to send their children to the Carlisle school, especially the girls; that he had sent some of his girls away to school, where they had been taught the white man's ways. They could read and write and had been taught to sew, keep house and cook, and when they returned to the agency they were well dressed, better looking and were all well married, some of

them having married white men. He further said that
when those girls went away to school they were worth only
two or three ponies, but on their return they were worth
eight or ten ponies.

CHAPTER XLIII

INDIAN MEDICINE

ONE of my scouts named White Antelope had the jaundice quite badly and wanted to go to a medicine man for treatment. I told him no, that he must go in to the post hospital; that the doctor knew more about that disease than any medicine man; that he would get better care and it would not cost him anything. (A medicine man does not practise his profession for his health.) Antelope went into the hospital rather reluctantly. It did not seem to him that he was getting cured as fast as he thought he should and he kept asking permission to go to the medicine man. In fact, he was worrying so much about it that the doctor said it might be a good idea to let him go.

Antelope was gone two or three weeks and returned fully recovered in health. It appeared that the medicine man's treatment was white sage tea to drink, sweat baths, and in between times beating the tom-tom and singing. This was done to intercede with the Great Spirit to spare his life. I am quite sure that Antelope thought the incantations had more to do with his recovery than either the sage tea or baths.

At one time I had a trumpeter, a Carlisle boy named White Buffalo, who had more than ordinary intelligence. His hair was as white as snow, one of the very few white-haired Indians I ever saw. (In fact, I have seen only two

317

others, a brother and sister at Fort Washakie.) One day
I heard drumming and singing in the tepee of White
Buffalo and asked the cause. He said his wife was very
ill and that the medicine men were trying to cure her. A
few days later I asked him how his wife was getting on
and he replied, "All right"; that one of the medicine men
had sucked a bone out of her side as large as his thumb!
I tried to convince him that this was impossible but never
succeeded.

The Indians regarded sickness as the visitation of an
evil spirit, and like the Chinese and other Orientals, they
thought this spirit could be exorcised only by incantation
and by magic potions, the secret of which rested with the
medicine men, who enjoyed a high repute and did no labor.
Their profession, however, was a dangerous one, and unlike civilized doctors they were not supposed to make many
errors. The common people regarded them with great
awe and when they were superintending the mummeries
over a sick brave they were considered bigger men than
the head chief himself.

Before commencing his work the medicine man goes
through many fasts and vigils and many weird incantations.
It is doubtless this elaborate religious preparation that makes
the Indian think he is deserving of punishment if he fails.
The Yumas, as well as some other tribes, find many ways
of putting the medicine men away if they make too many
failures.

Many of these medicine men were wonderfully skilled
in treating all ordinary complaints. Their knowledge of
herbs was remarkable and they had sure cures for even
the bite of the deadly rattlesnake and venomous insects.
The weed used for the cure of such bites was usually
found where rattlesnakes abounded. It was applied
directly to the wound and drew out the poison. The medi-

cine men also brewed a tea that counteracted the poison.
The Mexicans also knew of this weed.

I learned this on an occasion when a party of them
were working on my ranch (Rose Creek Ranch) during
haying. One of the Mexican children was bitten by a
rattlesnake while trying to feed the reptile a grasshopper!
The snake evidently was coiled, as they do not bite except
when in that position. One of the Mexicans at once found
the weed in the creek bottom, made the tea and gave the
child some of it to drink, at the same time applying the
weed to the wound. The sufferer recovered. In cases
where some of my stock had been bitten by rattlers I have
applied common baking soda to the wound, which, in a
few cases, saved the animals.

When it came to contagious diseases, like measles and
smallpox, the medicine men were powerless. Consumption
has sapped the strongest of the Indians, who are pecu-
liarly susceptible to this dread scourge, quite contrary to
what one would infer, as their nomadic life of the old
days kept them in the open air. I think the reason this
terrible disease had such a telling effect on the Indians was
that they took very little precaution against colds or
coming into contact with victims of tuberculosis. I am
glad to state that mortality from this disease decreased
greatly after they were placed on government reserves.

In the manuscript notes left by W. M. Boggs the following curious story is recorded (p. 51.)*:

"William Bent had contracted a severe cold and sore
throat—putrid sore throat—and it became so bad that he
had ceased to swallow and could only talk in a whisper,
until his throat closed and his wife fed him with broth,
through a quill which she passed down his throat. I went

---

*From the *Kansas Historical Collections*, Volume XV, 1919-1922,
"Bent's Old Fort and its Builders," by George Bird Grinnell.

into his lodge to see how he was and he told me, by writing on a piece of slate that he had with him, that if he
did not get relief in a very short time he was bound to
die, and that he had sent for an Indian doctor called
Lawyer, and was expecting him every hour. The Indian
came while I was there, a plain-looking Indian without
any show or ornamentation about him. He proceeded at
once to examine Bent's throat by pressing the handle of a
large spoon on his tongue just as any doctor would do,
and on looking into Bent's throat he shook his head, got
up and went out of the lodge and returned very soon with
a handful of small sand burs. They were about the size
of a large marrowfat pea, with barbs all around, as sharp
as fishhooks and turned up one way. They were so sharp
that by pressing them they would stick to one's fingers.
He called for a piece of sinew and a lump of marrow
grease. He made five or six threads of the sinew and
tied a knot in one end of each, took an awl and pierced
a hole through each bur and ran the sinew through it down
to the knot, then rolled the bur in marrow grease until it
completely covered over the barbs of the bur; took a small
flat stick about like a China chopstick, cut a notch in one
end, wrapped one end of the sinew around his finger and
placed the notched stick against the bur, made Bent open
his mouth, and he forced that bur or ball down Bent's
throat the length of the stick and drew it out of the
throat and repeated that three or four times, drawing out
(on the barbs) all the dry and corrupt matter each time,
and opened the throat passage so that Bent could swallow
soup, and in a day or two was well enough to eat food.
And he told me that he certainly would have died if that
Indian had not come to his relief.

"The Indian was laughing while he performed the
operation. He was the most unassuming Indian I saw

among the Cheyennes, but was considered by all the whites that knew him the shrewdest doctor belonging to the tribe. No medicine would have had any effect in removing these obstructions in Bent's throat. It had become as dry as the bark on a tree, and but for this simple remedy Bent would have died. No one but an Indian would ever have thought of resorting to such a remedy."

CHAPTER XLIV

THE Cheyennes, Arapahoes and other Indian tribes, like some civilized people, believed that trouble and misfortune were visited upon them for their sins; that all the good visited on them came from the good spirit, and all the evil from the evil spirit.

Not many years ago these Indians held sun dances, at which time the male members of the tribe volunteered to submit themselves to torture and suffering, to satisfy the evil spirit. At these dances they usually erected a pole of some height, on which was placed a buffalo skull. They attached lariats made from buffalo hides near the top of the pole, for the ceremony. The dancers made two incisions three or four inches long and two or three inches apart, on their right and left breasts, or in the shoulder blades. In these slits lariats were fastened. At high noon the signal was given by the master of the ceremony and the dancers commenced to circle the pole, gradually leaning backward or forward with considerable force. While they did this the lariats quite frequently tore out, causing considerable suffering. If some of the dancers were about to succumb from the ordeal through which they were passing, their friends would seize them, pulling them from the lariats and tearing loose the slits. This was done to save the dancer from disgrace. If they succumbed from the ordeal it was considered bad medicine.

Warriors were supposed to resist all suffering. During

the dancing the tom-toms beat and the musicians sang, to keep up the courage of the dancers. The warriors were nude, except for the breech-clout, and their bodies were painted various colors, according to individual taste.

John H. Seger, an old friend of mine who has done much to educate and train the Cheyennes and Arapahoes in the white man's way, and who is more familiar with their history and customs than probably any other man now living, told me, in one of my interviews at his sub-agency, of a sun dance he witnessed many years before. I remember the substance of a prayer made by Raven, a celebrated Arapahoe chief and medicine man at the Red Hills.

It was high noon. Six warriors stood nude, save for the breech-clout. To their bleeding breasts was fastened a rawhide lariat. In the midst of these tortures, and while one warrior was dragging about a buffalo skull, the horns of which were attached to the lariat, old Raven stepped out and, raising his hands toward the sun, he addressed the Great Spirit, as he moaned:

"Many are sick and suffering from disease. The great buffalo are leaving us; the white man surrounds us like hunters around a herd of tired buffalo. We know this punishment is visited upon us for our disobedience to the wish of the Great Spirit. We are willing to suffer the just punishment from the invasion of the white man. We realize that the buffalo will disappear with the coming of the white man. What we ask is, that the Great Spirit will pity us and let the soldiers and young men bear the suffering for their people, which they are willing to do, as the Great Spirit can now see. We ask that the Great Spirit be satisfied with this voluntary suffering, and that the women and children, who are weak and tired, be spared from sickness and suffering. We ask that, as there is no hope for the Arapahoes, except to get their food from the earth as the white man gets it, the Great Spirit may so influence the young men and children that they may be willing to cultivate the earth and raise food to keep the people alive."

This prayer expressed the sentiment of the Arapahoes. When I was there again in 1892 I observed, and since then have been told, that they have been slowly but steadily advancing toward the fulfilment of their prayer.

The government put a stop to the sun dance many years ago.

The Hopi Indian believes that the souls of all deceased adults go to the Grand Canyon. When a man dies, a grave is dug. The nearest relative of the deceased carries the body to the grave, places it in a sitting posture, facing the Grand Canyon, erects a long pole between the legs, locks the dead man's fingers around it and fills the grave. To the top of the pole, protruding above the ground, he ties the end of a string, and leads the other end in the direction of the Grand Canyon. At the end of four days, it is believed, the soul leaves the body, climbs the pole, and, with the string to guide it goes to its eternal home in the canyon.

The Navajos, on the contrary, are very superstitious about handling dead bodies. They believe that the evil spirit that kills the person hovers around the "hogan," as the lodge is called, awaiting other victims, and a hogan in which a death occurs is never again occupied. Navajo hogans are always built with the entrance facing the east. When a death occurs in one of them an opening is invariably made in the north side. Therefore, when one sees a hogan with the north side knocked out, he may be certain some one has died in it.*

Some of the Cœur d'Alene Indians were among the

---

*Dillon Wallace in *Outing*.

HOCH-E-A-YUM, THE GREAT MEDICINE DANCE

This is a dance of endurance. Each dancer fixes his eye on the suspended image and blows continuously on his whistle. Each must keep up incessant whistling and unremitting motion, and continue the dance without sleep, food, or drink, until the Medicine Chief orders the suspension of the ceremony. The dance lasts from three to four days, and death frequently overcomes the dancers.

first to embrace Christanity. It came about in the following manner:

A party of semi-civilized Iroquois from Canada made their way to the country of the Cœur d'Alenes, fraternizing with them. They told them of the many wonders in the white man's land; how they lived; of the great things they performed; their countless numbers, and, chief of all, their manner of living and their manner of reaching the Happy Hunting Grounds after death. They told the Cœur d'Alenes that the white man had a book, a "medicine" (the Bible) that would show every Indian the true trail to the Happy Hunting Grounds, where he would live forever in perfect happiness. After much discussion, the Cœur d'Alenes resolved to procure a copy of this wonderful book, and a party was organized to go in search of it. They had no definite object in point, other than the vague East, where the Iroquois told them they could procure it. This little band after traveling a long distance came in contact with a war party, which attacked and killed some of them. The others escaped, and, returning to their own people, related what had happened. Another and larger party was formed to continue the search for the white man's Bible. This party succeeded in reaching Fort Benton, where they sold some of their animals and skins to pay the passage of a few of them to St. Louis on the steamboat. Wandering about the city, they met with Pierre Chouteau, an old trapper, and, by the use of the sign language, told him what they wanted. He took them to the Jesuit fathers, among whom was one Father De Smet. They related to him what the Iroquois had told them and enlisted his sympathy to such a degree that he asked and received permission from his superiors to accompany the Indians back to their country.

Father De Smet was one of the most remarkable men

of his day. A Belgian by birth, he came to the United
States when a young man and his entire after life was devoted to the spreading of Christianity among the Indians.
Lake De Smet, in Wyoming, was named for him. I knew
at Fort Washakie, Wyoming, a few Shoshone Indians
whom he had converted to Christianity.*

I gave the Indians at my post their first Christmas tree.
I asked the scouts to subscribe to the fund, which they did
very liberally, so that every woman and child received a
suitable present. I also gave each child a bag of nuts,
candy, cakes and some kind of fruit. Moreover, I had
Santa Claus come into camp with a sled loaded down with
gifts. I then explained to them in simple words about the
day and how Christmas originated. They never forgot the
day and very often referred to it.

*Facts taken from Humphreyville's *Twenty Years among Our
Hostile Indians.*

CHAPTER XLV

INDIANS are, as a whole, honest and upright in their dealings among themselves and with the whites. It seems to be the consensus of opinion among the American people that the Indians are dishonest, unreliable and thieving; but in my several years' experience among the different tribes I have always found them truthful and honorable, in all my dealings with them.

I once heard Bishop Whipple (at that time bishop of the Minnesota diocese, who no doubt has done more for the civilization of the American Indian than any other man) say that there was not a case on record where they had first broken a treaty with the United States Government or British America.

I was stationed at Fort Washakie more than two years and during that time was detailed to witness the issuance of beef to the Indians, also the payment of their annuities. I also did considerable work teaching them how to farm. There were about four thousand Shoshones, three thousand Arapahoes and some Utes and Bannocks there. No restrictions were placed on them about coming and going in at the post and the only guard we had on post was Number One, at the guard-house, and one sentinel over the storehouses at night. They were there more as a precaution against fire than anything else. Moreover, the officers did not make a practise of locking the doors of their quarters.

A great many Indians would come to see our commanding officer, Major John J. Upham, Fifth Cavalry, who had their interests at heart and had great influence over them. They were welcome at my quarters at all times and I used to buy a great many curios from them, so if they had anything to sell they were quite sure to come to me. Many times we could not agree about the price of an article. They had no idea of the value of money. If they wanted more for an article than I considered it worth I would tell them to take it away; or if they had something I was anxious to get for my collection I would count out my offer in silver dollars and lay it out for them to look at. As they could not tell the different denominations of paper money I used silver. If I had any business to attend to I would leave them to ponder over the matter, and when I returned I found either the money or the article bargained for.

Upon one occasion an Indian princess, daughter of a principal chief, had a beautiful set of saddle equipments which I had set my heart on obtaining, but she would not part with them. I told her if she ever decided to sell them, to come to my quarters and I would buy them. Several months afterward she came, and I offered her seventy-five dollars for them; but she wanted a great deal more than I could afford to give, so I placed the money on my desk, as I usually did in those cases, and told her whenever she was ready to accept my offer she would find the money on my desk, and if I was not there to take the money and leave the equipments. She would not accept my offer that day and took the articles away with her; but I did not give up all hope of getting them.

On ration day, every two weeks, I had to go to the agency to witness the issue of beef. At these times I would count out the seventy-five dollars and leave it on my desk as usual, hoping that some day she would accept.

Not long afterward, to my great surprise, when I returned from the agency I found the money gone and the equipments were there.

I relate these incidents to show that the Indians were allowed to come to my quarters at all times whether I was in or not, and I never lost a single article by theft that I am aware of.

J. K. Moore was the Indian trader at Fort Washakie for many years and was well known by many of the older officers. He told me that in all those years he never had anything stolen, to speak of it, in or around his premises; that he would let the Indians have goods on credit, with the understanding that they were to pay for them when they brought in their furs and that they rarely failed to settle with him.

At one time I was stationed at Fort Robinson, Nebraska, for a year or more, near which place were located the Cheyenne and Sioux agencies. There were several thousand Indians there, and they had the reputation of being honest and trustworthy. I found the same thing to be true at Darlington, Indian Territory, where I was an Indian agent for a short time.

In their own villages they had no means of guarding their personal property. If an Indian wanted to leave the village and his lodge for a few days he would notify the chief of his band, or some friend, that he was going to be absent. He then locked up his belongings in his tepee by placing a log or some brush at the entrance. Their tribal laws were not many, but what they did have their people were taught to respect. If a man or woman was caught stealing the matter was investigated by some of the head men, and if guilt was proved he or she was taken out and publicly whipped.

Bishop Whipple told the following story:

"While visiting an Indian village in one of the Dakotas, many years ago, I rode up to the head chief's lodge, where I was expected to remain for the night. The chief came out and received me, while, at the same time, his squaw unsaddled my horse and placed the equipment alongside their tepee. I asked the chief if they would be safe there, whereupon he observed, 'Yes, there isn't a white man within two days' ride of here.'"

During all the four years or so that I had charge of my Indian scouts, numbering from thirty to one hundred, I never had a complaint that anything had been stolen.

I am very sorry to say that since the whites have come in contact with the Indians the latter have become addicted to many of the vices of the former; principally, not paying their debts and drunkenness. However, it is not among the older Indians, as a rule, but is confined to the "rising generation." While they like "firewater," the majority of them do not drink. I had some drunkenness among my scouts, but it was mostly among the young men who had been away to some Indian school. Of my non-commissioned officers I had only one who drank, and he but periodically. One of the scouts, Yellow Bull, told me that many years before, when he was a young man, he was with a war party that captured a Mexican wagon-train, down on the border. They found in the wagons two or three barrels of whisky on which they all got drunk. He said it made him very sick and that he never had been in that condition since.

CHAPTER XLVI

T HE reason an Indian would sacrifice everything to remove the body of one of his tribe who had been killed in battle was to prevent the taking of the dead tribesman's scalp. The belief of the Indian was that a man who was scalped could not enter the Happy Hunting Grounds, but was doomed to wander in outer darkness forever. For that reason he always scalped his enemy, so that when he, himself, reached Indian heaven he would not be bothered by a lot of his enemies whom he had killed during his lifetime. Naturally, it was a point of order for him to get the body of his friend away, so that he would not be debarred from the Happy Hunting Grounds. Sometimes an Indian did not scalp an especially brave man. (General Custer was not scalped.) It was the belief of the Indian that if he killed a man in battle and did not scalp him he would be the slave of the unscalped one in Indian paradise.

Scalping is not necessarily fatal. There are several cases on record where men and women have been scalped and have survived the operation. In April, 1868, Thomas Cahone and Willis Edmonton, employees of the Union Pacific Railroad, were fishing near Sidney, Nebraska, and were attacked by a small party of Sioux who swooped down on them. They rode up alongside these men and shot eight arrows into Cahone and four into Edmonton. The latter was not scalped, but Cahone was. At no time did he lose consciousness. He stated that when he was being scalped he closed his eyes and expected each instant to have his skull crushed or feel the knife plunged into him. He recovered in a few months, and went back to his old position of passenger conductor for the railroad company. He never suffered from his wounds or from the scalping.

Another way an Indian can be cut off from the Happy Hunting Grounds is by strangulation. He believes that the soul escapes from the body by the mouth. Should death occur by strangulation the soul can never escape but must always remain with, or hovering near, the remains, even after complete decomposition.

As the soul is always conscious of its isolation and its exclusion from participation in the joys of Paradise, this death has peculiar terrors for the Indian, who would much prefer to suffer at the stake than die by hanging, even if the strangulation may be a mere matter of accident. The unfortunate one might be a person of integrity and wisdom, a woman of virtue or an innocent child, but should one or the other chance to become entangled in the lariat of a grazing horse and strangle, the soul would never enter the Happy Hunting Grounds, or Indian heaven.

Among the Cheyennes and some other tribes, a murderer is not allowed to attend any of the ceremonial feasts.

Suicide, though not common among the Indians, is considered "big medicine," a high religious act. Through it the man rises superior to his gods, whatever the special religion of an Indian may be in regard to the taking of the scalps of slain enemies. Colonel Richard Irving Dodge, probably one of the highest authorities on the customs of the American Indians of his day, states in his most valuable work, *Our Wild Indians*:

"I have never yet known a single case where the scalp of a suicide was taken, and in many cases the superstition is so strong as to prevent the Indian from even touching the body. If an unscalped body is found with many terrible wounds, gashed and mutilated, it was the deliberate purpose of the Indians to torment the soul; if it be found with but one mortal wound it is a case of suicide."

Colonel Dodge relates several cases which confirm his opinion that a suicide was never scalped. I will briefly relate one of these, which personally came under his own observation: In 1855 the post of Fort Davis, Texas, was established. He was acting quartermaster. The post guide, Sam Cherry, and an escort of one non-commissioned officer and three men were sent out in search of timber suitable for some logs. That night the party did not return. Next morning early, the wagon-master of a train came into the post and reported that the dead body of a man and horse had been found in the road about six miles from the post. A company of infantry was immediately ordered out and proceeded to the spot, where they found the body of Sam Cherry, pinned fast to the ground by the dead body of his horse. The search was continued and in a lateral canyon were found the bodies of the sergeant and the three privates, riddled with bullets, mutilated and disfigured, but giving every evidence of having sold their lives as brave men should. The trails were examined, and the whole story was worked out. The party had traveled along the road nearly to the entrance of the canyon, known as the "Wild Rose Pass," when suddenly about thirty mounted Indians dashed from the bushes along the stream, cutting off their retreat toward the fort and driving the men up the lateral canyon. Suspecting a trap, Sam Cherry dashed through the lines of the Indians, regaining the road, and ran for life away from the post, followed by a number of yelling savages. He was evidently doing well, when his horse stumbled and fell, breaking its neck and pinning Sam's leg to the ground. In an instant he was surrounded by the exultant Indians. Raising himself slightly, Sam fired five shots at his enemies, then turning the muzzle of his pistol against his own temple he escaped the torture of their vindictive rage by his "last shot."

The baffled and terrified Indians went away as fast as their ponies would carry them, not even touching the body nor taking Cherry's arms.

Custer's body was found unscalped and unmutilated. Colonel Dodge's knowledge of Indians convinces him that Custer also died by his own hand.

CHAPTER XLVII

WHILE I was officer of the day on one occasion at Fort Washakie, Wyoming, a prisoner escaped from the guard-house during the night. The matter was not reported to me by the sergeant of the guard until reveille. We had some Bannock prisoners, so I sent for one known as Bannock Frank, who could speak some English, and told him that a prisoner had escaped from the guard-house.

I told him I wanted him to go and get two or three good trailers and that if they caught the prisoner I would pay them a reward. He secured the trailers and they circled the guard-house, which was located on the banks of a stream, but could not find any tracks which indicated that the prisoner had left the guard-house. Two of the Indians then crossed the stream and followed it up the banks, the other two following on the opposite bank. This was on their own initiative.

They soon discovered where the prisoner had broken off his shackles a few hundred yards up the river, and a short distance farther found where he had come out of the water. The sergeant of the guard, who accompanied them, came back and reported that the Indians had found the trail, and wanted some horses with which to follow it. I told the sergeant to go to the troop stables and get a mount for each of them. They followed on the trail, trotting most of the time, and finally located the prisoner trying to hide in the mountains about ten miles from the post.

335

The sergeant said he could not see a sign of a trail, but the Indians had no trouble whatever in following it.

While the scouts were serving at Fort Elliott, Texas, a soldier deserted from one of the infantry companies. I was not notified of the desertion until guard mounting, about nine A. M., so the deserter had had several hours' start. The scouts had some trouble in finding his trail because of the many footprints around the garrison, and it was no sure thing that he had left the post on foot. They finally found the trail about a half mile from the garrison. Following it up several miles, it led to the door of a ranch house. Entering they found the deserter hiding under the kitchen table.

While I was stationed at Fort Reno, Indian Territory, a prisoner, while at work, escaped from the guard. Lieutenant Wilhelm, my assistant, happened to be in the post and picked up Sergeant Goodman, a scout, and started out after the escaped prisoner. They found him hiding in a near-by ravine, whereupon he started to run up a gulch with Goodman after him. The man would not halt, so the sergeant shot at him, knocking him over. "My God!" exclaimed Wilhelm, "you have killed him!" Goodman smiled. "Nothing in it; nothing in it," he grunted, at the same time grinning from ear to ear. Suddenly the prisoner jumped up, in a dazed manner, and exclaimed, "Lieutenant, I thought I was killed sure." Goodman had placed a blank cartridge in his gun, and as he was quite close to the prisoner, the wax holding the powder in the shell hit the man in the back of the neck. Wilhelm felt very much relieved that the man had not been killed.

My captain, Taylor, told me that while in Arizona his command was in the mountains after some renegade Apaches, and was marching at night on an old trail. Striking of matches and smoking were, of course, forbidden. Suddenly the scouts reported that something had been walking in the trail. The command was halted, a match was carefully struck and it was discovered that a bear had come into the trail, taken a few steps along it and then left it. It was found that one of the scouts had stepped into the bear's track while passing over it.

The Navajos are wonderful trailers. Not many years ago a murder was committed on the reservation and the murderer had several hours' start before the Indian police took up the trail. It happened that the fugitive's unshod pony had one nicked hoof. This mark the Indians followed swiftly, even where the murderer had cunningly followed a bunch of ponies, thinking, no doubt, to make the hoof-prints of his mount unrecognizable. But within a day after they had struck the trail the Indian police had run down the murderer in a stronghold in the mountains.

Runners have been known repeatedly to travel one hundred miles in twenty-four hours or less without stopping on the way for sleep or nourishment. Their gait at such times was a swinging trot. They have been known in many instances to go without food two and three days and utter no complaint. On such occasions to still the gnawing hunger they were accustomed to wrap a thong several times around the waist. It should be added, however, that in all such cases of special exertion or denial full compensation was made.

The Apaches are a tribe capable of standing great fatigue under a sweltering sun and will follow a trail as unerringly as a bloodhound. When old Geronimo was on the warpath and scalping settlers in the Salt River Valley, Arizona, it was necessary that word be sent immediately from the garrison at Fort Yuma to a detachment of cavalry under Captain Lawton, a hundred miles to the northwest.

The country was dry, rugged and hot. No horse could travel it nor could it be done by relays, as there were only blind trails. A young Apache scout agreed to carry the despatch. Stripped to the loins and with a water bottle and some parched corn and dried meat, he left the fort at four in the morning, on foot and alone. He arrived at Lawton's camp about eight that same evening. He had covered the one hundred and three miles over a rough country, and much of the time with the thermometer at a hundred degrees in the shade!

The following paragraphs are quoted from Lieutenant Clark's book:

"There is, of course, great difference in the capacities of individual Indians as trailers, some being no better than many white men, while others are astonishingly capable. In 1874 troops were sent out from Fort Keogh, Montana, to intercept some Cheyennes who had been reported by an officer as crossing the Yellowstone below the post. After the troops had been two days out from the fort a Cheyenne scout called Poor Elk was sent out with despatches. He had ridden all night and his pony was very tired when he joined the column at about ten in the morning, but he managed to keep his pony alongside the troops. The country had been overrun by great herds of buffalo, the grass had been eaten and broken down. Some excellent white and Indian scouts were with the command but nothing had been discovered, when suddenly Poor Elk stopped (he was riding about the middle of the column), and, going a little distance to the right to more thoroughly scour the country, came back and reported that he had found the trail of the Indians.

"It crossed the direction of the troops at right angles and one-half of the command had already passed over it. Poor Elk followed it for about a mile, to where the pursued party had camped. He brushed away the ashes from the dead fires and felt of the earth underneath, examined the droppings of the animals, counted the number of fires and noticed, by marks made by the pins, the size of the lodges; carefully scrutinized some moccasins, bits of cloth, etc., that had been thrown away; noticed that the moccasins were sewn with thread instead of sinew and were made as the Sioux made them; discovered that the calico was not as is used at the agencies, and found a bit of hair braid, such as Sioux Indians fasten to the scalp lock. A sweat-lodge had been built, indicating that they had remained in camp at least one day, and the droppings of the animals determined that the stay had been but one. The position of the camp, the tying of the animals near the tepees and wickiups, the number of lodges, the care taken by the Indians in leaving, all these things furnished evidence as to the number of Indians and animals and the number of days since they had camped there. Though moving steadily, yet they were in no special hurry; were Sioux and not Cheyennes, as stated; had recently left an agency; had not crossed the Yellowstone at the time reported, but two days previously; were evidently a party of Sioux who were on the way to join the Indians north of the British line. In fact, the record left by these Indians was as complete as though it had been carefully written out.

"In following the trails of animals the knowledge of their habits and peculiarities is of the greatest assistance. Troops frequently go through or across country; Indians take the line of the least resistance and war parties keep concealed. A broken blade of grass, a bead or feather dropped, a moccasin track, and the story is told. White horse thieves on the frontier frequently disguise themselves as Indians and 'run off' stock, but as a rule they make a trail which can be easily detected. The Indian whips and other articles which they drop are placed where they are sure to be seen by the pursuers, thin moccasin tracks are made in the snow or soft earth where they will be distinctly outlined; in fact, they overdo the business, and yet they have deceived many good white trailers."

CHAPTER XLVIII

THE "ghost dance" is comparatively modern, having originated with the Piute Indians in Nevada about 1889. It was the outcome of a religious belief that a Messiah was soon to appear who would rid the land of the white man, and restore to the Indians all their rights.

During the so-called ghost dance excitement in the latter part of 1890, Sitting Bull, an Arapahoe (who must not be confounded with the famous Sioux medicine man of the same name), came to our agency at Darlington, near Fort Reno, Indian Territory, and commenced preaching about the coming of the Messiah. He was from the Shoshone agency, Wyoming, where I had known him very well. He came to my quarters quite frequently. His wife gave me a very pretty pair of moccasins.

Sitting Bull claimed that he had had a dream in which he was told that he must go and find the Messiah, and that he had followed a star for eighteen days through a barren country, and that wherever he camped, a pool of water would form to quench his thirst. This star, he said, went before him until it came and stood over the entrance of a cave, where he saw Christ and was invited to become the first and greatest apostle, and that he must go south to the Arapahoes and Cheyennes and prepare them for the coming of the Messiah.

Sitting Bull declared that the Messiah was to expel the whites from the country, bring back the buffalo and restore

340

to the Indians their hunting grounds of former days.   He said that the ghost dances must be kept up night and day until Christ came.

The Indians did keep up the dancing for several months. At our agency they were divided up into relays, one party relieving the other when fatigue overtook them.   I have seen them drop, perfectly exhausted.   A blanket would be thrown over the prostrate forms, and they would be allowed to remain until they had recovered from their swoon.   I have seen two and three hundred dancing and singing in a ring which they had formed.   They would fold their arms across their breasts, clasping one another's hands, which brought their bodies close together, and men, women and children would form these dancing squads.

I told some of the Indians that there was plenty of water in the country Sitting Bull had passed over and that he could not have died from want of water if he had tried ever so hard.   To this they would shake their heads, saying: "It must be so if the Arapahoes say that it is so."

Their faith in one another was great, owing to their childlike simplicity.   Then several other shrewd men among them, seeing how Sitting Bull had prospered by reason of presents given him by his converts, also commenced to have dreams and see visions.   In time, therefore, quite a number were preaching about the coming of the Messiah.

I allowed my scouts to attend these dances, because I realized that it would be difficult for me to keep them away. Furthermore, if I had forbidden it, it would only have fanned the prevailing excitement of the moment.   I was quite sure the agitation would die out in time and that if we attempted to stop it, it would only make matters worse.

During the Messiah craze, my Indians were very much interested in the new religion.   Lieutenant Wilhelm, who was afterward killed in the Philippines, was my assistant, and One Horse, one of my scouts, told him that the Messiah was coming, that the old days would come back, and with them the buffalo and other game which the Indians had enjoyed, and that all the white people would start back across the ocean, and when they reached the middle of the "big pond," the Great Spirit was going to put down his hand and sink all their vessels and this country would then all be turned over to the Indians again.

Wilhelm said to One Horse, "Do you think it is right for the lieutenant and myself, who are friends of yours, to go with the rest of the whites and be drowned? Here we are, doing all we can for you."

Old One Horse, with tears in his eyes, said that the scouts were very fond of us and that he was very sorry, but, nevertheless, we would have to go, too. Then pondering a moment, he added that he would see what he could do for us; that he would go down and talk with the other Indians and possibly we could be adopted into the tribe.

In a few days he returned, saying that the Indians had had some sort of a council and that Wilhelm and I would be adopted into the tribe, and therefore, we would remain with the Indians. However, he added, we must marry into the tribe, and they had selected our wives!

This interesting part of the ceremony never came to pass, as, following the battle of Wounded Knee, December 29, 1890, the Messiah craze gradually died out.

One of the strangest as well as one of the saddest ceremonies that I ever witnessed was in connection with these great dances. It was a variation from the usual method of conducting these religious assemblages.

An Indian well along in years, nearly nude, stood perfectly motionless for an hour or more, his hands raised toward the sun, as if in supplication to the Great Spirit. It was wonderful how he could remain in that tiring position so long. Near by were other old men of the tribe, with vessels containing meat cut into small pieces. They gave this meat to the other Indians, talking all the time, while the medicine man remained in his tiresome position, his eyes wide open, gazing at the sun. I was told that the meat given to the Indians was buffalo meat which Sitting Bull had brought from the north. That could not have been, as the buffalo had all been killed off many years before.

Suddenly, and apparently without a signal, the whole multitude rushed toward this man, and, falling down at his feet, set up a loud lamentation. It seemed to be as if all the sorrows of the North American Indian were concentrated in that wail! Tears were streaming down their copper-colored faces, and some of the women were weeping as if their hearts would break.

Calling Fanny Flying Man, an intelligent Indian woman, the wife of one of my scouts, I asked:

"Fanny, what do they say to you?"

"Oh," she soberly answered, "they were talking about our people." That was all the information I could get from her.

Then I asked others. The general reply was "Nothing," accompanied with a shake of the head.

After all, when one considers their treatment at the hands of unscrupulous whites, these poor victims of civilization were not to be blamed for their dream of the coming of the Messiah and their hope and anticipation for better days; nor for the belief that the white men were to return across the ocean whence they came and that the buffalo would return, nor for their superstition concerning the resurrection of their "great chief," an Indian long since interred.

CHAPTER XLIX

VARIOUS INDIAN WAYS

IN THE ensuing pages, I have set down some random notes on Indian customs, manners, etc. Some of them are not well known to the white man, and will, I believe, interest my readers:

Twins.—Twins are usually regarded by Indians as unearthly, and are rather feared as possessing occult power. Among some of the Oregon and other Pacific Coast tribes they are regarded as abnormal, and one or both are killed. This is not so with the plains Indians or the Shoshones and Bannocks. I knew a brother and sister at Fort Washakie who were twins, and both were regarded as being unusually fortunate in anything they undertook.

"Red men."—It is thought by many who have studied Indian lore that the Indians were first called "red men" because of the universal custom of painting their faces and bodies, and for this purpose they used fine clays containing different kinds of iron which they themselves had found. Since the establishment of the trading stores, they bought these ochers to a great extent. Michelle, chief of the Pen d' Oreilles, said to my dear friend, Lieutenant Philo P. Clark, author of *The Indian Sign Language*: "I do not know exactly why we use paint. When I was young many kinds were used, black, yellow, red, and so on. We know by its use when it is hot—we do not feel the sun so severely; and when cold, the winds are not so keen and painful.

"The priests tried to stop its use. I asked them if it

was any worse to paint the face than it was to paint the church and if the church would last longer by being painted, why should not the Indian? I think God made all things to be used—the paint for the Indians; and this is why we use all kinds of color on face and hair when we go to war, and it gives us good luck."

Black paint is used by many tribes after returning from an expedition, that being the color for rejoicing; red paint is used in profusion in any excitement, either in war or love.

The squaws usually used red for the cheeks to enrich their beauty. War paint, so called, is only an excessive use of any color. When painting for war they use many stripes and rings of different color; but on returning only black paint is used. For courting they paint themselves as handsomely as possible.

In the religious and ceremonial dances various kinds of fantastic designs were exhibited.

Pipes.—The Indians' pipe has been the symbol of peace and friendship, and has always played an important part in the religions, war and peace ceremonies. To smoke the pipe of peace was essential to the preparation of every compact of friendship or treaty entered into by these people and they usually have a pipe made and used only for this purpose, the stem being from two to three feet long, one-half inch in thickness, and from one and one-half to three inches wide, decorated with eagle feathers, brass tacks, porcupine work, horse hair and ribbons. The red sandstone, procured from the pipestone quarry of Minnesota (from which the county is named), is undoubtedly the finest material for Indian pipes. When we were living in Minnesota my father visited these quarries and brought home some of this stone, from which he made pipes, paperweights and other articles. He spoke of some of the wonderful carvings on the quarry walls,—lizards, snakes and other Indian gods, rabbits with cloven feet, muskrats with human feet, reptiles, etc., which required much artistic skill and a great deal of time and handwork.

Eagle Feathers.—The tail feathers from "the chief of all birds," as they call the golden eagle, are highly prized, and are the chief and talismanic decoration of war bonnets. These feathers are fastened in the hair and also in the manes of their war ponies. Some tribes only allow a man who has killed some one in a fight to wear a feather of this kind on the head; that is, stuck in the scalp lock. Should two or three be worn there they indicate the number of persons killed by the wearer. Some Indians claim that this bird was created and given them by the Great Spirit (God) for its beauty, for decorating themselves, and for a special charm in battle. The Indians regard the golden eagle as an emblem of strength and courage. The wings of the bald eagle are prized for fans, and the large bones of eagles' and hawks' wings are used for whistles, the eagle wings being most highly prized. The whistle, when skilfully played upon, has a sound exactly like that made by the bird itself, as in the case of a turkey. It is like the plaintive note of that fowl.

Scalp Lock.—The plains Indians braid that portion of the hair contained in a circle about two inches in diameter, at the crown of the head. The braid is formed of three strands, and the circle is marked by pulling out the hair, and this little circular part is painted, usually with red ocher. The hair of the head is parted in the middle and the parting extends to this circle. The scalp lock seems meant to be a mark of manhood and defiance.

Poisoned Arrows.—Poisoned arrows were not commonly used by the North American Indians. Lieutenant Philo Clark states that the Shoshones admitted to him that before they met the whites they used poisoned arrow-heads. For this purpose the arrow-heads were dipped in a compound made of ants pounded to a powder and mixed with the spleen of an animal. The mixture was then placed in the sun and allowed to decay partly. The result was such a deadly poison that if the arrows broke the skin in touching a person it was sure death. They also said the plains Indians never used poisoned arrows.

Tepees.—Tepees are called "lodges" and "wigwams." From fourteen to thirty poles are used in a tepee, and one or two for the wingpoles on the outside; these latter for adjusting the wings, near the opening at the top of the tepee, for the escaping of smoke; the wings are kept at such angles as to produce the best draft. The best poles are made from slender mountain-pine, which grows thickly in the mountains. The women cut and trim them and carefully peel off the bark. They are then partly dried or seasoned, which requires some little time, and are first pitched for some time without covering of canvas or skin. By being thus slowly cured they are kept straight. The length depends upon the size of the tepee and varies from sixteen to thirty feet. A set of tepee poles is valuable and is worth several ponies. The Indians have a smaller lodge used while on their hunts, which is carried on the travois.

When a lodge is to be pitched, three of these poles are tied together near the top and set up like a tripod. The cord with which the three poles are tied is sufficiently long for the ends to hang to the ground. The other poles, save one, are successively set up, the top of each resting against the first three, while the lower ends form a circle from twelve to seventeen feet in diameter. The tops are then bound together securely by means of the pendent cord. One edge of the tepee cloth is now made fast to the remaining pole, by means of which it is raised and carried around the framework, so as to envelop it completely. The two edges of the cover are closed together by wooden pins or keys, except three feet at the extreme top left open for a smoke hole, and an equal space at the bottom for an entrance. The spare pole is attached to one edge of the cover at the top, so that the smoke hole may be closed or opened at will.

The skin of some animal, a piece of canvas, or a blanket or two are fixed to the outside of the lodge, above the entrance, so as to hang down over the latter as a sort of door. Inside, the fireplace occupies the center of the lodge. Cooking is generally done outside, except in rainy weather. When mosquitoes are unusually numerous smudges are built in the lodges. About the fireplace are spread mats, which serve as seats by day and couches by night. In permanent camps they quite frequently put up raised platforms, about fourteen inches from the ground, for couches and other purposes.

The covering of a lodge is one continuous piece, made of buffalo skin (or canvas), nicely fitted together. In tanning, the skins are dressed so thin that sufficient light is transmitted into the interior even when the lodge is tightly closed. When new they are quite white, and a village of them presents an attractive appearance. Sometimes they are variously painted, according to the tastes of the occupants.

In moving the village the large tepee poles are fastened at their smaller ends by a rope or a rawhide thong which passes over the pony's back, and the large ends of the poles drag on the ground. The poles become shafts and behind the animal the load is fastened. Small children are frequently placed in a wicker work basket fastened to these poles; and for transporting the sick and wounded the skin of a freshly killed animal, a robe or blanket, is fastened to the poles, forming a bed upon which the sick or wounded person reclines; two poles, as a rule, are used for the purpose.

Disappearance of the Buffalo.—Surgeon O. C. McNary states in *The Campfire*:

"In the fall of 1885, when I, as a young acting assistant surgeon, United States Army, was stationed with A Troop, Fifth Cavalry, [my regiment] for a short time at Cantonment, Indian Territory, we had several bands of Cheyennes under our care. Among the chiefs we had Stone Calf, Little Robe, Spotted Horse and White Horse. Having learned the sign language, I had many talks with these Indians.

"Stone Calf and Little Robe were greatly troubled over the disappearance of the buffalo. They told me that the great spirit created the buffalo in a large cave in the Panhandle of Texas; that the evil spirits had closed up the mouth of the cave and the buffalo could not get out. They begged me to get permission from the great father at Washington for them to go and open the cave, and let the buffalo out. They claimed to know the exact location of the cave. They even wanted me to accompany them."

[Chief Whirlwind of the Cheyennes told me the same story when I was in charge of the scouts.]

Death of a Great Chief.—Cochise, the great war chief of the Chiracahua Apaches, died at Camp Bowie, Arizona Territory, June 8, 1874. He had been sick for about six weeks and was reduced to a mere skeleton. He had an idea that he was bewitched and in order to break the spell the war chiefs and others, under the direction of the medicine man, kept up all the noise they could, by singing, and drumming on beef hides stretched over sticks, night and day, during his entire sickness.

He said that the spirits of the white men he had killed were haunting him. There is little doubt that his disease originated from drinking tizwin, made from ground corn, fermented and drunk in large quantities on an empty stomach. Indians frequently fast forty-eight hours before indulging, that the liquor may have the desired effect.

The morning after his death, Cochise was washed, and painted in war style, placed on his favorite horse in front of one of his sub-chiefs, who supported the body, his four most noted sub-chiefs preceding and his family and others of the tribe following. They marched twelve miles to his grave, no one but those who were of the tribe's blood being allowed to attend. The grave was very large. On the bottom were laid blankets and the chief was rolled up in a pair of very handsome ones of forty-two pounds weight, which had his name woven in the texture. The sides of the grave were walled up about three feet with stone. His rifle and arms, as well as other articles of value, were laid beside him. Above his body were placed more blankets, then mescal poles, resting on the walls of his grave. Covering these were skins, to prevent dirt falling through. Then the grave was filled with stones and dirt. His favorite horse was shot within two hundred yards of the grave; another horse was killed about one mile distant and a third about two miles away, the idea being that he would find a horse when he needed one in the spirit land. The family and relatives destroyed all the clothing that they had, and the tribe destroyed all the stores on hand, so they were without food for about forty-eight hours.*

The Indian Census.—The census taken in 1920 shows a decrease in the Indian population as enumerated. Nearly ten per cent. is probably to be accounted for in part by the enumeration as Indians in 1910, and as white in 1920, of certain persons having only slight traces of Indian blood.

---

*From the *Army and Navy Journal* of July 11, 1874. At one time I owned the cane which General O. O. Howard gave Cochise in 1873, after one of their treaties.

In 1910 a special effort was made to secure a complete enumeration of all persons having any perceptible amount of Indian blood, for the purpose of perpetuating a special report showing tribal relations, purity of Indian blood, etc., and it is probable that for this reason a considerable number of persons who would ordinarily have been reported as white were enumerated as Indians. The assumption is borne out by a comparison of the totals shown for the Indian population the last four times the census was taken, the only ones at which a complete enumeration of the Indian population has been attempted.

There were, in 1920, 242,950 Indians in the United States; in 1910, 265,683; in 1900, 237,196; in 1890, 248,253. Of the total decrease in the Indian population between 1910 and 1920, amounting to 22,733, the greater part took place in Oklahoma alone. The only prominent increase was reported for North Carolina, from 7,851 to 11,824. The only states which had, in 1920, a thousand or more Indian inhabitants, and which reported increases in Indian population were Louisiana, Texas, Montana, Oregon and California.

There are Indians in every state in the Union. But Delaware, Vermont, New Hampshire and West Virginia, each have less than fifty.

The Indian has made vast strides in agriculture in the past ten years. The early explorers of this country found the Indian cultivating the soil, although the women did most of the work, the men being engaged in hunting and fishing when not on the warpath. Of later years, the women have confined themselves largely to household affairs. The census report for 1920 states that 36,459 Indians cultivated 762,126 acres of land, produced crops worth $11,037,589, as compared with 28,051 Indians who cultivated 558,503 acres in 1912, worth $3,250,288. In the opinion of the author, this all would have been accomplished years ago if the Indian question had been judiciously handled.

The figures of the Indian census taken in 1920 are of great ethnological interest, and I wish that I could devote more space to it and go into the matter more thoroughly.

The following Indian names are copied from an old property return which I have had for nearly fifty years. They are all Shoshones:

1—Pe-ah-sop (Big Belly)
2—Te-nap-it-sy (Boy)
3—Pi-ko-mot-st (Sorrel Pony)
4—Won-go-dzock-ah (Breaks down Pines)
5—Joh-e-yuh (Wolf Fat)
6—No-nem-be (Little Devil)
7—Quar-ro-shon-gatz (Like an Antelope)
8—No-ton-no (Bottom Log)
9—No-pi-she (Foolish)
10—To-nam-be (Black Foot)
11—Ash-we-yoh (Roan)
12—Meh-dzot-se (Cactus)
13—To-ash-shu-a (Calf Skin)
14—Wash-wiich-y (Rotten Log)
15—Ha-de-pe-wag (Blubs)
16—Ga-nog (Lodge)
17—To-yah-wo-mit-see (Mountain Log)
18—Poh-que-mannof (Green Sage)
19—Te-hah-rah-gweski (Sweating Horse)
20—Pah-n-hak-naret-so (Elk Water)
21—Ty-bo-ro-ce-do (White Man's Toe Nail)
22—Werk-ip (Burnt Robe)
23—Mo-vch-we (Cat Fish)
24—Naa-kie (Packs on his Horse)
25—Zag-ware (Sits Dignified)
26—He-vat-see (Woodpecker)
27—Pe-yah-n-bo (Big White Man)
28—Ho-see (Dog Urine)
29—Pop-pag-go-wat (Budding Willow)
30—Pe-yah-en-gok (Big Red)
31—Wap-wot-see (Two Knives)
32—En-goh-won (Red Pictures)

33—Pan-dem-mos (Dam)
34—To-ne-vooh (White Bob-tail)
35—Go-ro-ko (Necklace)
36—Ton-wos (Writes on the water)

PROPER NAMES

American Horse
Whistling Elk
End-of-the-Woods
Running Horse
Spotted Weasel
Bad Wild Horse
Count-Coup-One-by-One
Dog-Walks-on-the-Ground
Spotted Tail
Crazy Horse
Man-Afraid-of-His-Horses
Little Warrior
No Neck
Long Neck
Thundering Eagle
Bald Eagle
Waiting
Touch-the-Clouds
Swift Bear
Pretty Lance
Sitting Bull

These Indians are mostly Cheyenne and Sioux. Credit goes to *The Indian Sign Language*, by Lieutenant Philo Clark.

PART SIX: SERVICE IN PORTO RICO
AND RETIREMENT

CHAPTER L

BUILDING IN PORTO RICO

IN 1892 I was appointed Indian agent by President Cleveland for the Cheyennes and Arapahoes, being stationed at Darlington, Indian Territory, but held the appointment only a short time, having to resign because of ill health. This I regretted very much.

On being relieved as Indian agent, I joined my new troop, G, Fifth Cavalry, at Fort Brown, Texas, remaining there more than four years.

A short time before leaving Darlington agency, on one of the ration days, when several hundred women and children were drawing rations, one of the squaws asked me if I intended to leave them, and when I told her that I was obliged to go on account of my health, she informed me that the Indians were all very sorry that I was going away because I had been good and kind to them. She then told these people and they all commenced to moan and cry, which, needless to say, made me feel very bad.

I had previously asked to be relieved because of my ill health, and a reply came from the Interior Department advising that they were disinclined to relieve me, and urged me to stay, stating that I had excellent control over the Indians. I then sent a second letter, supported by certificates from two physicians, to the effect that my health was such as to compel me to go.

At the outbreak of the Spanish-American War, in April, 1898, my regiment, the Fifth Cavalry, was stationed at Fort Sam Houston, Texas. We were ordered to New Orleans, camping there on the race course. We were there several days and were then ordered to Mobile, Alabama, by water. About two weeks later we were ordered to report to General Joe Wheeler at Tampa, Florida. My troop, G, and three others were ordered to Cuba with General Shafter's expedition. Not having sufficient transportation, we were unable to go, to our great regret. We remained at Tampa until nearly one-half of the regiment was on the sick report, with malarial fever and some typhoid. We were then ordered to Huntsville, Alabama, for recuperation. We were there nearly three months, when we were ordered to Porto Rico, sailing from Savannah, Georgia, on the cattle-ship *Michigan,* arriving at San Juan in November. My troop, G, was ordered to Aiboneto, a town of two thousand two hundred inhabitants, situated on the military road, about half-way between San Juan and Ponce.

I was in Aiboneto during the hurricane of 1899, in which my barracks, stables, hospital and storehouse were blown down. They were all new buildings. The walls of the barracks were eighteen inches in thickness. Fortunately, no one was injured. In the town and vicinity one hundred and twenty-eight persons were killed and seriously injured. When my barracks were about to collapse, I ordered my men to save themselves. Some of them went to town and did noble work in saving the people. They carried several women and children into the church. When I visited it in the evening it contained about a thousand persons. I had charge of issuing the rations and clothing to the destitute. My districts were Aiboneto, Barranquitas, Barrios and

Camero, which contained a population of about seventy-five thousand. The industries in my district were principally coffee and tobacco. I put up nearly one hundred houses, repairing many others, and built a hospital to hold thirty-two beds. I was in Aiboneto in 1916 and found the hospital still in use. I paid for the labor and material by issuing rations to the men employed and also gave rations for the lumber. I had similar work at Barranquitas and Barrios. Sergeant Patrick Collins of my troop had charge of the rations at Barranquitas. He did splendid work, receiving a vote of thanks from the citizens. I had a detachment of men stationed at each of these places and had to inspect them frequently. There was only a trail leading to Barranquitas and Barrios and everything to and from those places had to be transported by pack animals. The trail in many places during the rainy season was almost impassable.

I suggested to the alcalde (mayor) the proposition of putting a few men at work on the bad places and I would pay for their labor in rations. My proposition was readily accepted. Upon inspecting their work, I found they had done so well that I gradually increased the number of men to over a hundred. I allowed only one or two men or boys in a family to work, and they were allowed to work but a week. I did this in order to spread the work around so as to give the greatest possible number, who desired, a chance to earn the rations.

Shortly after the rations gave out Governor Allen made an extended trip through the island, and I accompanied him. The people of both towns gave him a big reception and presented a large petition pleading for a road. The Spaniards some years previous had surveyed a road but did very little work on it. The governor told them it was a question of money as they were spending large sums in public improvements. He told them that if I would take charge of the

BARRAQUITAS
Showing road built by Captain Wheeler

work (having seen what I had accomplished with only the tools that the natives brought with them), he would try to help them out. He could not promise to complete the road, but would give them some money to furnish the people with employment. Shortly after, I was notified that a certain amount of money would be placed to my credit. The money was received and I went to work. The funds came along in driblets and then I was notified that no more funds could be supplied me at present; so I turned in my tools that had been furnished by the public workers, and made my arrangements to leave the island. This was in May, 1900. Just as I was about leaving I was informed by the board of public works that they could spare me a little more money. I decided not to return, which I have always regretted for no more work was done on the road for several years.

During my work on the road the Fifth Cavalry was ordered to the States, and I remained behind at the request of Governor Allen. Before I left I was given a reception at Barranquitas. A brass band and the city *concejales* (council) met me at the outskirts of the town and escorted me to the public building where the school children had assembled in charge of their teachers, and where they sang a song, written for the occasion, and commending my work on the road. I should judge by the throng that there were fully a thousand people assembled. Speeches were made and a banquet was given me, followed by a dance that evening. I was also given a set of resolutions signed by a great many women, thanking me for my work for the hurricane sufferers and for my road work.

The following letters and newspaper clipping speak for themselves:

WILLIAM H. ELLIOTT

DEPARTMENT OF THE INTERIOR OF PORTO RICO. OFFICE OF THE COMMISSIONER SAN JUAN

April 9th, 1901.

PERSONAL.

My Dear Captain:

Upon the eve of your departure from Porto Rico I deem it not only incumbent upon me, with knowledge of the character and good results of your efforts to better the condition of the people in the vicinity of Aiboneto, where you have been stationed, but esteem it a pleasure, to bear testimony to the value of your services.

I sincerely regret that it was not possible for this department to place at your disposal means sufficient for you to complete the construction of the road between Aiboneto and Barranquitas, a work in which you took deep interest and prosecuted with rare intelligence and economy. But I am pleased to assure you that the highway will be finished at an early date and the people will know that the forwardness of the work as left by you has made it possible for it to be completed.

Wishing you a safe voyage, an enjoyable leave of absence and good fortune wherever you may go, I am,

Very respectfully,

(Signed)   WILLIAM H. ELLIOTT.

Capt. H. W. Wheeler, 5th U. S. Cavalry,

San Juan, Porto Rico.

A TRUE COPY:

Captain 11th Cavalry.

The secretary of the Town Council of Barranquitas hereby certifies:

D. José Felix Colon
—Alcalde—

—Concejales—
D. Manuel Yorres
D. Felipe Colon Hoyos
D. Placido Roduques

D. Luciano Collaso
D. Juan Bta Pagan
_____

Secretario
D. Pio Colon Ortiz

That in the session of said Council which took place to-
day, the gentleman named in the margin being present, the following ordinance was adopted:

A petition signed by a large number of citizens was presented and read. It was requested that the council
change the name of "Comercio street" to "Captain
Wheeler street," as a slight token of gratitude to that
gentleman for the great work he has done in behalf
of the town.

The Council made said petition an ordinance, and
adopted it unanimously. Comercio street will hence-
forth be called "Captain Wheeler street."

It was further agreed that a copy of this ordinance be
presented to the Captain.

In complying with this and with the endorsement of the
mayor, I hereby signed the above.

(Signed)   Pio Colon,
                                           Secretary.

José Felix Colon,
    Mayor.
A TRUE COPY:
    Captain and Adjutant 11th Cavalry.

CLIPPING FROM THE *RAILROAD GAZETTE*
NOVEMBER 23, 1900

Extract From *American Road-Builders Porto Rico,* By
Albert Wells Buel.

_____

(This work was done during the first occupation of
Porto Rico by United States troops in 1898-'99.)

Besides the work already described, there has been a
certain amount of rough grading, paid for in rations,
(known in the vernacular as "relief beans") by the Commissary Department of the United States army. The best
piece of work of this work was done by Capt. H. W.
Wheeler of the Fifth Cavalry, who attacked the wretched

mountain trail, difficult even for ponies, between Aiboneto, Barranquitas and Barrios, and succeeded in putting through a graded road on the whole distance of about sixteen miles, except for about three miles in one place and half a mile in another. The hiatus exists solely because the "relief" was withdrawn. Some of the energy and push which must have been back of this effort may be conceived when it is understood that practically all of the work was performed with hoes, which the peons possessed, since Captain Wheeler had but twelve shovels available and no other tools or plant of any sort. This road is marked on the map as "relief beans."

The standard sections for typical locations show very heavy work, and highways in Porto Rico can not be built for much less than $15,000 a mile. The maximum gradient on the mountain roads is 7 per cent. and the minimum curvature 60 feet radius; that portion of the road between San Juan and Ponce, which was built before the American occupation, has gradients of 8½ and 9 per cent.

ITEM FROM *NEW YORK EVENING POST,*
SEPT. 23, 1911
POST TRADER TO COLONEL

Colonel Homer Webster Wheeler, an additional officer in his grade in the cavalry, leaves active service on his own application next Saturday. Colonel Wheeler is not a West Pointer, nor did he serve in the ranks in the army, but was a post trader in Kansas when he received his appointment as a second lieutenant. He was born in Vermont, May 13, 1848, and removed at an early age to Kansas, where he soon won favorable attention by frequent volunteer service with the regular troops in their campaigns against hostile Indians. His most important service was with Captain Henry C. Bankhead's expedition, which was dispatched to the rescue of Major George A. Forsyth's command on the Arickaree Fork of the Republican River in the fall of 1868.

In April, 1875, General John Pope, who had his headquarters in Fort Leavenworth, was advised that a party of Cheyennes had crossed the Arkansas River west of Fort Dodge and were attempting to make their way across the Platte into the Sioux country. In this band were some of the Indians who had murdered part of the Germaine family a year before. A detachment of soldiers under Lieutenant Austin Henely, Sixth Cavalry, was sent out after the Cheyennes. Colonel Wheeler was then the post trader at Fort Wallace. He left his business and volunteered to accompany the detachment as guide. This young post trader located the Indian camp, being the first to discover it in the morning, and, although not expected to take part in the fight, was always on the skirmish line and showed great courage and activity. He was highly commended in department orders for good judgment and conspicuous gallantry on that occasion, and having shown willingness to surrender his tradership at Fort Wallace for a commission in the army, President Grant appointed him a second lieutenant in the Fifth Cavalry in October, 1875.

Lieutenant Wheeler joined his company at Fort Lyon, Colorado, in December of that year, where he had station, with occasional tours of field service, until July, 1876, when he was transferred to Fort Robinson, Nebraska. He joined the Powder River expedition in November, 1876, taking part in the action at Bates Creek, where he was conspicuous for gallant and valuable services. He had station at Fort D. A. Russell until May, 1877, when he entered upon a tour of field service in northern Wyoming. Lieutenant Wheeler participated in the operations against the hostile Nez Percés and served with the escort for Lieutenant General Sheridan from Fort Washakie, Wyoming, by way of the Big Horn Mountains, to Fort Custer, Montana. While stationed at Fort Washakie in the spring of 1879 he captured the remnant of the Bannock Indians remaining at large at the end of hostilities with that tribe.

From fighting Indians he was sent to the infantry and cavalry school, from which he was graduated in 1883. He became a first lieutenant in 1884, captain in 1893, and major Ninth Cavalry in October, 1902, after a service of twenty-seven years in the Fifth Cavalry. He did not remain with the Ninth Cavalry very long, as he was transferred to the Eleventh Cavalry in December, 1902. He became lieutenant-colonel of the Fifth Cavalry in 1910, and received his colonelcy last March.

THE END

INDEX

INDEX

365